ESTRANGED TWINS

The Praeger Special Studies
Series in Comparative Education

General Editor: **Philip G. Altbach**

Published in Cooperation with the
Comparative Education Center,
State University of New York, Buffalo

(continued on last pages)

ESTRANGED TWINS

Education and Society in the Two Germanys

Sterling Fishman and Lothar Martin

(Praeger Special Studies in Comparative Education)

PRAEGER

New York
Westport, Connecticut
London

Library of Congress Cataloging-in-Publication Data

Fishman, Sterling.
   Estranged twins.

   (The Praeger special studies series in comparative
education)
   Bibliography: p.
   Includes index.
   1. Education—Germany (East) 2. Education—
Germany (West) 3. Comparative education. I. Martin,
Lothar II. Title. III. Series
LA722.F53 1986   370'.943   86-21211
ISBN 0-275-92460-2 (alk. paper)

Library of Congress Catalog Card Number: 86-21211
ISBN: 0-275-92460-2 (alk. paper)

First published in 1987

Praeger Publishers, 521 Fifth Avenue, New York, NY 10175
A division of Greenwood Press, Inc.

Printed in the United States of America

The paper used in this book complies with the Permanent
Paper Standard issued by the National Information Standards
Organization (Z39.48-1984).

10 9 8 7 6 5 4 3 2 1

CONTENTS

LIST OF TABLES AND FIGURES

TABLES

FIGURES

LIST OF ABBREVIATIONS

BRD   Federal Republic of Germany (West Germany)

CDU   Christian Democratic Party (East Germany)

CDU   Christian Democratic Party (West Germany)

FDGB   Free German Workers' Union (East Germany)

FDJ   Free German Youth Movement (East Germany)

EOS   Academic Senior High School (East Germany)

GDR   German Democratic Republic (East Germany)

GEW   Union of Scholars and Teachers (West Germany)

LPG   Agricultural Production Cooperatives (East Germany)

SED   United Socialist Party (East Germany)

SPD   Social Democratic Party (West Germany)

PREFACE

This is a book about estrangement. It tells the story of how countrymen have been rent asunder by politics and ideology. It details the end of that brief and tragic period when Germans were united in a single state — Germany endured for less than 75 years. It also shows that where formerly the German people were divided by regional and religious differences into small political fiefdoms, today they are being estranged because the frontier between two hostile world camps goes right through their territory. Today, not only is the country divided by an ugly scar, but the aspirations of its people are being gradually twisted apart as well.

This book is also about reconciliation. The authors of this work were both young boys in a world at war. The older relatives of each bore arms against the other's country. They grew up as enemies. Then, following the end of actual hostilities, each of them received an opportunity to study abroad in the other's land.

Lothar Martin was given an opportunity to leave his devastated homeland and to spend a year in the multinational community of a small college in upstate New York. It was a formative time in his life, and the amiable atmosphere of earnest study and college life gained a friend for the United States. This visit was to become the first of many to the United States; it helped Martin to define his career in education. In the field of comparative education and as a member of the international counseling movement, he has dedicated his work to the advancement of human services and international understanding.

Sterling Fishman's situation was somewhat different. His parents had fled as children from the religious persecution of Eastern Europe. His parents and relations then watched with horror and profound sadness as their coreligionists were hounded across Europe and exterminated. As Fishman became conscious of nations and politics, the word "holocaust" received its present coinage and was linked forever with Germany. Many years later it was a Gratitude Fellowship from the West German government that brought him to study at the University of Munich and to know Germans. Making lifelong friends in Germany has not caused Fishman to forget the victims of Nazi oppression, or the darker side of the human soul, but has rather led him to appreciate the complexities of the human condition. Like Martin, he has devoted his career to promoting international understanding through his work on European culture and education.

The authors of this work came to know and value each other through a series of cooperative ventures carried on by their respective institutions. In researching and writing this work, they have both been impressed by the tremendous effort and investment it has taken to divide peoples in the East and West. Wherever possible, misunderstandings have been magnified for the purpose of alienating the Germans and the two hemispheres. A climate of fear and suspicion prevails as a result of this effort. Fortunately, the violence of words has not yet led to more frightful forms of violence. Yet, the authors are keenly aware of how small the cost would be to the various states to produce wellsprings of friendship and cooperation. Estrangement requires billions to sustain, while reconciliation costs the price of a student fare.

ACKNOWLEDGMENTS

The authors gratefully acknowledge the assistance provided them by various grants and stipends from the universities of Bonn and Wisconsin. They would also like to thank colleagues and friends who have listened and responded to them. They express special thanks to Stephanie Stone in helping to prepare this work for publication. This book is dedicated to our wives, Nancy and Gisela.

Lothar Martin
Bonn, West Germany

Sterling Fishman
Madison, Wisconsin
USA

1

A TWIN STUDY OF A DIFFERENT KIND

> But twins have a special claim upon our attention; it is, that their history affords means of distinguishing between the effects of tendencies received at birth, and of those that were imposed by the special circumstances of their after life.
>
> Sir Francis Galton

Twins have been objects of fascination throughout human history. They occur repeatedly in the myths and folklore of virtually every culture. The Romans, for example, dated the founding of their city to the struggle between Romulus and Remus, the twin sons of Mars. The Bible has its twins as well. Jacob and Esau, the twin sons of Isaac and Rebeccah, played a significant role in the history of the Israelites. And, of course, twins have proven to be an effective literary device, especially for comedies such as Shakespeare's "Comedy of Errors."[1]

In the last hundred years, however, twins have come under the scrutiny of scientists. Since the work of Sir Francis Galton, scientists have gathered data concerning the effects of "nature versus nurture." Nowhere can the differing effects of social environment versus heritability be better observed and measured than with twins. Given the difficulties of controlling such factors in research on humans, is it any wonder that twins have attracted such diverse researchers as geneticists, pathologists, psychologists, and educators.

The question then arises: would it be possible to find two *societies* that could be paired for purposes of this kind of comparison? Could a social scientist, for example, find two societies whose inherited

1

characteristics — language, history, culture, and birth dates — were similar enough to make a "twin study" feasible? If such a pair could be found, then the complex effects of a variety of factors might be studied and measured.

Obviously, the situation that has developed in Germany since the end of World War II offers instructive possibilities for such a study. A highly developed European state was divided, and the two parts, which once shared a common culture, traditions, language, and institutions, were then exposed to differing values, and political and educational institutions, and incorporated into two competing hemispheres. This would seem to offer a rare opportunity for a twin study of a different kind, a "macro" comparison of two societies.

In the past, fields such as comparative education and others involving the comparative analysis of societies have grappled with the problem of finding meaningful bases for comparison. What sense does it make, for example, to compare the judicial systems of Denmark and Spain, or the educational systems of Hungary and Australia? One might expect to learn little more than that states with different histories and cultures have different laws and schools. The German situation, on the other hand, is unique among the developed states of the world. This singularity, it would seem, would attract the attention of a variety of scholars, but especially those interested in the controversies and dilemmas of modern education. Where else might one better observe the effects of schooling on successive generations of a population?

Yet, a twin study of the two Germanys offers even more possibilities than one might expect. East and West Germany may also be observed as representative prototypes of the two ideological blocs to which they belong. West Germany is committed to a Western capitalist, pluralistic, and democratic mode of life, while East Germany is devoted to a Marxist–Leninist world view.

In addition, history and geography have placed these two states in the central arena of two competing hemispheres. Their friends and allies are especially sensitive to political and educational developments in these two states. As the ancient maxim goes: *Quod licet Galliae non licet Germaniae*. This means that if France, or Poland or Rumania, deviates somewhat from the acknowledged value structures of the Western or Eastern worlds, this is tolerable, but not so in the Germanys. Each must be a model, a *Musterknabe,* for the others; each must set a worthy example in the great struggle between East and West.

To summarize, then: this is a study of society and education in those estranged twins, East and West Germany. In the course of this work, we hope to generate an understanding of the interrelationship between political and economic systems on one hand and the aims and achievements of schools on the other. We hope to shed light on the ways various factors affect processes of education-curriculum development, modes of instruction, and guidance procedures, among others.

Methodologically, these two states lend themselves to systematic comparison because of their common history, language, and culture as well as their similar durations of existence. Both states publish a huge quantity of material about their educational systems: — some in glossy and colorful formats in which every child is portrayed as diligent, happy and "above average" and every teacher an exemplar of the profession; some in lengthy statistical tables and dry, official prose; and some in harsh criticism. Each Germany is eager to find the shortcomings of the other and quick to publicize them.

This study should enhance not only our understanding of these two states and their efforts to perpetuate their societies through education; it should also reveal some of the educational achievements and deficiencies in capitalistic, pluralistic democracies and Marxist communist societies in general.

Two final technical notes: First, in rendering German words we have dispensed with the umlaut and have transcribed the umlauted a, o, and u as ae, oe, and ue. Unless otherwise noted, all translations are those of the authors. Second, we have throughout the text referred to the western country as West Germany or the BRD (Federal Republic) and to its eastern counterpart as East Germany or the GDR (German Democratic Republic).[2]

NOTES

Epigraph to Chapter 1 is from *Inquiries into Human Faculty and Its Development* (London, 1883), p. 155.

1. For the Biblical account of the birth of Jacob and Esau, see Genesis 25:19–34. An excellent discussion of the subject of twin studies can be found in Peter Mittler, *The Study of Twins* (Middlesex, England, 1971).

2. BRD, the abbreviation for *Bundesrepublik Deutschland* (Federal Republic of Germany) is used less often than GDR, the abbreviation for the German Democratic Republic.

2

THE TWO GERMANYS

Unity and right and freedom
for the German fatherland!
Let us all strive after that
brotherly with heart and hand!

Hoffman von Fallersleben

THE BIRTH OF TWO NEW STATES

Twins are never equal, even identical ones. The circumstances of their birth will inevitably differentiate them. One will precede the other into life; they will be received in the world in different ways. The same holds true in our analogy of the birth of two new states. However similar their lineage, the two Germanys were born in vastly different and complicated circumstances. Unlike mammal twins who are born from the same mother, the Federal Republic and the GDR resulted from a more primitive kind of reproduction, "cell division." And instead of being the offspring of a normal birth trauma, the German states grew out of a tremendous worldwide catastrophe.

World War II left incredible carnage in its wake. Not only had millions of soldiers and civilians died, not only had great cities become piles of rubble, but entire states and ways of thinking perished as well. The leading belligerents, Germany and Japan, whose vast empires had sprawled across Europe and Asia, lay in ruin. They were prey to their long tormented enemies who now occupied and ruled them. Political ideas as well as states were casualties of the war. Not only did the idea of

4

a Third Reich and a New Asia die, but older concepts like colonialism and Europe also suffered mortal wounds. Previously powerless peoples threw off their colonial yokes while, at the same time, two superpowers asserted their hegemony over Europe. The military and moral power of Europe had disintegrated.

In the middle of Europe lay a defeated and prostrate Germany. Occupied at first by its allied enemies, whose armies had met at the River Elbe, it would soon be controlled by suspicious and hostile rivals. Germany's quest for unity was once more interrupted. Actually, the German state had had only a brief history, lasting from 1871 to 1945; otherwise Germany had never really existed as one political unit. Jealous local princes and prelates, abetted by powerful neighboring states, had kept the German-speaking peoples fragmented into many political pieces. Indeed, many of the leading figures of German cultural unity — Lessing, Goethe, Kant, Grillparzer, Keller — were all citizens of different states.

But the new division of Germany following 1945 was different in many ways from the divisions of the past. First, the Germans had experienced more than 70 years of unity prior to this rupture. Second, the new division resulted from a horrendous catastrophe that left the country ruined. Third, the boundary between the two Germanys became increasingly impenetrable as barbed wire, walls, and minefields marked its course. And fourth, the citizens of the two Germanys were subjected to the education and propaganda of two competing ideological and cultural systems.

Something too must be said about the Nazi era that brought Germany to the nadir of 1945. Whereas Germany had in the nineteenth century been known as a country of poets, composers, and philosophers, a country of *Kultur* and universities, by the end of World War II it appeared to many as the land of the SS, book burning, racial hatred, and extermination camps. The Germans had allowed themselves to be ruled by a man who, according to Golo Mann,

> lived by a few simple ideas: Nature is cruel. As part of nature man is justified in being cruel. Life is war. There is always war, only its form changes. As a predatory animal lives at the expense of other animals a nation lives at the expense of other nations. What it wants to enjoy it must take away from others. If it wants to enjoy safety it must either exterminate its neighbours or at least render them permanently impotent. Compassion, charity, truthfulness, loyalty to obligations, all the Christian virtues are inventions of cowards and weaklings. Nature does not know them; the strong man does not

observe them. He kills the weak; he lies and breaks treaties where it is to his advantage.[1]

Both Germanys fell heir to the moral trauma of Nazism. However much the rest of the world had tolerated the *Anschluss* with Austria, the occupation of Czechoslovakia, the 1938 pogroms against the Jews, the Germans had perpetrated these outrages. These, of course, were only harbingers of what soon would follow; war and hideous crimes beyond civilized comprehension. Germany will forever be linked in history not only with places like Wittenberg, Weimar, and Oberammergau, but with Auschwitz and Dachau as well.

There are many people who felt that Germany therefore deserved the destruction and chaos that followed the war. Cold and hunger amid the rubble was the lot of practically every German. In the East, Poland and Russia annexed old German provinces, and perhaps 12 million Germans were displaced and crowded into the defeated Fatherland. Furthermore, the victorious Allies now began to quarrel about, among other things, what to do with their former enemy.

The Soviets, who had suffered so immensely, had no desire to assist Germany in reconstructing itself and instead wanted reparations. In addition, they wanted to destroy the capitalist economy and the social class structure, which they felt had helped to cause the war. This meant not only the industrial denuding of their eastern zone of occupation, but the confiscation of large estates, banks, and the remaining industries as well.

The Western occupying powers, on the other hand, reasserted their faith in private property and a pluralistic society. The social structure was essentially left intact. The currency reform of 1948 underscored Western policies and confirmed the division of the country that had already occurred. The political partition that followed a year later was entirely logical, given the ideological differences which by that time existed between East and West. Milovan Djilas, the Yugoslav communist, reported that Stalin predicted as much in 1948, when the Soviet leader said, "The West will take over Western Germany and we shall make East Germany into our state."[2]

The Germans themselves could play only a relatively passive role in the division of their country. Despite declarations about future reunification in the founding documents of the Federal Republic, the fate of Germany was sealed for the foreseeable future. Separate administrative and legal systems, separate currencies and economies, and separate political parties made the division permanent.

Not merely two states, but two cultures seemed to be developing in the Germanys as well. Each Germany claimed to be the true and legitimate heir to the German mantle. Each viewed the past with a different lens and from a different perspective. Massive and comprehensive efforts to separate the German twins would now begin. Having sprung from the same seed, the twins would have to be reared and educated in different nurseries and separate schools. "Two separate peoples shall issue from your body," God had said to Rebeccah in Genesis. As in the many studies of individual twins that have been done, the question is very much the same with our twin nations: what roles do education and socialization play in forming two separate identities?

THE UNEQUAL HERITAGE OF THE GERMAN TWINS

Institutions never exist in a vacuum nor are they created from nothing. Unlike Athena, who sprang fully formed from the head of Zeus, institutions, even newly created ones, are derived from a wide variety of sources. Certainly, they may reflect a vision of the future, but they are always beholden as well to the present and the past. Economic factors, for example, limit what even the most ambitious politician may accomplish, and we have learned that the most inspired revolutionary leaders may not ignore the cultural traditions and folkways of a people's past. Equally as important as other factors in determining institutions are geographical ones. These, combined with economic and sociocultural forces, have helped to create the German estrangement.

The Federal Republic of Germany, often called West Germany, inherited the western portion of the German "Reich" (approximately 96,000 square miles), an area about as large as Great Britain (89,000 square miles) or two-thirds the size of California (159,000 square miles). The country extends from the Alps in the south to the North Sea and the Baltic in the north. Its varied topography, combined with its generally mild maritime climate, supports a wide variety of agricultural and recreational activities. Viniculture flourishes in the deep valleys, while pine forests cover the numerous hills and mountains. In addition, some mineral resources, especially coal, help to support traditional industries such as steel and chemical manufacturing, as well as the production of automobiles, textiles, and electrical instruments and equipment.

Geographical factors affect a society and its culture in a direct as well as an indirect fashion. Nothing is irrelevant. Resources, combined with climate, help to determine the density of population. The density of population, combined with topography, influences the nature and quality of the transportation system, which in turn greatly affects the educational system. The Federal Republic has a road and railroad network that is the envy of even other wealthy, industrialized states. This makes it possible to have highly differentiated schools with specialized curricula. In addition, schooling is fairly evenly distributed throughout the country (although this has not entirely muted the controversy over rural-urban distribution). The population density of the Federal Republic is 247 persons per square kilometer. The total population of the country is approximately 61 million.

Located in the center of Europe, West German cultural life reflects a rich and wide variety of origins. Germany itself became a center of humanist studies during the Renaissance. The German love affair with Greek and Latin began very early and has survived, like German universities, the vicissitudes of many wars and changing educational fashions. German intellectual life has both enriched and been enriched by English and French literature and thought, even, at times, at the cost of rejecting autochthonous culture. Frederick the Great's court at Sans Souci spoke French and copied French and Italian music and culture. The study of foreign languages has remained central to the German school curriculum down to the present; two are still required for university admission. Thus the strong cultural ties of the Federal Republic with Western Europe do not stem from postwar political developments, but derive from a long tradition.

This many-faceted cultural tradition has created some especially vexing educational problems. For example, there has been a long-standing commitment to a unified curriculum in order to overcome cultural diversity. Contrariwise, however, the creation of a unified curriculum is a conundrum, as so many cultural values compete with one another for a place in the curriculum.

Yet, to most people, the Federal Republic brings to mind an industrial and economic vision rather than a cultural one. The West German "economic miracle" (*Wirtschaftswunder*) following the utter devastation of the war astounded the world. Forty-two of the largest cities of the Federal Republic had suffered more than 50 percent destruction. Factories with their heavy machinery lay in ruins. Fueled by the Marshall Plan, the West Germans reconstructed their industrial economy and stood third in world trade by 1960, following the United States and Britain. Five years later, West Germany replaced Britain in second place.

This remarkable industrial growth, however, could not be sustained. Recently West Germany has begun to suffer from many of the same economic problems as other advanced industrial states. Domestic coal has largely been replaced by costly and less dependable foreign energy, thus making the economy more volatile. In addition, the high standard of living that West German workers attained caused many industrial products to suffer in worldwide competition. This led to the export of a good deal of production to developing countries, which, along with automation, has produced increased unemployment in the Federal Republic. The world economic crisis of the 1980s has resulted from such factors.

This economic reconstruction did not occur in isolation, but as part of the West German integration into the Western European community of nations. Nor were these links only economic, but have been political and cultural as well. For example, in order to overcome long-standing feelings of hostility between their countries, Konrad Adenauer and Charles de Gaulle initiated a variety of political, cultural, and educational exchanges. West Germany has made similar efforts with respect to other Western countries as well.

The interrelationships of industrial and educational systems is much debated by experts in the field. Economics of education, as a separate discipline of study, is a relatively new field. Experts from East and West have encountered serious methodological difficulties in formulating theories and testing hypotheses when dealing with education as a form of investment and capital.[3] Yet, no one doubts that much of the Federal Republic's remarkable economic success in the 1960s and 1970s must be attributed to its well-trained pool of engineers and skilled workers, people who gained their knowledge in West German schools. Economic growth and educational expansion proceeded side by side.[4]

This does not necessarily mean that the economic miracle was a direct result of educational investment. Growth in education, it appears, may have an opposite effect as well. What can safely be said is that the demands of industry and business have had a tremendous impact on education, whatever the reverse may be. Many educational planners have tried to reorganize schools and revise curricula on the basis of anticipated industrial and business needs of the future.

The German Democratic Republic (GDR) or East Germany has inherited a very different set of geographic and economic circumstances.

It is by far the smaller of the "twins," with an area that comprises less than half the size of its neighbor (41,500 square miles); this makes it slightly smaller than its southern neighbor, Czechoslovakia (49,000 square miles), and slightly larger than the state of Ohio (41,000 square miles). With the exception of a highland in the south, the GDR is relatively flat, forming part of the plain that stretches across much of central Europe. Whereas the borders of the Federal Republic are largely historical (the common border between the Germanys being the exception), the boundaries of the German Democratic Republic are recent. The Oder–Neisse border in the east, for example, separates the GDR from Poland. In so doing, it mutilates the older German provinces of Pomerania and Brandenburg and virtually cuts off all of Silesia.

The western border of the GDR was the original line of demarcation between the postwar Soviet zone of military occupation and those of the United States, Britain, and France. As the postwar crisis between East and West deepened, Winston Churchill dubbed it the "Iron Curtain." Meanwhile, Greater Berlin sits as an island in the midst of East Germany. It was not included in any of the postwar military zones of occupation and is currently divided by the Berlin Wall. The eastern portion is under GDR control, while its western arc is closely connected with the Federal Republic, however isolated it may be geographically. The population of the German Democratic Republic is approximately 17 million, or less than one-third that of the Federal Republic.

In terms of natural resources, the two Germanys are also markedly different. Although this does not apply so much to agricultural production, where conditons are similar, it does apply to mineral resources and the subsequent structure of industry. The GDR did not inherit the hard coal and iron deposits of the old Reich; they fell to West Germany and Poland. As these resources provided the basis for heavy industry, the GDR instead developed light industries such as the manufacture of textiles and clothing, optical instruments, precision tools, and porcelain. Abundant supplies of soft coal and potash also formed the basis for a chemical industry in East Germany. Overall, the GDR is much less blessed than the Federal Republic with natural resources.

In their desire for reparations, the Soviets stripped their zone of occupation of virtually all of the industrial equipment that survived the war. Factories and even railroads were dismantled and moved to the east. Between 1945 and 1953 the Soviets transported an immense amount of equipment, goods, and money from their zone to the Soviet Union.

Thus, with fewer resources and no foreign assistance, the denuded and newly created German Democratic Republic had to make heroic efforts not only to rebuild itself, but merely to survive. Stringent economic measures as well as strenuous efforts to train and use every calorie of human energy must be seen, therefore, in the light of necessity as well as Marxist-Leninist ideology. The introduction of "polytechnic education" made good economic sense, while also underlining the dictum of Blonskij that "industrialism is the greatest victory of man over nature."[5]

With respect to cultural ties, geography combined with politics in determining the orientation of this new German state. Whereas West Germany remained contiguous to and in contact with traditional sources of German cultural exchange in the West, East Germany was now isolated from France, Britain, Italy, and the other Western countries. In addition, the GDR became increasingly isolated from West Germany as well; what began as a political separation soon became cultural. East Germany was increasingly incorporated into the Eastern European, Communist bloc of states, which was largely Slavic in language and culture and Russian dominated. Indeed, Russian became the required second language of young East Germans.

Thus the political separation of Germany, which was eventually sealed with a wall, became a cultural rift as well. The official ruling party of the GDR, the all-powerful SED (United Socialist Party), sought to control the cultural life of the country by forming official organizations of writers, artists, and scholars. State-controlled publishing houses and bookstores carefully determined what citizens could read; books and magazines could not be mailed to or carried into the GDR. Radio and television broadcasts were and are state controlled; viewing and listening to West German programs is discouraged.

On the other hand, cultural contact with the socialist "brother nations" of the East, especially the Soviet Union, is strongly encouraged and officially supported. For example, the "Society for German-Soviet Friendship" (DSF) claimed in 1978 a membership of 5.5 million members, or one-third of the total population. Its official motto is: "Learning from the Soviet Union Means Learning to Be Victorious." The society owns a publishing house and edits weekly and monthly magazines; it also supports "Circles for Learning the Russian Language" and "Circles for the Utilization of Soviet Experiences," among others. Membership in such an organization not only counts as minimal proof on the part of any citizen of necessary "societal involvement," but also satisfies one of the necessary prerequisites for admission to universities.[6]

Other indicators of Eastern bloc cultural orientation are numerous. Young people in the GDR who want to visit foreign countries are directed to the eastern European socialist states exclusively. In 1977, 4,200 students from the GDR were studying at Soviet universities, while *Jugendtourist,* the official tourist agency for young people, arranged 125,000 tours to allied socialist states.[7] The curriculum of East German schools not only requires the study of Russian, but also gives Soviet history and literature a preeminent place. And GDR universities maintain numerous friendship agreements with partner institutions in the East: 63 with the USSR, 50 with Poland, 44 with Czechoslovakia, 44 with Hungary, 17 with Bulgaria, and 11 with Rumania (1978).[8] According to the official cultural-political handbook of the GDR, cultural policy is determined by the necessity to "create the fundamental preconditions for the gradual transition to Communism." This requires a "continuously deepening friendship and cooperation with the Soviet Union and the other countries of the socialist community of states."[9]

Of course, official cultural policy does not solely determine the cultural tastes and inclinations of people. Cultural traditions as well as the presence of the other, larger German twin beyond the Elbe and Werra (and in West Berlin) constantly challenges the geocultural orientation of the GDR. Although censorship is strict in order to maintain the cultural separation, Western radio and television broadcasts as well as Western visitors and mail thwart official policies.

According to East German authorities, however, this cultural rift is nothing new. If, at present, it takes the form of a separation between the capitalist Federal Republic and the socialist GDR, previously it existed in a different form, in the culture of the proletariat. As Erich Honecker, the East German head of state, described the situation in 1973, "Look at the history books in the two German states: there are two histories. A common culture? There have always been two cultures in Germany: that of the ruling class of exploiters and that of the laboring masses."[10]

However, a Marxist view of history does not solely determine East German cultural policies. Witness, for example, the 1983 commemoration of the birth of Martin Luther 500 years earlier. Most of Luther's life had been spent in what is now the GDR: Eisleben, where he was born, Wittenberg, where he taught; and Wartburg, where he took refuge. The East Germans celebrated the anniversary as though Luther was a patron saint of communism. They restored important locales in the life of Luther, sponsored international meetings of Luther scholars, mounted important commemorative exhibitions, and published documents and encomia. Virtually no mention was made of the traditional Marxist view of Luther as the "gravedigger of German liberty" or the "greatest spiritual figure of the counterrevolution." Friedrich Engels, Marx's colleague, had castigated Luther in his study of the Peasant's War as not only the enemy of the true revolutionary, Thomas Muenzer, but also the man who betrayed the German peasants to the German princes and landlords.[11]

Yet, the GDR has now fully rehabilitated Luther as a national hero. Between 1965 and 1980 he was gradually reinterpreted and then fully integrated into the revolutionary tradition. Erich Honecker himself led the way and took the chair of the Martin Luther Committee, which consisted of 100 important officials and celebrities representing every aspect of GDR political and cultural life. The Committee not only planned the state festivities in honor of Luther's 500th birthday, but launched the new Marxist image of Luther as well. Luther was now hailed as a genuine revolutionary figure whose deeds, such as the posting of his 95 theses on the door of the Wittenberg Cathedral, earned him an honored place in East German historiography. He was even praised as the man who helped to ignite the Peasant's War of 1524–1525, rather than as the reactionary who helped to suppress it. As the official party organ of the SED noted: "With the victory of the working class and its allies, with the founding and building of Socialism, the conditions have now been created for a complete and just scholarly appreciation of Martin Luther. We honor those who have struggled in past generations under personal risk to bring about progress and enrich culture. . . . This is particularly true with regard to Martin Luther. . . . Martin Luther's progressive heritage is preserved in the socialist German national culture."[12] Indeed, Erich Honecker invited Karl Carstens, the president of West Germany, to come to Eisleben with him on November 10, 1983, to celebrate the day of Luther's birth. Carstens refused the invitation.

There are many other geocultural factors that divide the two Germanys; we have mentioned only some of the salient ones. For example, we have not described regional or folkloric differences that have loomed large in Germany's divided past, nor have we discussed the extent of religious differences; traditionally most of the GDR was Protestant, while the Federal Republic was about one-half Protestant and one-half Catholic. We have been able, however, to indicate that the German twins, although born of the same trauma, received different birthrights from the moment of their appearance. And, as we shall now describe in the pages that follow, they received different foster parents as well.

DIFFERENT FOSTER PARENTS

Following the defeat of Nazi Germany, the leaders of the victorious Allied powers met at Potsdam and agreed to suppress completely every vestige of fascism and militarism in their former foe. To this end, the victors concurred that "German education shall be so controlled . . . to make possible the successful development of democratic ideas."[13]

But the Allies, however much they agreed on what they opposed, could not agree on what was meant by "democratic ideas" or how these ideas should be implemented. Given the vast differences that existed between the political and educational systems of the triumphant states, lack of agreement on how to democratize Germany should have come as no surprise. In the months and years that followed, the educational authorities in the military zones of occupation relied on their own experiences as the means of implementing the Potsdam agreements. U.S. "education officers," for example, had usually attended comprehensive public high schools (or private boarding schools) before receiving a college or university education. Their British counterparts, on the other hand, had most likely spent several years in the exclusive precincts of a grammar school or public school such as Eton or Harrow, and then gone up to the hoary halls of Oxford and Cambridge. Soviet educational administrators were probably much less formally educated, since the Soviet Union had suffered such severe disruption during the war and Soviet educational goals were far from being realized in any case. Even as late as 1958, Nikita Krushchev complained that only 80 percent of Soviet children were completing the "Seven Years' School," which had long been mandatory. In any case, Soviet authorities were undoubtedly selected and trained as convinced communists.

Certainly the occupying powers exerted a great influence on educational institutions and goals as they were established in the years following the war. Yet deep-seated educational traditions gradually reasserted themselves, especially in the case of the Federal Republic.

Although the West German state was founded in 1949, the Allied high commissioners preserved some influence until 1955. The overall situation in that first decade following the war was not unlike that of three disagreeing teachers trying to control a very willful child. The Americans favored a six-year elementary school and a comprehensive, differentiated secondary school for all students in grades seven to twelve, thereby integrating the elite *Gymnasium* with more vocationally oriented secondary schools. The "American way" meant making all secondary education courses equally accessible to all students, no matter what their social class background. It also meant giving social studies a greater emphasis in the curriculum and encouraging more student self-government.[14] All of these measures were seen as promoting democracy in a society that was viewed as class-ridden. Ironically, however, U.S. planners also showed much sympathy for the development of private schools, which undoubtedly says something about the educational backgrounds of some of the U.S. officials.

The British educational authorities also favored the democratizing of German schools, but were less avid and programmatic than their transatlantic allies. Under the British plan, the traditional four-year German elementary school would also be extended to six years, but thereafter German youths would be directed into one of three secondary schools, according to the abilities and career goals of the students. On the much disputed issue of whether to establish denominational schools (Catholic or Protestant), the British preferred to defer to "local educational authorities," as was generally the case in England.

As might be anticipated, the French, in their zone of military occupation, undertook the re-education of the Germans as a *"mission civilisatrice."* Assuming strict control of the school system, they sought to increase German appreciation for "liberté," individualism, and clear, self-reliant thinking. They believed no better vehicle existed for inculcating these values than the French language; its study became mandatory on a daily basis, while Latin was deleted from the first three years of the *Gymnasium* (grades five to seven). Some expansion of curriculum choice was also introduced at the upper levels of the same school.

Such broad differences of opinion virtually invited resistance from the German people. Like any determined student, it knew all the arguments and answers. Who among the Allied powers could really reject appeals to the "Christian-humanist tradition," on which German schools were supposedly based prior to the Nazis? Or who could gainsay such time-honored concepts as parents' rights to choose an appropriate education for their children, the effectiveness of "inner reforms" as opposed to structural changes in schools, and a commitment to quality education? Various West German interest groups had little difficulty in using differences and ambivalences among the occupying powers in order to achieve their goal of reconstructing the traditional German educational system in the Federal Republic.

This does not mean that most Germans opposed democratization of education. Many traditionalists merely favored a return to pre-Nazi norms, however elitist these may have been. Broad support for such norms came from middle-class parent organizations, conservative political parties, and elite teacher organizations, many of which became stalwart partners of Allied military governments. Essentially, these groups favored a return to a universal, four-year comprehensive elementary school, followed by a differentiated system of middle and secondary schools. The academic elite would matriculate in a language-oriented, humanistic *Gymnasium* (grades five to thirteen), similar to those that had traditionally inspired (or repelled) so many Germans of earlier generations. The working class, however, would receive a short, basic upper-elementary education (grades five to eight) and then enter apprenticeships while continuing in part-time vocational schools. Pupils who fell between these two educational tracks, often the children of lower middle-class parents, would attend a six-year middle school (grades five to ten) before entering vocational schools or joining the labor force. Such a tripartite system had the weight of tradition behind it and was not seriously discredited by any association with Nazism. Indeed, the Nazis had rejected much of this system as too academic and not sufficiently practical.

The dilemma of allied educational reformers went even deeper: was not the idea of *imposing* democracy on a people itself a contradictory notion? It was one thing to expunge Nazism; it was another to compel Germans to accept an educational system that fit Allied ideals, especially when the victors could not themselves agree on the best system for the Germans.

In the end not even those goals to which the Allies unanimously subscribed, such as the compulsory six-year elementary school, ever reached fruition. The willful German child got its way.

Two additional factors, it should be mentioned, mitigated against full implementation of Allied re-education plans. First, given the dire economic straits of Germany during the early postwar years, ever greater attention was diverted to economic reconstruction rather than re-education. By the time the Marshall Plan had stimulated an economic recovery, a rather traditional school system was already well established.

Second, the Western Allies came to favor a decentralized system of educational control, vesting power in the German states (*Laender*) rather than in a centralized ministry of education. In so doing, they responded to the brief period in German history, when under the Nazis, coercive centralized power had been employed for destructive goals. Unintentionally, thereby, the Western "foster parents" strengthened the conservative structure of West German school systems. They became insulated against reform initiatives from below (which is frequently the origin of reforms in Britain and the United States) or reorganization from above (as is usually the case in states such as Sweden).

Thus, the Western democracies, in the end, did not provide any uniform educational plan for democratizing the larger German twin. In piecemeal fashion, the various German states made minor modifications in order to satisfy the demands of the occupying officials. Genuine educational reform would only occur later, in the 1960s and 1970s, when German citizens began to demand greater possibilities for social mobility.

By contrast to the discordant Western foster parents, the Soviet "parent" appears much firmer, more certain, and self-assured. And it would seem, therefore, that the smaller Germany, the GDR, would have benefitted thereby from more consistent parenting. This was not entirely the case, however.

Indeed, the Soviet leaders had little doubt that democratization meant inculcation of the principles of Marx and Lenin as they understood them, but at first they had no clear idea of what this meant with respect to school reorganization in their zone of Germany or exactly how re-education would proceed. Even in the Soviet Union itself the educational system was still in a state of flux. Following the Revolution of 1917–21, radical experimentation had given way to narrow traditionalism. In postwar Russia, an unswerving ideological commitment had to be combined with pressing demands for economic reconstruction.

Nevertheless, the Soviets had developed a number of clear ideas for their zone of Germany regarding school organization, curriculum, and methodology. They had also trained the nucleus of a teaching corps among emigrant German communists who had fled to Moscow during the Nazi period. But most important of all, the Soviets were more single-minded and forceful in imposing their influence and will on the vanquished East Germans. In this respect, they differed dramatically from their Western allies.

Notably, not all of these clearly defined educational principles can be traced to Moscow. The Germans, too, had a Marxist pedagogical tradition that could be called upon for guidance and precedents. In fact, the standard history of education used by the GDR makes special note of this tradition, going well back into the nineteenth century for inspiration, but giving special honors to communist educators of the Weimar period, some of whom now emerged as pedagogical leaders in the postwar period.

Among the most inviolable principles upon which East German education would be based were the following:

- School education is the monopoly of the state; there shall be no private schools, no religious education nor any religious influence within the school system
- The preeminent role of the working class must be taken into consideration in the reorganization of the schools. The rule of the bourgeoisie must be broken and all fascist influences must be eliminated
- The principles of Marxism–Leninism must take precedence in the schools, as well as friendship with the Soviet Union.

From these principles it followed logically with respect to school organization and curriculum that:

- Schools had to be organized into a uniform, comprehensive, and undifferentiated system in order to integrate all social and ability groups and to give working-class children optimal opportunities in education.
- The curriculum would have to be unstratified and compulsory for all in order to guarantee a "harmonious, well-rounded, general education" in accordance with party and state plans.

Of course, the development of a school system was only one part of a larger, long-range plan for building a new socialist-communist society in the Soviet zone of Germany. As noted above, a number of communist refugees had been prepared for the task of repatriation, and immediately assumed leading roles in the occupation, most notably among the "Group Ulbricht," whose motto was: "Everything must appear democratic, but we must hold all power in our hands."[15]

Under the Soviet Military Administration, one reform quickly followed another: large landed estates were broken up and redistributed in 1945; the older Social Democratic and Communist parties were merged into the new SED (United Socialist Party) under Communist Party control in 1946; judicial reforms with the appointment of "People's Judges" and assumption of control of the law courts by the SED took place in 1945–46; industrial reforms were initiated in 1946; and a "Democratic Bloc" was organized in 1948 to include all political parties and mass organizations. The Democratic Bloc (which became the "National Front" in 1949) organized public elections by preparing an *Einheitsliste* (unified list), which guaranteed each party and mass organization a predetermined number of seats in the *Volkskammer* (Assembly). This effectively meant that all political groups had to accept the primacy of the SED and its Central Committee and Politburo.

The growing rift between the Soviet Union and its former Allies soon cast every "reform" in a Cold War context. The blockade of Berlin in 1948–49, the birth of the two Germanys in 1949, and the integration of the new states into East–West blocs gave every action of the Allied powers a permanency and significance that might not have originally been intended.

As early as 1946, however, the Soviets had carried out broad school reforms independent of their former Allies. Under the "Law for the Democratization of the German School," the Soviet Military Administration decreed an absolute state monopoly over education and established an eight-year, tuition-free, compulsory elementary school. This was done while the Americans, British, and French were still debating the extension of the traditional German four-year Basic School (*Grundschule*) to six years. Contemporary East German historians have lauded this unilateral action on the part of their Soviet foster parent. As one noted, "The Law established a unified, eight-year elementary school for all children, whose level of instruction was considerably higher than that of the old German *Volksschule*. This was accomplished during a time of dire distress and would not have been possible without the generous assistance, material as well as otherwise, of the Soviet Military Administration."[16]

The same historian has also praised the enthusiasm and efficiency of "some 40,000 politically reliable (*integer*) new teachers (*Neulehrer*), young workers, employees, and other members of the working class, who very frequently following brief training, filled the places left vacant by dismissed ex-Nazis and other missing teachers."[17]

Indeed, it appears that such terms as "de-Nazification" and "democratization" were also code words for "dethronement of the bourgeoisie" and the establishment of socialist-communist schools.[18] This was especially so with respect to teachers. Approximately 70 percent of all teachers in the Soviet Zone were replaced by "politically reliable members of the working class," who were initially trained by "trustworthy" experienced teachers either in part-time seminars or directly on the job. Later this was done in ideologically refurbished pedagogical institutes and universities.

From the outset, teacher training was not only decidedly anti-fascist, but was also critical of the educational programs of the Weimar Republic as well. It emphasized the ideology of Marx and Lenin and closely followed Soviet educational philosophy and teacher training programs. In defining the role of the "new teacher," the Executive Committee of the SED asserted:

> The teacher must be a fighter for the goals of the political leaders. He must support the National Front. . . . Every teacher must be a friend of the Soviet Union. As a friend of the Soviet Union, he must study the knowledge and experiences of the Soviet Union.[19]

Indeed, in Thuringia by 1947, 63 percent of the newly recruited teachers were members of the SED, and 77 percent were members of the official union (FDGB).[20]

Thus, the German Democratic Republic, founded in 1949, could then continue to build on the ideological base that the Soviets had created for education in their zone of occupation. In 1952 the SED adopted as its primary educational goal the "building of the foundations for socialism." More specifically, this meant the well-rounded education of citizens who are "able and prepared to build up Socialism and to defend the achievement of the workers to the utmost."[21] In that same year the GDR moved decisively in the direction of centralization. First, it abolished the *Laender,* thus making East Germany a homogeneous political unit, and, second, it adopted the Soviet model of "democratic centralism," which became the instrument of Party control in all sectors of public life, including education. Meanwhile, the German Central Paedagogical Institute, which had been founded in 1949, continued its revision of curriculum and textbooks along Marxist-Leninist lines, while the Socialist youth organization (FDJ), following the model of the Soviet Komsomol, added another element of control to the lives of young East Germans.

In summary, then, the German twins, heavily influenced by their respective parents, developed in almost opposite directions. The Western sibling grew into a many-headed thing — pluralistic, federalistic, and capitalistic. Under the discordant tutelage of the Western Allies, the Federal Republic spawned an educational system that contained all the strengths as well as the weaknesses of a Western democratic system:

• Control by the *Laender* has made it possible for diverse factors (historic, cultural, economic, etc.) to influence education while, at the same time, limiting the possibilities for centralized synchronization. This has probably made schools more conservative with respect to making changes in school organization, curricula, etc.

• Diverse interest groups such as churches, political parties, trade unions, and teachers' organizations have exercised an influence on education, which has thereby furthered democratic participation and shared responsibility. But this has also resulted in a competition for influence in which power, money, and access to the media have become critical for success. Needless to say, these are the very things that foreign workers, minorities, and the poor are least likely to have.

• The great variety of schools and curricula make it possible for all children to develop personal interests and abilities in a heterogeneous and culturally diversified setting, although it happens that children of the upper half of society are better able to use these opportunities than children of the lower half.[22]

Similarly, the East Germans, under the tutelage of the Soviet Union, have created a system following the ideological and institutional patterns of the USSR:

• A homogeneous, centralized, and unified school system with a required curriculum for all children, yet one that is easily changed according to the "needs of the society" as identified by its political leaders.

• A so-called high-level general education for all, giving special attention to working-class children, which in practice turns out to be an instrument of propaganda for the SED and "our friend, the great Soviet Union." Students, therefore, who hope to succeed and gain university admission, must be loyal and active adherents to the prevailing Marxist-Leninist creed. Individual needs and goals may be served — as long as they are compatible with socialist ideology and the economic needs of society.

Thus the German twins, born of the same seed, have grown apart under the guardianship of Eastern and Western foster parents. The divergent societies that have resulted are based on different social and economic philosophies; education has been shaped to serve these two systems. It will be our task in the following chapters to describe the educational estrangement of these twins and its consequences.

NOTES

Epigraph to Chapter 2 is from the national anthem of the Federal Republic of Germany, Hoffman von Fallersleben (1794–1874).

1. Golo Mann, *The History of Germany Since 1789,* translated by Marion Jackson (New York, 1968), p. 435.
2. Cf. Minna Regina Falk, *History of Germany* (New York, 1957); William Lawrence Shirer, *The Rise and Fall of the Third Reich* (New York, 1960); Alexander Abusch, *Der Irrweg einer Nation,* 8th ed. (Berlin, 1960); Alan John Percivale Taylor, *The Origins of the Second World War* (London, 1961); Esmonde Manning Robertson, ed., *The Origins of the Second World War* (London, 1971); Maurice Baumont, *The Origins of the Second World War,* translated by Simone De Couvrer Ferguson (New Haven, 1978).
3. Elchanan Cohn, *The Economics of Education,* rev. ed. (Cambridge, MA, 1979); Organization for Economic Cooperation and Development, *Planning Education for Economic and Social Development,* edited by Herbert S. Parnes (Paris, 1963); Hasso von Recum, *Bildungsoekonomie im Wandel* (Braunschweig, 1978).
4. Between 1960 and 1980 the percentage of 16-year-olds in full-time education increased from 25.2 to 63.3; the percentage of graduates from secondary schools who qualify for college/university increased from 7.3 to 22 percent of the age group. In 1960 only 79,400 new students entered higher education (27 percent women); in 1980, 216,000 (40.1 percent women). Bundesminister fuer Bildung und Wissenschaft, *Grund- und Strukturdaten* (Bonn, 1982–83).
5. Pavel Petrovich Blonskij, *Trudovaja skola* (Moskva, 1919).
6. Bundesminister fuer innerdeutsche Beziehungen, ed., *DDR Handbuch,* 2d ed., rev. and enl. (Koeln, 1979), p. 467f.
7. Ibid., p. 1085f.
8. Ibid., p. 1107.
9. Manfred Berger, ed., *Kulturpolitisches Woerterbuch,* 2d ed., rev. and enl. (Berlin, 1978).

10. E. Honecker, in his presentation to the 9th SED Convention, May 1973.

11. Abusch, *Irrweg einer Nation*, pp. 23, 27; Frederick Engels, *The Peasant War in Germany*, translated by Moissaye J. Olgin (New York, 1966), pp. 50–73.

12. *Einheit: Zeitschrift fuer Theorie und Praxis des wissenschaftlichen Sozialismus*, Vol. 9 (Berlin, 1981).

13. U.S. State Department, Office of Public Affairs, *Germany, 1947–1949* (Washington, D.C., 1950), p. 49.

14. For details see Arthur Hearnden, *Education, Culture and Politics in West Germany* (Oxford, 1976).

15. *DDR Handbuch*, p. 500.

16. Helmut Klein, *Bildung in der DDR* (Reinbek, 1974), p. 50.

17. Ibid., p. 50f.

18. Cf. Johannes Niermann, *Lehrer in der DDR* (Heidelberg, 1973), p. 22ff.

19. Ibid., p. 35.

20. Ibid., p. 40. FDGB stands for *Freier Deutscher Gewerkschaftsbund* (Free German Workers' Union).

21. Arthur Hearnden, *Education in the Two Germanies* (Oxford, 1974), p. 64.

22. For an excellent description of education in West Germany in English, see *Between Elite and Mass Education: Education in the Federal Republic of Germany*, translated by Raymond Meyer and Adriane Heinrichs-Goodwin (Albany, 1983). This work also contains a thorough bibliography of other works in English and German.

3

PUBLIC AND PRIVATE
VALUES
IN THE GERMAN
DEMOCRATIC REPUBLIC

My partner for life should be . . . tender and amorous. He also
must view our world with a Marxist-Leninist perspective.

From a letter of a 20-year-old woman
printed in *Junge Welt*

OFFICIAL COMMANDMENTS AND PLEDGES

Are you prepared as true patriots to continue deepening our close friendship
with the Soviet Union, strengthening our brotherhood with socialist
countries, struggling in the spirit of proletarian internationalism to protect
peace and to defend socialism against every imperialist aggression? If so,
answer "yes, we pledge to do so."[1]

Each spring, in what amounts to a rite of passage, the 14-year-olds of
the German Democratic Republic are officially admitted into the society of
their elders. Approximately a quarter of a million boys and girls gather in
public places and solemnly pledge their fealty to their state, its allies, and
the principles of international socialism. In this ceremony, known as the
Jugendweihe (Ordination of Youth), the young people declaim four
pledges, the last of which we have quoted above.

Perhaps no better source of public values exists for a society than the
oaths that it extracts from its young people. Certainly this is true for the
GDR, where public statements of loyalty and enthusiasm command great
respect. In their annual ceremony the East German teen-agers promise
above all to support the "great and noble cause of Socialism" and "the

revolutionary heritage of the people." This means vowing to strengthen bonds of friendship with Eastern bloc countries, especially the Soviet Union, and fighting the enemies of socialism, whether they be domestic dissidents or alien imperialists. In addition, these loyal sons and daughters of the workers' state (*Arbeiter-und-Bauern-Staat*) promise to strive for excellence in "education and culture," "to learn unflinchingly," not so much for personal development, but for the "realization of our great humanistic ideals." They pledge to unite their personal happiness "with the struggle for the happiness of the nation."

The question is, of course, how deeply the values contained in these official pledges penetrate the psyches of the pledgers. No one truly knows. The distinction between public and private value systems, difficult to discern in an open society, remains even more occluded in a closed one. Yet, since such oaths form an important part of life in the GDR and other socialist countries, it is relatively easy to describe the "official values" in these states. Not only do 14-year-olds make their pledges, but so do newly trained workers, for example, about to enter the labor force. Moreover, such public proclamations of fealty are only the final stage of a long period of preparation, during which these values are inculcated in an extended series of political education sessions.

Walter Ulbricht (1893–1973), a "grand old man" of German communism and president of the GDR from 1960 to 1973, delivered his "Ten Commandments of Socialist Morality" to the Fifth Party Congress of the SED (United Socialist Party) in 1958. Although Ulbricht never claimed to have received these on a socialist Mount Sinai, the tone is Mosaic. They were adopted as part of the official SED program in 1963 and are worth quoting at length:

1. You shall always support the international solidarity of the working class and of all working people as well as the inviolable solidarity of all socialist countries.
2. You shall love your Fatherland and always be prepared to use all of your power and abilities for the defense of the Workers' State.
3. You shall help to abolish the exploitation of man by man.
4. You shall accomplish good deeds for socialism, because socialism leads to a better life for all working people.
5. In the building of socialism, you shall act in the spirit of mutual help and friendly cooperation, respect the collective, and take its criticism to heart.
6. You shall protect and increase the people's property.
7. You shall always strive to improve your performance, be sparing and strengthening socialist work discipline.

8. You shall train your children in the spirit of peace and socialism so that they will become well-rounded [*allseitig gebildet*], high-principled, and physically strong.
9. You shall live in a clean and decent way and respect your family.
10. You shall practice solidarity with peoples who are fighting for their national liberation and those who are defending their national independence.[2]

Of course, a number of questions immediately arise: What are the ideological origins of such commandments and pledges? Do they represent an alien set of doctrines that people such as Ulbricht and his successors are trying to impose on East German citizenry? Or do such values have German roots that give them popular legitimacy and acceptance? Will the officially propagated value system ever truly coincide with popular values? After all, the entire structure of the GDR — its schools, its laws, its institutions, and the media — are dedicated to translating these publicly proclaimed values into popular currency. As stated in GDR rhetoric, these are the values that represent the *genuine* strivings of the people and will in the end liberate them from capitalist (i.e., bourgeois) domination. For all of these reasons, it is worth examining these doctrines more carefully. Let us begin by discussing those principles most frequently articulated in GDR litany.

FREEDOM FROM EXPLOITATION

Freedom is a magical concept, clearly one of the most appealing of all human ideals. Heroes and heroines die for freedom; the founding documents of every state extol it. And yet freedom remains an ambiguous concept. In Western liberal societies, political philosophers and citizens have most frequently defined it in individualistic terms. Characterized by an absence of constraints, freedom in these societies permits people to pursue personal goals and to act according to their own self-interests. And yet even the most ardent advocates of laissez-faire liberties acknowledge that their notion of freedom is not an absolute one. Freedom is limited by natural and material resources, circumscribed by physical and psychic powers, and abridged by the rights of other people as well as moral laws.

Freedom therefore remains a problematic value. At various times and places, people have cherished and defended many different kinds of freedom: the freedom to travel, the freedom to worship, the freedom to speak openly, the freedom to accumulate property, and the freedom to choose one's own government; and as many as are the forms of freedom for which people strive, so numerous too are the kinds of constraints that inhibit or prevent their realization. Slavery crudely inhibits freedom, but so too does poverty. Various subtle forms of mind control and manipulation also limit freedom. One person exercising his or her freedom may in turn prevent others from doing likewise. Freedom may also be seen as a cultural concept, defined differently by various nations and cultural groups.

In Germany, for example, the idea of freedom has had a different history than in Britain and France.[3] Whereas the great British and French political philosophers defined freedom in terms of individual rights and even in some memorable instances, justified revolution as a means to gain such rights, their German counterparts usually described obedience to moral principles embodied in the state as the means to gain freedom. John Locke, the great English political philosopher, justified revolution in the name of "inalienable rights." His successors, Adam Smith and John Stuart Mill, further extolled and enshrined individual rights in the economic and political spheres. In France, freedom became associated with the *philosophes,* the revolution, and slogans such as "liberté, egalité, et fraternité." In Germany, on the other hand, where statism has had a powerful and persistent history, terms such as "inner freedom" and "German freedom" came into usage. Friedrich Schiller's (1759–1805) variation on Rousseau's famous line expresses this difference quite well: "Man is free even if born in chains."

The German Enlightenment philosopher, Immanual Kant (1724–1804), ponderously defined freedom as obedience to universal moral laws. Kant, who remained throughout his life a loyal subject of the absolute Prussian monarchy, never did justify revolutions as a moral human right, however immoral the government under which one lived. Reform, he insisted, is a duty "not of the citizens but of the head of state." Kant quoted Frederick the Great of Prussia: "Argue as much as you will and about what you will, but obey."[4] The individual must be compelled "to obey a general will under which every man could be free."[5]

George Wilhelm Friedrich Hegel (1770–1831), the other monumental German political philosopher of the age, even more explicitly declared that individual freedom could only be realized in conjunction with the state. He praised the state as "that form of reality in which the individual has and enjoys his freedom; but on the condition of his recognizing, believing in, and willing that which is common to the Whole."[6]

Political thinkers in the GDR, therefore, may even make a strong claim that their state represents a truer embodiment of the German idea of freedom than the Federal Republic, which has tried to adopt and adapt alien traditions. In innumerable speeches and publications, the West is castigated not only for its "capitalism," but for its "licentious individualism" as well.

Yet, freedom in the GDR means, foremost, "Freedom from Exploitation," which emanates from Karl Marx rather than any particular German or non-German tradition. Marx had described in *Das Kapital* the exploitation of human productivity and the existence of private property as two of the most significant impediments to human freedom. These are clearly embodied in the third and sixth of Walter Ulbricht's commandments: "You shall help to abolish the exploitation of man by man," and "You shall protect and increase the people's property."

According to Marx (and Ulbricht et al.), private ownership of property and resources leads to private exploitation of productive labor. This in turn results in the deprecation of human dignity. Productive labor after all is the "life activity" that provides the producer with dignity as well as goods. Hegel had argued, and Marx concurred, that produced property is the "embodiment of personality, through which alone personality achieves objective reality."[7] The worker, Marx added, "sees his own reflection in a world which he has constructed." In perverting the process of production, capitalism deprives the worker, not only of his goods, but of his dignity as well.[8] The true freedom of the worker cannot be restored until capitalism is superseded by socialism, until a system based on "unlimited individualism" and "cut-throat competition" is replaced by one based on cooperation.[9]

According to the official doctrines of the GDR, capitalism thus alienates the worker: (1) from his labor and product, (2) from his fellow workers, and (3) from himself. In the end it "produces man as a spiritually and physically dehumanized being."[10]

If capitalism exploits the labor of the workers and alienates them, socialism, as it is officially defined in the GDR, ennobles the workers' labor and helps them to give genuine meaning to their lives. This leads us to the concept of *work* in the GDR.

WORK

The official daily party newspaper of the GDR is *Neues Deutschland.* Frequently in its pages, the exploits of workers, as models of socialist behavior, are reported at length. For example, in the March 13, 1983, issue, Gunnar Schrank, a highway construction worker, plays this role. Schrank, who is also a delegate to the Congress of Young Workers (*Arbeiterjugend*), exemplifies the worker who subordinates himself to his collective. Through "strong wind, gusts of snow, ankle-deep mud . . . day by day the 26-year-old comrade must endure special trials with his collective. . . ." He seeks neither privileges nor the role of a leader: "the collective aims high, which demands his full commitment." Schrank embodies in himself the goals of the FDJ, the state youth organization, whose members pledge to achieve the "highest efficiency every day" and to save time, energy, and material and make maximum use of technology. "With his readiness to undertake unusual tasks, the young comrade causes his group to exceed what is required."

Gunnar Schrank is of course reminiscent of Alexei Stakhanov, the Soviet miner whose feats of labor have been used to inspire others in the USSR since 1931. Like Stakhanov, Schrank does not labor for personal gain, but for his collective and the GDR. Surpassing his 1983 quota means more apartments, Schrank explains: "The housing program of our party is outstanding in German history . . . it is wonderful to help build happiness for the people."

In his encomium on Gunnar Schrank, the reporter for *Neues Deutschland* employs both contemporary socialist rhetoric as well as quotations from Friedrich Engels: "'There is only one way of overcoming the housing shortage: to do away with the exploitation and oppression of the working class altogether.' In our Republic this has been accomplished. . . . The capitalistic exploitation of society has been overthrown and socialistic conditions have been achieved which allow us to tackle the housing problem as a social task."

The example of Schrank reifies several of those values that appeared in Ulbricht's "Commandments of Socialist Morality." Unlike the alienated workers in a capitalist society, Comrade Schrank fully understands that "good deeds for Socialism . . . lead to a better life for all working people" (fourth commandment). He will have fulfilled his pledge to "use all his knowledge and abilities for the realization of our great humanistic ideals" (second commandment).

Labor, therefore, is the single human activity that permits the worker to gain self-realization while contributing to social progress. In addition, it serves an important educational function and provides a crucial component in the curriculum of every classroom of the GDR.

It must be noted, however, that Marxist theories of labor and history fully embrace the industrial system. There is no trace of nostalgia for pre-industrial artisan work. As early as 1848, Marx and Engels in their *Manifesto of the Communist Party* declared that industrialization, however much it may appear the cause of misery and oppression, will eventually provide the remedy for poverty and class exploitation: "The advance of industry, whose involuntary promoter is the bourgeoisie, replaces the isolation of the laborers, due to competition, by their revolutionary combination, due to association."[11]

Industrialization itself involves ever more efficient application of natural laws in machines and factories, which is seen as one of man's noblest endeavors. And industrial labor not only solves the problem of commodity production, it also satisfies other basic human needs as well. It compels men to reorganize for cooperation and will eventually leave no room for selfish class antagonisms. Industrialization produces both goods and values. It eventually restores human dignity, which had become a casualty of history.

This theory, therefore, helps us to understand the immense effort being made in the GDR and other communist countries in the fields of science, technology, and industry. It accounts for the enormous pride of achievement in such areas as space exploration. It explains the elevation of Comrade Gunnar Schrank to the rank of "hero." Virtually self-taught, Schrank had qualified himself for an important technical position in his *Kombinat* (collective) and now helped to build "housing and happiness" for his countrymen and comrades.

The extraordinarily high value placed on productive industrial labor also explains its inclusion in the educational curriculum. The term that describes this is *polytechnic education,* a group of subjects, and beyond that, a leading principle of all instruction (see Chapter 8).

Understandably, the growth of the computer age has taxed the imagination of Marxists and GDR theorists as the center of gravity in industrial production has shifted from traditional engines and machine tools to computers. The computer engineer and specialist have begun to challenge the primacy of the factory worker in the industrial system. This development has profoundly influenced the political-economic ideology of the Eastern bloc states as well as their educational philosophies.

Ideologists now label this the "Scientific-Technical Revolution" and must make room for the new breed of electronic specialist alongside the machine worker. They, too, perform socially useful labor. An updated version of Gunnar Schrank in GDR media wears a smock coat rather than overalls and has clean hands rather than grease-daubed ones; he performs heroic deeds for society at the console of his computer.

Failure to appreciate fully the implications of these changes in the area of work was one of the causes that led to the fall of Nikita Krushchev in the Soviet Union in 1964. His reforms in education had emphasized industrial training in factories and agricultural collectives as part of polytechnic education, while neglecting the rise of the new "Scientific-Technical Revolution."[12]

The rise of cybernetics has led to other ideological tensions among communist theorists as well. In stressing the importance of the electronic specialist and "intellectual worker," the electronic revolution promises to transfer ever more power to an intellectual elite. The traditional communist promise of resolving the conflict between the intellectual worker and the manual worker becomes ever more elusive to achieve. Management of the means of production seems even less likely to be vested in the hands of industrial workers. As one critic has noted: "The economic and political orders come from a functionary [political and technological] elite who have appropriated control over all relevant economic and political processes."[13] The workers' alienation from their labor, from one another, and from themselves has taken on a new and more efficient form.

Our purpose in this chapter, however, is not to examine the recent difficulties of communist ideologists in the GDR, but rather to explore the value structures of both German states and their effects. With that in mind, let us return to work and the formidable role that it plays in the value structure of the GDR. Having discussed the meaning of this term and its idealized manifestations (e.g., Gunnar Schrank), we must now turn to the particular qualitative aspects of work in the official litany of the GDR. In this regard, three qualities especially stand out: (1) the quality of work as experienced by the workers, (2) the quality of its results, and (3) the qualitative link between the two, which is called "socialist work morale."

With respect to workers and their work, communist theory from Marx to the present has been unswerving in its commitment to dissolving the alienation that exists between the worker and his/her labor. Ideally, unalienated work is "a man's life activity." Once alienation is ended, as in socialized factories or LPGs (Agricultural Production Cooperatives), communist theorists maintain even the hardest and most grueling labor becomes an entirely different and more satisfying experience for the worker. Gunnar Schrank, it should be recalled, did not strive to earn more than his comrades as he would have in a capitalist system, but gained satisfaction in striving for his "highest efficiency every day," whether in "storm, snow or knee-deep mud," thus causing his comrades as well "to achieve more than is ordered."

The net result of socialized working conditions and unalienated labor, according to Marx, Lenin, and their followers, will be an increase in efficiency and productivity on the part of workers. And socialist workers in the end, with their higher productivity, will triumph over exploited capitalist labor. Krushchev's famous dictum made in 1960 on an Iowa farm, "We will bury you!" meant just that. Soviet labor, not Soviet bombs, would eventually triumph over capitalist labor. Precisely the same assertions emerge from numerous GDR texts. "In the final analysis it is the higher work productivity that will — as Lenin taught us — be decisive for the ultimate victory of socialism over state monopolistic capitalism."[14]

The triumph of socialist labor will not occur, however, without great efforts by all concerned. The iron laws of history, according to Marxist theory, do not operate automatically, but only as a result of a heightened state of consciousness. And consciousness grows in a dialectical relationship with changing realities. The task of those in positions of influence, therefore, is to urge every comrade "to strive to improve your performance" (Ulbricht's seventh commandment). Indeed, GDR workers are continually implored, and most especially at year's end, through every means of mass communication, to produce higher-quality goods, to work longer hours, and to fulfill and even exceed their quotas.[15] No Western worker is ever subjected to so much of this kind of propaganda. It can only be compared to the hard-sell advertising in capitalist countries that urges everyone to consume more products.[16]

If productive labor in the GDR is powerfully oriented toward high achievement, so too is the rest of society as well. Life is suffused with pledges and proclamations to this effect. In their second pledge, every eighth-grader promises: "To strive for excellence in education and culture, to become masters of our fields, to learn unflinchingly, and to use all of our knowledge and abilities for the realization of our great humanistic ideals." The report on Gunnar Schrank in *Neues Deutschland* is only one small link in an unending chain. Olympic heroes and heroines, along with "best workers," deliver inspiring speeches; and pledges and promises to fulfill quotas are made in every farm, factory, and school from the Baltic Sea to Silesia. Yet, despite intense efforts, not every citizen of the GDR has been able to achieve the desired result, to combine hard work with personal satisfaction.

"Socialist work morale" or "communist work morale" should transcend "employee morale," because the worker is the owner of the means of production. This is an essential element of the "socialist personality" and therefore a fundamental, officially propagated value of the GDR. It involves a willingness to work indefatigably and "a sense of duty to accept every task that the society deems necessary." Marxist theoreticians and educational philosophers regard this as their most significant goal — a society in which workers gain both subjective and objective satisfaction in their work. To the Westerner, the recitation of seemingly dreary production statistics during prime time television hours is puzzling and inexplicable. To GDR officialdom it is all part of their charge to create a "culture of labor" and a new moral order.

THE COLLECTIVE

"A team is greater than the sum of its parts," concludes a U.S. television announcer who is trying to explain the success of Japanese goods in the U.S. market in competition with American-made goods. The explanation, according to the broadcaster, lies in the team spirit of Japanese workers, which U.S. workers should emulate.

This well-known notion may help us to understand the high importance of the collective in the communist hierarchy of values. It provides the guiding principle for the organization of all aspects of life in the GDR and other Communist bloc states. According to the fifth commandment in the GDR panoply of socialist morality, every member of society should always "act in the spirit of mutual help and friendly cooperation, respect the collective, and take its criticism to heart," and constantly act to enhance collective solidarity with workers, the party, the state, and other socialist countries. "Personal happiness should always be merged with the struggle for the happiness of the people" (Pledge 3 of the *Jugendweihe*).

What then is the socialist collective to which everyone in the GDR is expected to pay allegiance? It is an idea and an entity that is loosely defined: a group of workers, a school class, the family, a youth group, a football team. The socialist collective also refers to larger entities as well, such as the factory collective, the agricultural cooperative, or even the Party. In its broadest usage, this even refers to an entire system of collectives which unite to form the state, the working class, or the "Brotherhood of Socialist Countries" under the leadership of the great Soviet Union. Every member of society therefore — from childhood until old age — is expected to identify with a variety of collectives and to participate actively in the development of the collective or socialist spirit on which the entire collective structure is based.

The idea of the socialist collective, however, transcends most Western notions of mutual organizations where individuals cooperate to help one another. The socialist collective, at its best, contains a mystique that brings individuals to a higher reality, and permits them to improve themselves immeasurably. The collective is the means as well as the end of communism. For this reason, the idea of the collective dominates and influences all education in the GDR, that is, "education in the collective, by the collective, and for the collective."

Given such an exalted place in the value structure of the GDR, the collective must be taken seriously by everyone. Collective criticism must be acknowledged and taken seriously. The collective not only represents one of the highest ideals of socialist morality, it clarifies and produces moral values in its own right. In order to attain this optimal sociopsychological level, the collective must demand discipline and a high sense of responsibility from its members. It must constantly clarify the perspective of those whose vision is blurred or short-sighted. Its active core of highly principled members must provide ideological leadership and set ever higher goals for the society. Communist theorists even claim that the collective has opened the way to scientific study of morality, and the structure and make-up of the conscience.[17]

Of course, the collective serves practical as well as ideological goals. It helps to maintain and increase productivity while serving as a means of social control and propaganda. Is it any wonder that it is so highly prized in Communist societies! Nor is it any wonder that Anton S. Makarenko (1888–1939), the educator who did most to develop collective education in theory and practice, is prized above all other communist educators.[18] As we shall see, principles of collective education exercise a profound influence on every aspect of schools and learning in the GDR.

OFFICIAL AND PRIVATE VALUES
IN SOCIALIST EDUCATION

By and large, people living in Western democracies have great difficulty in even imagining the totality with which communism claims to evaluate and regulate every phase and aspect of public and private life. We have dealt here with those overriding values (work, freedom from exploitation, and the collective) that suffuse life in the GDR and the Eastern bloc. But this does not yet tell the entire story. The pledges and commandments of socialist morality, which we have not discussed, further express ideals and modes of action that citizens are expected to incorporate into their daily lives. The general pledge, for example, "to work and fight for the noble cause of socialism" (Pledge 1) is closely connected to more concrete instructions contained in Pledge 4: "to deepen the friendship with the Soviet Union, and to strengthen the brotherhood with the socialist countries, and to struggle in the spirit of proletarian internationalism to protect peace and socialism against imperialistic aggression." In every classroom, in every youth group meeting, these ideas become part of the daily agenda of young people. Their ideas and feelings are subjected to constant scrutiny and influence.

The question must then be raised: How deeply do the officially propagated ideals and values of the GDR penetrate the lives of people? How many people continue to hold values that are contrary to the official ones? And how much are these private values cherished and nurtured, and how are they expressed?

If you believe GDR media, people young and old do identify themselves with official values. To prove this is one of the functions of their "letters columns." *Junge Welt,* the official organ of the FDJ, published the following reply to a query about what qualities to look for in a marriage partner: "My partner for life should be interested in nature . . . have much understanding for my occupation and problems . . . be tender and amorous. He also must view our world with a Marxist-Leninist perspective."[19]

West German officials, party spokespeople, and many private citizens do not take such letters in the censored GDR press very seriously. They frequently point to the millions of GDR citizens in their midst who fled from the East prior to the building of the Wall in 1961. These refugees, they maintain, along with the Wall itself, offer proof that the citizens of the GDR reject the values of the socialist state. Hundreds of thousands of West Germans who have visited friends and relatives in the GDR since

1961 would testify that anti-official attitudes have not altered significantly since that time either. A number of books by prominent GDR writers who have left the East, would further confirm this assertion. Although much of this proof is anecdotal, it does contradict the official claims of the government of the GDR, which points to more rallies, economic achievements, and official documentation as evidence of general enthusiasm for communist ideals.

The television viewing habits of East Germans may also provide some evidence of their private value preferences as well. In East Berlin and many other areas of the GDR, television viewers may receive West German broadcasts quite easily. Apparently, Western programs are so popular as to cause GDR authorities to resort to a variety of measures to interfere with their reception. Members of the Free German Youth Movement (FDJ) have even been used to remove antennae designed to receive Western programs. Yet, television viewing is, at best, only a marginal indicator of values. Television programs, however value laden they may be, are probably selected by viewers because they are entertaining and well produced.

Perhaps a better indicator of personal value commitment is religious affiliation and church attendance. Communism is pointedly atheistic, and it would appear that the continuing appeal of religion in the GDR would provide proof that the official inculcation of values has failed. But, as with television viewing, the evidence is not as entirely convincing as it might appear at first. Communism certainly rejects any notions of the divinity of Christ and the Bible. If Christian values are seen as emanating from either the Ten Commandments or Christ, then communism and Christianity are alien to one another. If, on the other hand, one asks the question, as J. Somerhouse does: "Are 'Christian values' rejected by Marxism?" one might conclude otherwise.[20] Marxism not only accepts such Christian tenets as brotherly love, charity, honesty, and respect for the rights of others, it stresses them.

The GDR does, however, actively exclude any Christian education from the schools and the youth groups, and has sought to replace Christian instruction and confirmation by the Communist Youth Ordination (*Jugendweihen*). In addition, the government has confined all Christian activities to church-owned premises, and discriminates against applicants for higher education and government positions who are overtly Christian.

Yet the ambiguities persist. Under Article 39 of the GDR Constitution of 1968, every citizen is guaranteed the right to his/her religious belief and participation in religious activities. And at various times in this complicated relationship, the government of the GDR has tried to win the active support of practicing Christians by emphasizing the identity of communist and Christian values. Furthermore, the Christian churches have even received a limited amount of government support: priests and ministers are educated at the six older universities; Christian books and periodicals are published; and even a few religious radio and television programs are broadcast on the state-monopolized media. In addition, some of the traditional charitable activities of churches (e.g., hospitals and homes) have even been incorporated into state planning.

In the final analysis, the GDR would undoubtedly like to replace Christian values with socialist ones at the earliest possible moment. That about one-half of its citizens still retain church membership (six-sevenths Protestant, one-seventh Catholic) and that 100,000 Christians participate every summer in the annual Church Days must rankle many Party leaders and government officials. Even the former leader of the small and officially tolerated Christian Democratic Party (CDU), Otto Nuschke, once proclaimed: "We are without reservation a socialist party."[21] This is the official position, not only in politics, but in all matters.

With respect to education, the question of whether values antithetical to the official ones exist is moot. The state exercises a real monopoly over every aspect of education, including teacher training, curriculum, textbooks, examinations, and so on. There are no private or independent schools. Even on the informal level the ever present influence of the Party and Socialist Youth Organizations relegates any nonsocialist values to invisibility as well as insignificance. The GDR may tolerate some competing sources of allegiance where it must, as in the case of churches, but in the field of education in schools, it reigns supreme at all levels.

IDEOLOGY AND LEGAL NORMS
IN A SOCIALIST/COMMUNIST SOCIETY

At this point, critical readers may question how much we can confidently infer about the values of a society from: the pledges taken by its citizens, a combination of principal doctrines of Marxism and Leninism, and an article or two from the official newspaper, *Neues Deutschland,* or *Junge Welt.* Are we really doing justice to the GDR? What kind of valid conclusions can be drawn from these materials?

Would any serious observer of a pluralistic society dare to make far-reaching generalizations about the society after analyzing the oaths of its young people and a party program?

The answer we offer is that the relationship between political ideology, implicit values, and legal norms in a socialist/communist state such as the GDR finds no parallel in a Western pluralistic democracy. A further examination of GDR ideology as it pertains to its legal norms should provide additional evidence to prove this point.

Frequently in the GDR, the term *einheitlich* is used to characterize the activities of the citizens: to describe the various organizations to which people belong, the educational curriculum of the schools, and even the process of thinking itself. The word is one of those difficult to translate German expressions that connotes "unified" and "homogeneous," perhaps even "centralized" and "standardized." The dominant political party, for example, is the SED, the Socialist *Einheits* Party. Furthermore, in order to guarantee the *Einheit* of political thinking and political power, the traditional German political parties have not been dissolved, but are combined in the *einheitliche* National Front under the permanent leadership of the SED. The Politburo of the SED and the government are, as in the Soviet Union, not identical, but cooperate in order to ensure an *einheitliche* policy. Schools form the *einheitliche* socialist educational system; the curricula are *einheitlich*. Teachers and administrators cooperate with the various youth organizations such as the Free German Youth (FDJ) and the Pioneers, as well as the parents' organizations, production units, and neighborhood social groups in order to provide *einheitliche* political and educational activity.

More than anything else, this general standardization of all publicly organized activities allows us to use the pledges recited by children and articles from the official daily newspaper as valid indicators of the value system in the GDR. Unlike the programs of political parties in Western societies, which are merely programs, the program of the SED states the official norms of the GDR. It does more as well; it also states the legal norms of the society. To understand fully the *einheitliche* nature of official political values and legal norms (and how they pertain to school laws), we must briefly describe the political structure of the GDR.

At the political center of the state stands the SED or *Sozialistische Einheitspartei* (United Socialist Party). Official documents refer to the SED as "a new type of party," "the party of the working class and the entire working population," and the "Marxist-Leninist Party."[22] In fact, the term *party* is totally misleading as it might be applied in the Federal Republic or most Western states. In pluralistic democracies, political parties are free associations of citizens with similar political ideas. These ideas are usually stated in a party program. Parties then function "to assist in the formation of the political will of the people,"[23] to compete in free elections, to form governments when successful, and to act in opposition when unsuccessful. On the other hand, the SED, like the Communist Party of the Soviet Union, functions as the single, all-powerful organization for the exercise of political power in the state. According to the distilled doctrines of Marxism-Leninism, such a party is "the highest form of the class organization of the working class." It has simultaneously integrated all of the "progressive forces" of the society while functioning, until the final state of communism, as the "dictatorship of the proletariat." It not only "represents the interest of the whole society," but also "personifies the future of mankind."[24]

Nor is the primary political role of the SED left to electoral choice; the Constitution of 1974 explicitly guarantees the position of this party. The Constitution recognizes the National Front, dominated by the SED, as the "alliance of all powers of the people" (Article 3). The Central Committee of the Politburo of the SED, along with the Secretariat of the Politburo, functions as the chief political organ of the GDR. The most powerful political figures in the state hold memberships in both these bodies. Furthermore, the Constitution not only guarantees the rule of these central bodies, but also, under the principle of "democratic centralism," excludes organized opposition as part of the established political process. The central organs of the SED and the government determine policies and programs which are in turn implemented at every level, and in every institution, by the approximately two million Party members and functionaries. In the factory, on the farm, in the school, or in the neighborhood council, the decisions of the SED prevail.

How the preeminence of the SED works can be seen in the educational system. The most recent Constitution of the GDR (1974) decrees that while all citizens have an equal right to education, education is defined as "continuous socialist education" in order to produce the "socialist personality." This equates closely to the educational ideals of the SED as does Article 25, which provides for compulsory attendance in the state-run Polytechnic High School as well as prescribing that "all young persons have the right and duty to learn an occupation."

The General School Regulations define this relationship even more explicitly. In the preface to these regulations, the duties of the school principal are clearly delineated: "The school principal is obliged to carry out his activities of school management based on the decisions of the United Socialist Party (SED), and the laws and other legal regulations"

(Paragraph 3).[25] The laws themselves, to which the legislature (*Volkskammer*) normally gives its unanimous consent, are submitted by the central bodies of the SED. Indeed, the teachers and educators share the task of "the improvement of the communist education of school youth" with the school Party organization of the SED, as well as the SED-controlled State Labor Union and youth organizations (the FDJ and Pioneer Organization Ernst Thaelmann).[26] Even the SED-controlled people's production units share in the political education of young students. Thus, we see that on every level of educational decision-making and implementation, the SED plays a dominant role. This is truly the ruling party, recognized as such by the Constitution, and providing de facto guidance in the entire educational system.

The principle of *Einheitlichkeit* thus replaces political competition as the hallmark of politics in the GDR. Whereas in Western pluralistic democracies, the political process is advanced by the struggle between parties to attract voters, in the GDR the political process consists of struggles within the party itself. According to official GDR doctrines, divisive political activity outside the Party is a phenomenon of a lower, earlier stage of historical development. The role of the SED now transcends such bourgeois traditions. With respect to education, therefore, the West German practice of democratic participation in school administration with parents, teachers, student representatives, and administrators struggling as interest groups to resolve difficult educational problems, is seen in the GDR as antiquated and anachronistic. Moreover, any notion of parental rights that might be defended in court against the school authorities or the state is regarded as irrelevant. As a recent commentary on GDR family law noted:

> The educational goal of Paragraph 42 FGB (Family Law Book) derives from the common basic interests of family and society. It is guided by Socialist Humanism and aims at the total development of the socialist personality of the children. The essential sameness [*inhaltliche Uebereinstimmung*] of the principal educational goal of the society, the societal institutions of education, and the family derives from the character of socialist society.[27]

Although the official School Regulations explicitly provide that the school and the parents bear a "joint responsibility for the complete communist education of the children," in the final analysis the SED and its Central Committee decide what that education will be.

On the constitutional level, therefore, personal rights as opposed to the state's rights are negligible. Rights are granted and guaranteed on the basis of socialist/communist principles as defined in the Constitution.

Courts are bound to exert "socialist partisanship." Whereas in West Germany a Supreme Court (the *Bundesverfassungsgericht*) exists to defend personal rights against the administrative or legislative powers of the state, in the GDR such a court would violate the spirit of the Constitution. The complete integration of the individual into the state makes individual rights superfluous. And it is the SED that guides the apparatus of the state. The SED controls the legislature (*Volkskammer*), and its leading council (Staatsrat; chair, Erich Honecker), and it decides which laws and regulations are constitutional or not (Articles 74 and 89 of the GDR Constitution). The SED is the fountainhead of public and private values; it is the source of legal norms; and it is the promulgator of official regulations.

And one might ask why is the SED so all-powerful? Why does it stand at the center of the East German state? The answer would be that history has decreed it so. In its decision-making capacity, "the party of the working class" is the voice of history.[28]

NOTES

Epigraph to Chapter 3 is from Norbert Haase, Lothar Reese, and Peter Wensierski, eds., *VEB Nachwuchs: Jugend in der DDR* (Reinbek, 1983), p. 111.

1. Akademie der Paedagogischen Wissenschaften der DDR, ed., *Das Bildungswesen der Deutschen Demokratischen Republik*, 2d ed. (Berlin, 1983), p. 72.
2. Autorenkollektiv: Bernd Bittighoefer et al., *Moral und Gesellschaft*, edited by Bernd Bittighoefer and Juergen Schmollack (Berlin 1968), p. 30.
3. Leonard Krieger, *The German Idea of Freedom* (Chicago, IL, 1972).
4. Kant quoted Frederick the Great of Prussia in "Beantwortung der Frage: Was ist Aufklaerung?" *Berlinische Monatsschrift* 4 (December 1784).
5. See Krieger, *German Idea of Freedom*, p. 90.
6. Georg Wilhelm Friedrich Hegel, *Philosophy of History*, rev. ed., translated by J. Sibree (New York, 1956), p. 38; Krieger, *German Idea of Freedom*, p. 132.
7. Georg Wilhelm Friedrich Hegel, *Philosophy of Right*, translated by T. M. Knox (Oxford, 1942), pp. 35, 51.
8. See Richard Schacht, *Alienation* (Garden City, NY, 1970).
9. These quotations are from Margot Honecker, GDR Minister of Education; *Erziehung Sozialistischer Persoenlichkeiten*, edited by Akademie der Paedagogischen Wissenschaften (Berlin, 1976), p. 25.
10. Bertell Ollman, *Alienation* (Cambridge, 1971); Karl Marx, *Das Kapital* (Hamburg, 1867-1894).
11. Karl Marx and Friedrich Engels, *Basic Writings on Politics and Philosophy*, edited by Lewis S. Feuer (Garden City, NY, 1959), p. 17ff.
12. Gerda Achinger, *Die Schulreform in der USSR* (Muenchen, 1973).

13. Dirk Bode, *Polytechnischer Unterricht in der DDR* (Frankfurt/New York, 1978), p. 54f.

14. *Moral und Gesellschaft*, p. 45.

15. For instance, on March 15, 1985, *Neues Deutschland* appeared with the main headline of the front page, EVERY DAY HIGHEST PERFORMANCE IN RESEARCH AND PRODUCTION, and the subtitle B Y THE 40TH ANNIVERSARY MORE THAN ONE DAY AHEAD OF SCHEDULE — THUS COLLECTIVES HONOR THE LEGACY OF OUR LIBERATORS AND STRENGTHEN OUR REPUBLIC.

16. See Paul Hollander, *Soviet and American Society* (New York, 1973), p. 118ff.

17. See *Moral und Gesellschaft*.

18. Fedor Filippovich Koroljow and Vladimir Efimovich Gmurman of the Academy of Pedagogical Sciences of the USSR praise him for "overcoming traditional pedagogy, which dealt primarily with the influence of the individual education on the individual pupil, by an education that emphasized the communistic education in the collective and the development of individuality within the work collective of children." *Allgemeine Grundlagen der marxistischen Paedagogik* (Pullach bei Munchen, 1973), p. 85; See also James Bowen, *Soviet Education* (Madison, WI, 1962).

19. See above, Note 1.

20. John Sommerville, *The Philosophy of Marxism* (New York, 1967), p. 184.

21. *DDR Handbuch*, pp. 238f, 586ff.

22. Bundesminister fuer innerdeutsche Beziehungen, ed., Statutes of the SED of 1961; See also *DDR Hendbuch*, pp. 927–52.

23. This is, for example, the definition of the function of political parties in the *Grundgesetz* (Basic Law or Constitution) of the Federal Republic of Germany, Article 21.

24. Waltraud Boehme et al., eds., *Kleines Politisches Woerterbuch*, 2d. ed. (Berlin, 1973).

25. Ministerium fuer Volksbildung, ed., *Sozialistisches Bildungsrecht, Volksbildung: Allgemeinbildende polytechnische Oberschulen* (Berlin, 1982), p. 20.

26. Ibid., p. 20f.

27. Anita Grandke et al., "Zur Wirksamkeit des Erziehungsrecht des FGB," *Neue Justiz* 8 (1979): 345.

28. For good accounts in English of the GDR, its founding, and how it functions, see: John H. Backer, *The Decision to Divide Germany* (Durham, NC, 1978); Martin McCauley, *The German Democratic Republic Since 1945* (New York, 1983).

4

EDUCATIONAL VALUES AND THE LAW IN THE FEDERAL REPUBLIC OF GERMANY

> And when all is over — ; when all this has come to a standstill:
> ... the ecstasy of appearing in masses ... and waving flags
> in groups, ... then someone will come who will make a
> thundering discovery: he will discover the individual person. He
> will say there is an organism called man, who really counts. And
> if he/she is happy that is the question. That he/she be free that is
> the goal.... What matters is not that the state may live —
> what matters is that man may live.
>
> Kurt Tucholsky, 1890–1935

THE CASE OF *PARENTS VS. HESSE*

In the East the sardonic picture of life in a collective society that Kurt Tucholsky painted more than 50 years ago has come to pass, at least officially. Citizens of the GDR seem to "delight" in collective values and undertakings and "joyfully" wear the blue shirt of the official youth organization. In mass formations they "wave the national flag in bliss." In the West, one might ask, has the time arrived, when, as Tucholsky predicted, the thundering discovery of the individual will be made, when personal freedom and private happiness will be rediscovered?

There are critics of the Federal Republic who say otherwise. For example, in a recently published book on the youths of the GDR, the editors assert: "It's the same German traits that dam up [*verbauen*] our future in both states and that make life so difficult: order and diligence, work and family; *Bier ist Bier und Schnaps ist Schnaps*" (in some sense a popular version of Immanuel Kant's quotation from Frederick the Great: "Argue as much as you want, but in the end obey"). In both German republics, the editors continue, young people long for a life style that is different from the prevalent modes in either country, a life style not based on values such as "faster, higher, wider," or as the motto of the Tenth Party Congress of the SED states: "Achieve so that you will be able to indulge yourself" (*Leiste was, damit du dir was leisten kannst*); rather a life style based on humane values.[1]

Yet, of course, it would be easy to exaggerate such critical sentiments. The young people who hold such views are rebelling against an older generation as well as their national heritage. Prussian values of order, obedience, and hard work have all but disappeared. West Germans fill the sunny beaches of southern Europe and North Africa, they pamper themselves with consumer goods, and support a prosperous chain of Beate Uhse sex shops. It would almost seem that hedonism, individualism, and moral relativism have triumphed in the Western twin rather than the values of work and self-discipline.

Compared to the GDR, the political, legal, and social systems of the Federal Republic appear at first as incredibly chaotic. No single pledge taken by the teenagers of the country, no official statement of values can describe the multifarious nature of this society. Instead of one dominant political party, there are several. Efforts to create a two-party system modeled on England or the United States seem to have failed or at least are undergoing modifications. Young people divide their allegiance in many ways — among political parties, religious groups, and counterculture groups, all of which may express different norms. In addition, the various individual states (*Laender*) that form the Republic may enact laws that are different from those of other states and which, at times, may even conflict with the basic federal laws (*Grundgesetz*). In the latter case, resort to the Supreme Court of the Federal Republic (*Bundesverfassungsgericht*) may provide the only resolution. West Germany is remarkably pluralistic even for a West European state. In this sense, it more nearly resembles the United States than many of its sister democracies. It certainly bears virtually no resemblance in this respect to the GDR.

Take, for example, the case of *Parents vs. the State of Hesse,* which was decided by the Supreme Court on December 6, 1972. As in the United States, where the Supreme Court has played an especially important role in shaping educational policy by virtue of its decisions, such has also been the situation in the Federal Republic. The facts in this landmark case demonstrate what happens when efforts to initiate educational reform by the state conflict with personal freedom.

The Parliament (*Landtag*) of the state of Hesse enacted legislation in 1969 designed to "integrate" grades five and six of the public school system. Traditionally (since 1919) in Germany, the first four elementary school grades have included all students, whatever their intellectual abilities, in mixed or integrated classes. In the fifth year, when most youngsters have reached the age of 10, pupils have been divided according to ability (social class, say the critics) and thereafter sent to one of several secondary schools. Certainly, in the past, this has frequently meant that the professional or vocational destiny of young West Germans was decided prior to the fifth year of school. Following World War II, the U.S. Military Administration's efforts to alter this system by the establishment of a six-year primary school generally failed. (Would or could anyone in East Germany have rejected such proposals had they been made by the Soviet Military Government in the Soviet zone of occupation?) Yet the progressive state of Hesse has continuously tried to democratize its schools by integrating all young Hessians for two additional school years, the fifth and sixth (the so-called *Foerderstufe*) in order to permit disadvantaged students to catch up and to prepare all pupils for the various secondary schools. This led to a number of experiments and finally to the 1969 legislation.

The plaintiffs in this case consisted of a group of parents, grandparents, and children who claimed that the *Foerderstufe* Law violated their constitutional rights, particularly the right of parents to choose the school appropriate to the needs of their children. They also charged that these integrated classes tended to reduce individual differences and thereby "leveled" gifted children. The plaintiffs also alleged that the state of Hesse, by mandating *compulsory* attendance in the *Foerderstufe*, violated the rights of parents to send their children to private or denominational schools following the fourth school year.

On December 6, 1972, the Federal Supreme Court handed down a split decision in this case. On one hand, it upheld the right of the Hessian Parliament to create the *Foerderstufe*. This, it maintained, did not violate parents' or children's rights to select an education appropriate to the abilities of the child. However, the Court also ruled that Article 7 of the Constitution (*Grundgesetz*) did guarantee students the right to attend a private school following the four-year compulsory primary school. In addition, the Court maintained that during the period of transition to the new system, students could choose to attend a traditional secondary school in a different school district. Thus the Supreme Court struck down portions of the Hessian school law as unconstitutional. A closer look at the decision offers an even better opportunity to see how the values and legal norms of the Federal Republic are expressed and to compare this process with what we have observed in the GDR.

First, the Supreme Court, in its decision, raffirmed the power of the West German States (*Laender*) in matters of educational policies: "The Constitution has ... relegated school education to the exclusive jurisdiction of the States. ... As a result, the States have far-reaching freedom to determine educational principles and the content of instruction. ... The state of Hesse has made use of that freedom in an appropriate manner in Article 56, Paragraph 1, Sentence 2 of its Constitution; it has dealt with school education as an affair of the State. This is in accordance with Article 7, Paragraph 1 of the Federal Constitution, which places the entire school system under the supervision of the state."[2]

Given the nature of this particular case, and the decision it was about to render, the Supreme Court clearly felt the need to elaborate even further on the broad educational powers of the states: "Supervision of the schools ... includes the right of the State to plan and organize school education with the aim of guaranteeing a school system which avails all young citizens of educational opportunities according to their abilities and corresponding to current social conditions." This meant that the states could make decisions regarding the "organizational articulation of the school," content of courses, objectives of instruction, school admission policies, and whether "the student has achieved the instructional objectives."

But what limitations are there then on the power of the states with respect to education? What about the rights of parents? The Court then addressed these questions: "Even though the organization of school education has to a large extent been assigned to state legislation ... the Constitution has not declared school education as exclusively a state matter. In this area, the state shares the task of supporting and advancing the child in the development of a self-responsible, social personality with other agencies of education [*Erziehungstraeger*]. Especially, it is the parental rights in educational matters, as provided in Article 6, Paragraph 2, Sentence 1, of the Constitution, which limit the power of the State in school education."[3]

The particular provision to which this decision refers defines "the care and education of children as the natural right and a particular duty of parents." In its elaboration of this principle, the Court ruled that although the responsibility for educating the child falls on both the state and the parents, the aim of education "is the forming of a *single* personality." This goal cannot be divided into separate competencies and "has to be undertaken in a meaningful cooperation." The Court continued: "In the school, therefore, the state must respect the responsibility of the parents for the overall planning of the education of their children and remain amenable to a variety of views on educational matters, so long as these are compatible with an orderly state school system. The state may not regulate the entire school career of the child by means of school organization." The Court then forcefully concluded that the state must "provide a school system which, while leaving room for the development of different abilities, does not aim at management of potentialities. . . . It is the right of parents to plan freely the school career of their child."[4]

The Court rejected those portions of the Hessian School Law that extended *compulsory attendance* at state schools for an additional two years and which also forbade students from attending traditional secondary schools in neighboring school districts. The Federal Constitution has guaranteed the right of parents to send their children to private schools, albeit state supervised, following the first four elementary school years. The Court, however, did recognize the right of Hesse to extend comprehensive education for two additional years to meet individual and societal needs. In its mixed decision, the Supreme Court concluded: "However, the diagnosis of abilities and prognosis of education by the state would be unconstitutional if it determined once and for all the students' future role in the community or state, thereby eliminating the parents' right to do so."[5]

Clearly, this entire judicial process could not have occurred in the GDR. Legal norms are not decided in the East by adversarial confrontation in the courts. Nor does the GDR Constitution provide for the largely autonomous state school systems as does the federated political system in the West. In fact, the federal government of West Germany is, on the contrary, constitutionally prohibited from centralizing control of education.

In the GDR we have observed that the ultimate aim of schooling is the creation of the "socialist personality," which is predetermined and predefined by the "working class" and its leading party. In the Federal Republic the aim of education is the "self-responsible personality," the bearer of which will be capable of self-direction and, no less important, will know when and how to resist the authority of the state. In the case of *Parents vs. Hesse,* we have seen precisely such a situation.

PERSONAL FREEDOM

As we have seen, the West German *Grundgesetz* defines and guarantees the basic rights of its citizens. In so doing it especially focuses on ensuring personal freedom in the face of any possible government infringements. It is a document that grew out of the Western liberal tradition as well as the visions and nightmares of the recent German past. It owes an intellectual debt to John Locke and the U.S. Declaration of Independence, as well as to the Weimar Constitution and the European Convention of Human Rights (1950).

Like most Western constitutions, however, it does not define and guarantee social and cultural rights with the same alacrity and precision as it does personal freedom. For example, it does not guarantee, in the same way as it does personal freedoms, the right to a job, the right to enjoy social and medical benefits, nor even the clear right to a particular kind of education. The *Grundgesetz,* like its Western brethren, is certainly vulnerable to the censure often leveled by socialist and communist critics: What good are such personal freedoms as free speech when you are sick and unemployed? What good is freedom of the press when you are cold and hungry?

Clearly the notions of the role of the state and the rights of the individual, as defined in the two Germanys, are at odds here. Yet the *Grundgesetz* does not solely reflect a different intellectual tradition; it is also the product of practical considerations as well. The founding fathers (and mothers) of the Federal Republic did not want to prejudice or preclude a future union with East Germany. To have defined social and cultural rights more explicitly and fully might have made a future constitution for a reunited Germany all the more difficult to create. Many of the authors of the *Grundgesetz* wishfully (and wistfully) hoped that their endeavor would be a provisional one. To provide a detailed document, especially in those areas where East and West were most likely to differ, might help to ensure the future division of their country. This they sought to avoid.[6]

Of course, the rift between East and West has kept Germany divided and has rendered constitutional issues for a united Germany purely academic or as a matter of political lip-service. Yet the view of personal freedom embodied in Articles 1–19 of the *Grundgesetz* certainly underlines the fundamental differences between the two societies. In the *Grundgesetz* the function of the state is to respect and defend the "inalienable dignity of man."[7] "Man" is here defined as an *individual* human being whose self must constantly be safeguarded under all conditions, even as a convicted criminal, a patient in a mental institution, or as an unborn child.

Here, too, we confront not only basic ideological differences between the Marxist-Leninist GDR and the liberal, pluralistic Federal Republic, but we also see these differences manifested in interpretations of the catastrophe of recent German history. In the East the Nazi era and its attendant horrors are regarded as the outcome of a liberal, bourgeois period when selfish class interests reigned, when the moral tone of society was individualistic rather than collective in its orientation. The so-called collectivism of the Nazis was just an extension of class rule; not an aberration, but the logical outgrowth of bourgeois capitalism. A socialist-communist society, according to this ideology, provides the best antidote to future fascism because it creates a wholly new moral atmosphere. The abolition of unemployment and economic and social misery will remove the conditions that foster fascism, while the growth of a genuine collective spirit will provide a moral innoculation against future systems based on greed and hate.

In the Federal Republic the Nazi era is regarded differently. It is seen as a time when extremists of the Right gained control of the state and ruthlessly abolished personal freedom and individual rights. According to this interpretation, the state as Leviathan or behemoth is to be feared, especially if it falls into the hands of extremists of the Right or Left. West Germany must guard against resurgent fascism, but should be equally as alert to dangers from the Left. In recent years, the latter, in the form of terrorists such as the Baader-Meinhoff Gang, has provided a more potent threat than the former. The best protection against the abridgement or reduction of personal rights resides in constitutional and legal guarantees, hence the construction of the system based on the *Grundgesetz*.

This then is what sets the German "twins" apart: a decidedly collectivist orientation to the value systems on the one side, with some concessions to assertions of personal freedom; while on the other side, a personalistic value structure with some regard being paid to collective social obligations. Thus the "free development of the personality," which Article 2 of the West German *Grundgesetz* guarantees, stands in sharp contrast to the development of the "socialist personality," which is the goal of East Germany. The Federal Republic is forbidden to hinder freedom of choice in education, work, travel, religion, or sexual preference without compelling justification. Articles 4 and 5 of the *Grundgesetz* further guarantee a "free spiritual life," meaning not only freedom of religious belief, but ideological as well. Freedom to express opinions in the press and other media as well as to engage in research further supports the claims of a free spiritual life. A "free spiritual process" is guaranteed, "in which decisive value concepts shall have a chance to develop free from government influence." Even the right to refuse military service for reasons of conscience is constitutionally ensured (in the GDR, conscientious objectors must enter a military conservation corps, the *Bausoldaten*).

If anything, the Federal Supreme Court of West Germany has broadened these rights rather than narrowed them. It has declared unconstitutional laws that would have permitted federal government interference in broadcasting companies, inhibited freedom of research and instruction in universities, compelled the press to reveal informants, forbidden members of the army from freely publishing their opinions, or denied the rights of prison convicts.

As one might expect, the constitutions (and legal norms) of the two Germanys differ most dramatically and fundamentally in the realms of economics and politics. For example, whereas Article 12 of the GDR Constitution prohibits private ownership of mines and minerals, waterways, banks, transportation, and insurance, the Supreme Court of West Germany has repeatedly defended private property against encroachments on the part of governing bodies. Although Article 14, Paragraph 2 of the *Grundgesetz* does stipulate in a rather general fashion that the private ownership of property does carry with it a social obligation, private ownership has flourished in every realm of the West German economy. Indeed, the ownership and use of private property has provided the material basis and background for the development of the "free personality" that ultimately is one principal goal of West German society. Not only has private property and the profit motive produced prosperity, it has presumably fostered free initiative and personal responsibility as well. Furthermore, free labor unions have encouraged the development of these traits in the working population also, thus belying to some extent class criticisms made against this system.

Interestingly, even the Social Democratic Party (SPD) of the Federal Republic has become one of the pillars of a free enterprise and private initiative economy. This party, whose history has frequently been decidedly anticapitalist and which was once avowedly Marxist (see the Dresden Congress of 1903), has endorsed the private ownership of industry. Between 1969 and 1982, SPD chancellors essentially defended the system that their opponents in the Christian Democratic Party (CDU) had founded and put in place. Helmut Schmidt, the SPD chancellor from 1974 to 1982, regarded the "social market economy" as not only the source of private and public wealth in the Federal Republic and the vehicle of economic progress, but also the generating force of personal freedom and moral responsibility. Needless to say, the governing figures of the GDR have regarded the leaders of the West German "socialists" with all of the disdain that purists everywhere regard casuists. At best, the leaders of the SPD are seen as bourgeois liberals.[8]

The prevailing West German view of the relationship between a "free economy" and "personal freedom" has been excellently articulated by the Nobel Prize-winning economist, Friedrich A. von Hayek. In an essay in the *Frankfurter Allgemeine Zeitung* (summer 1983), Hayek describes private property as one of the motivating forces of human development and cultural progress. The free market has fostered the almost unlimited production and dissemination of ideas. It has provided a tremendous stimulus to human ingenuity that a highly planned, socialized economy does not. Indeed, Hayek claims that only a free economy can generate solutions to the problems threatening humanity today.[9]

Given the multifarious nature of West German society, this "liberal" view finds many opponents and detractors in the Federal Republic itself. There is, for example, a lively, and perhaps growing, neo-Marxist faction within the SPD. But private property and a free "social market economy" remain cornerstones of West German society. This is also reflected in numerous ways in the educational system.

LEGAL NORMS AND THEIR EFFECT ON EDUCATION

Is the West German twin then a stronghold of personal freedom and individual rights, a paragon of tolerance and pluralism? Some people might have doubts. Yet it is true that nothing differentiates it more dramatically from its Eastern sibling than the commitment to these values and, on the other hand, the collectivist orientation of the GDR.

Goethe, almost two centuries ago, declared that whoever promised freedom and equality simultaneously was a charlatan. This dictum may help us to realize that the Federal Republic pays a price for its emphasis on personal freedom in the form of dramatic economic and social inequalities. The struggle over the *Foerderstufe* in Hesse exemplified this. A coalition of middle-class parents, elite secondary school teachers, and conservative parties has thus far been able to preserve the right of parents to determine their children's schooling, but at the cost of lost educational opportunities for the economically and ethnically disadvantaged.

Recently (1984) the courts have re-opened the possibility of statewide establishment of the *Foerderstufe* in Hesse. Yet, even in Hesse, which has been continuously ruled by Social Democrats, this required that its prime minister (H. Boerner) gain the support of the small minority party of the Greens before it could be achieved. And even this "Final Foerderstufe Law" of 1985, too, has been attacked in the courts. In Western democracies, the chain of compromise always seems to add new links. Apparently every reform violates the interests of one group or another. A deadlock is frequently the outcome. Or, as the chair of the Union of Teachers and Scholars (GEW) described the confused situation with respect to grades five and six in the 11 *Laender:* "There federalism puts forth its greatest blossoms."[10]

Thus we see that the liberal and federal character of West Germany has often frustrated reformers and inhibited the development of a modern system to replace traditional forms of education. As with other Western countries, educational inequalities persist as the price that is being paid for regional and personal freedom. It is this which must be kept in mind as we continue to discuss the effects of legal norms on education in the Federal Republic.

Thus, educational policies and norms in West Germany are established by laws, but also by the conflicting claims of various interest groups which must frequently be decided in courts. The various *Laender* are jealous of their constitutional prerogatives and carefully guard, on the one hand, against possible encroachments by the Federal Republic and, on the other, against claims made by parents and special interest groups to educational rights. As in the United States, the Federal Republic constantly confronts the problem of educational equity and coordination among the *Laender*. What can the Federal Republic, which has no direct constitutional role in education, do, for example, about the mythical rural, Catholic farm girl from the hills who, for many years, was the educationally most deprived citizen in the country? Can the federal government find a way to intervene in order to narrow the educational gap between her and the son of a well-to-do official in Hamburg? Indeed, an even more educationally deprived group has emerged with the arrival of the children of foreign workers.

As we have noted, the *Grundgesetz* of the Federal Republic provides the federal government with no substantial influence on school education. Yet, the federal government has attempted with varying degrees of success to play a role in education. For example, under Articles 32 and 73, Number 1, of the *Grundgesetz,* the Federal Republic is assigned exclusive control of all matters pertaining to foreign affairs. Using this power, the government has concluded international cultural agreements and made various provisions for language teaching. The ever-anxious *Laender* have, in turn, questioned and challenged the increasing role of the federal government in such arrangements, seeing the diminishment of their own cultural sovereignty as a possible consequence.[11]

Considerably more controversial have been efforts made by the Bonn government in educational planning. Shortly after the establishment of the Federal Republic (1949), it became apparent that a certain amount of educational coordination on the national level was desirable, especially with respect to financing and equity planning. In 1953 the federal government signed an agreement with the ministers of culture (or education) of the various *Laender,* thereby establishing an educational advisory committee (*Deutsche Ausschuss fuer das Erziehungs-und Bildungswesen*). This led in 1965 and 1970 to the establishment of more ambitious councils and commissions (the *Deutsche Bildungsrat* and the *Bund-Laender-Kommission fuer Bildungsplanung*).

Membership and cooperation in the early committee had been purely voluntary on the part of the *Laender* and not always enthusiastic. As one member of the *Bundestag* observed, progress was determined "by the slowest ship."[12] Believing, however, that the time had arrived for a more ambitious effort at national planning, members of the *Bundestag* introduced a bill in 1968 which would have enabled greater planning and implementation at the federal level. Although the *Bundestag* passed the bill with a large majority, the various legislatures of the *Laender* rejected it, thus preventing its adoption. Instead, a Mediating Committee (*Vermittlungsausschuss*) was established which provided for voluntary cooperation between the *Laender* and the Federal Republic in the field of educational planning on the primary and secondary levels (*Grundgesetz,* Article 91b).

Under the provision of this agreement, cooperative planning has been spotty at best. A joint Federal-State Commission for Educational

Planning grew out of this agreement in 1970, with federal government officials getting 11 votes on this Commission and each of the 11 *Laender* having one each. The Commission members have divided dramatically on important issues, especially with respect to the establishment of Comprehensive Schools (*Gesamtschulen*) at the lower secondary levels (grades 5–10). Although a majority of Commission members voted in favor of establishing Comprehensive Schools, those *Laender* that were governed by Christian Democrats (CDU) have generally asserted their educational sovereignty by pursuing delaying tactics in instituting these schools, and threatening not to recognize the credentials of those who have attended them in *Laender* that have been more active in introducing them. This has not only frustrated the entire effort to democratize West German secondary education, but has also encouraged parents and teachers everywhere who opposed this reform. Thus even in the Federal Republic's most populous state, North Rhine-Westphalia, which was governed by Social Democrats, a coalition of opposition groups was able to collect enough signatures to cause the abandonment of an educational reform bill in 1978. In conservative Bavaria in the following year, government officials declared, "Bavaria will not agree to the establishment of the Comprehensive School as a regular school in Bavaria *or elsewhere.*"[13]

In the end, educational planning and cooperation between the *Laender* and the federal government has been generally ineffectual. Even the Federal-State Commission founded in the early 1970s could not be sustained in its original form. The *Laender* continue to exercise sovereignty in writing their own school laws and regulations and in exercising control over school finances, administration, curriculum, evaluation, and accreditation. They have agreed on some minor matters, such as staggering summer vacation schedules in order not to tax overcrowded *Autobahnen* (Interstate Highways) and tourist centers, but little else. If the establishment of Comprehensive Schools available to pupils of all nationalities (guest workers, for example) and social backgrounds can be considered progressive, then progress continues to be determined by the slowest ship in the Federal Republic.

Yet, as we have seen in the case of *Parents vs. Hesse*, the powers of the *Laender,* however considerable in their territory, are constitutionally limited in a number of ways. In particular, for example, the *Grundgesetz* guarantees the right to establish and maintain private schools which currently enroll approximately 5 percent of the secondary school population. Constitutionally, these schools are not permitted to promote segregation of pupils on the basis of social background (although, in reality, they often do). Yet they are seen as an essential element in a pluralistic society. Thus the educational monopoly exercised by the state in the GDR is attenuated by church groups and private school associations, such as the Waldorf School Association, which operate schools outside the state systems of West Germany. Private schools have served as a means both to promote and perpetuate conservative educational traditions, while at the same time providing an arena for experimental and free schools.

Given the high cost of maintaining such schools, the *Laender* provide subsidies to assist in their support. This practice has even been accepted as a legal obligation and is so stated in the constitution of the *Laender*. In fact, North Rhine-Westphalia has provided the most generous support to private schools of all the *Laender,* underwriting more than 90 percent of the expenses of these institutions. Indeed, when the legislature of this *Land* sought to reduce this support by 5 percent while enacting a recession-plagued budget in 1981, the Supreme Court of the *Land* decided that reductions could not be made that were not gradual and calculable.[14] Clearly, North Rhine-Westphalia was prevented from dealing arbitrarily or hastily with private schools' support, which might threaten their existence. It was prevented from possibly strangling, or at best, crippling its educational competition; a pluralistic system was thereby ensured.

This particular decision also reaffirmed another principle, namely that the state legislatures rather than the ministries of education should exercise final administrative and regulatory powers in education. As the Federal Supreme Court maintained, "The principles of a constitutional and democratic state require that the legislative branch decide the essential questions pertaining to schools rather than leaving them to the school administration."[15] By thus guaranteeing legislative involvement in school matters, the Court ensured that opposing views on important educational matters could be voiced in public debate. Considering the course of German history and how much had in the past been decided by administrative or executive fiat, this stands as an extremely important decision, in spite of its inhibiting educational reform.

As regards parental rights versus the state in educational matters, we have already seen how the Supreme Court guaranteed certain parental rights with respect to secondary education in *Parents vs. Hesse* (see above). Another equally significant case occurred in 1977, when groups of parents in the city of Hamburg (which is also one of the *Laender*) and the southwestern *Land* of Baden-Wuerttemberg sought relief for their children from certain portions of the sex education curriculum. In the main, the Court rejected the appeal of the parents and affirmed the right of the *Laender* not only to transmit information in schools, but to be concerned with broader aspects of personality development among its younger citizens as well, that is, with the development of emotions, attitudes, and values. Yet, however sweeping these powers might seem, the Court also warned the *Laender* that the power of personality development was a shared one, especially in such personal areas as sex education. Not only did parents still possess the overall right to determine the education of their children, they also possessed a special interest in such matters as sex education. Insofar as possible, therefore, the *Laender* and the parents should cooperate in this undertaking. "The joint task of education," the Court ruled, "whose goal is the formation of the *single* personality of the child, cannot be divided into separate components. It has to be conducted in a meaningful cooperation."

The concern of the Court was a cooperative approach in order to protect a society with a pluralistic value structure. "The school must avoid any attempt to indoctrinate students by advocating one particular kind of sexual behavior or rejecting another."[16] The *Laender* must respect the "natural sense of modesty of the children" and the various religious and ideological convictions of parents. Pupils could not be exempted from sex education, but neither could the sensibilities of parents and pupils be ignored by the state.

As might be expected, in one other area of great significance, religious instruction, the rights of parents and the *Laender* have clashed. Here, too, the courts have been called upon to adjudicate. It should be noted that in West Germany there is no tradition of separation of church and state as there is in the United States; quite the opposite is the rule. The authors of the *Grundgesetz* as well as the authors of the various *Laender* constitutions took into account the overwhelming Christian traditions of their predominantly Catholic and Protestant citizens in addressing their tasks. They undoubtedly also saw these Christian traditions as an antidote to Nazi rule and World War II.

Thus it should not be surprising that the Constitution of North Rhine-Westphalia specifies "reverence for God" as a goal of education (Article 7), or that it stipulates that "religious instruction is an ordinary subject in all schools" (Article 14). A plethora of such general provisions has meant, however, a rush to the courts for clarification and precise definition. Once again we observe the startling contrast between the GDR, where official ideology is clearly expounded, and the Federal

Republic, where it is adumbrated at best. In the East the courts are usually enforcers of orthodoxy rather than the interpreters of rights. In West Germany some parents have appealed to the Federal Supreme Court demanding stricter denominational education in public schools, while others have sought relief for their children from any religious instruction. This has meant that virtually every aspect of public schooling — organization, finance, and curriculum — has come before the Court in this context. Does the state, for example, have the obligation to establish separate schools for Catholics and Protestants in areas where the religious population is mixed? And what about virtually compelling non-Christian children to attend religiously oriented schools?

As a result of efforts both to protect the rights of parents and children as well as to establish schools that are both efficient and large enough to provide one class for each age cohort, so-called Community Schools (*Gemeinschaftsschulen*) have been established at the elementary level by most of the *Laender*. In some instances these are referred to as "Christian Community Schools," while in others they are not. The Supreme Court has confirmed the right of the *Laender* to determine the religious or ideological character of public school education, so long as the constitutional rights of parents and children are protected. The term "Christian" therefore should be interpreted as the historical, cultural, and educational heritage of the West German citizens rather than as indoctrination in a particular denominational belief, according to the Court. Minority rights and religious toleration must be regarded as paramount, even where religion is offered in a discrete denominational course; and no teacher may be compelled to teach such a course. In addition, parents of younger as well as older students may demand dispensation from denominational courses. Religious education in a stricter and narrower sense, as the Catholic church has frequently demanded, should be provided outside the public schools in a church or private school, according to the Court.[17]

One area in which West German courts have begun to venture boldly where previously they feared to tread is children's rights. In the early days of the Federal Republic, a traditional view of schoolchildren prevailed, that they did not possess the full constitutional rights of an adult. They lived in a special "authority relationship" (*Gewaltverhaeltnis*) and thereby did not exercise full religious freedom, for example, or full freedom of speech. School authorities could therefore exercise control over school newspapers, a problem area in many Western democracies.

During the last 15 years, however, the Federal Supreme Court has addressed the question of children's/students' rights in several contexts.

With respect to sex education, for example, in the case previously mentioned, the Court stated:

> Young people are not merely objects of parental or state education. Rather, they are from the beginning, and increasingly as they grow older, personalities protected by Article 2, paragraph 1 in combination with Article 1, paragraph 1 of the *Grundgesetz* (i.e., the right to "free development of personality" and the right to "inviolable dignity").[18]

Thus the Court has established a sliding scale with respect to the constitutional rights a child enjoys. The older a child becomes, the greater are his/her constitutional rights until the age of 18, when he/she achieves full citizens' rights. The school as well as the parents therefore exercise a diminishing degree of authority over the child as it grows older. At age 12, for example, parents must obtain the consent of a child before enrolling him/her for religious instruction. By 14 the child may decide without parental consent to petition for dispensation from religious instruction. Similarly, the Court has interpreted the child's right to free personality development to mean that corporal punishment is prohibited in schools, that children have a right to free expression in student newspapers, and that children have a right to free assembly and to demonstrate.[19]

This does not mean, of course, that these legal norms are accepted everywhere without protest or conflict. Legal norms do not necessarily coincide entirely with prevailing social norms. Yet, school laws and regulations must meet the standards set by the Supreme Court. Legal norms must be translated into legal imperatives.

In no area has the right of students been more jealously and zealously protected by the courts than in vocational choice. Under Article 12, Paragraph 1 of the *Grundgesetz,* students are guaranteed the right to a free choice of occupation and the right to gain the necessary education and training to practice it. It reads: "All Germans have a right to a free choice of their occupation, their place of work and the institution for their vocational/professional education and training."

For Americans, accustomed to an open society without a traditional elite or tightly controlled guild structure, this guarantee may seem unusual. For East Germans, on the other hand, accustomed to the strictures of state planning and "societal demands," this may even seem ludicrous or chaotic. The implications for higher education in West Germany are especially significant.

Traditionally, German university students have enjoyed a privileged position in German society. Once having passed a rigorous state examination, the *Abitur*, the door to any university, and any and every academic field of study, stood wide open. Furthermore, all universities are autonomous, although state-financed and tuition-free.

This favorable situation persisted in the Federal Republic until the 1950s, largely as a result of the highly selective nature of secondary education. The *Gymnasium*, which had provided the traditional path to the *Abitur* and the university, had maintained itself as an elite institution. Only about 25,000 students therefore began matriculation each year at universities in West Germany during the 1950s.

This situation changed rapidly, however, and by 1981, 155,000 young Germans were seeking space for the first time in German lecture halls and seminar rooms, an increase of more than sixfold.[20] As this increase coincided with both a time of fiscal pinch and overcrowding in many of the learned professions, several *Laender* sought to regulate university admissions. Initially the courts ruled that such efforts were unconstitutional. Eventually the *Laender* governments agreed to follow a central admissions policy for the entire Federal Republic and to distribute admissions according to available places in the various faculties. This almost immediately precipitated litigation on the part of excluded students. Once again the Federal Supreme Court was called upon to adjudicate. In cases involving efforts by Hamburg and Bavaria to regulate university admissions, the Court decreed:

1. That the constitutional right of students to choose their university must not be violated by university admission requirements;
2. That it is not permitted to use the regulation of university admission as a means of controlling the constitutionally guaranteed free choice of occupations;
3. That authorities are not allowed arbitrarily to exclude citizens from the advantage of a higher education and professional career.[21]

These principles certainly made it clear that the *Laender* of West Germany could not plan (and control) admission to the universities and various professions in the way that its socialist/communist counterpart could. The Federal Supreme Court, however, did not leave the *Laender* entirely helpless in the face of this crisis. It also recognized that overcrowding itself limited the right of students to make a totally free choice; therefore, the *Laender* were permitted ultimately to develop some criteria for regulating admissions in fields like medicine, dentistry, and biology, in which limited numbers of laboratory or clinical places are available. But the Court, ever mindful and watchful of students' rights, urged the *Laender* to expand the universities, provide counseling and then, when the only recourse was restriction of admission, to do so by means of establishing criteria that ruled out every conceivable bias (for example, social, geographical, etc.).[22]

Now that the crisis in higher education and the learned professions has in some instances grown worse, the Federal Supreme Court has, if anything, made it even more difficult for the *Laender* to restrict admission to study in these areas. For example, the glut of teachers in some fields caused the government of Baden-Wuerttemberg to deny university admission to a prospective student who wanted to become a history teacher. The Court ruled that it was unconstitutional for the *Land* to exercise this power; it could not use societal demand as a justification for restricting admission. The plaintiff must be permitted "to accept the risk of unemployment." The *Land* was denied the power "to limit the freedom of the individual to exercise personal responsibility and riskful self-determination in participating in the free competition for positions."[23] In this decision the Court not only protected the right of free choice in the professions, but also noted that "the self-discipline of applicants can guarantee a more reliable means of adjusting educational aspirations (*Ausbildungswuensche*) to the possibilities of employment than paternal interference on the part of the state (*Staatliche Bevormundung*)."[24] As a result students enjoy a virtually unlimited number of years (sometimes, ten or more) of tuition-free university studies.

The wide disparity that exists between East and West in the way legal norms regulate education is nowhere more vividly illustrated than in this case. Despite serious overcrowding in a number of professions, despite the tremendous cost of a university education, the Supreme Court has ruled that "human dignity" and the right to "free development of one's personality" outweigh all other considerations in mandating an open-door policy in university admissions. In the GDR, planning and societal needs take precedence over personal desires when learned professions and university lecture halls are full. Indeed, the number of university admissions and even the number of upper-secondary students have been rigorously limited in the 1970s and 1980s (see Chapter 6). The GDR Constitution and institutions guarantee that government and courts unite their power to ensure an *einheitliche* socialist/communist education unhampered by the "bourgeois interests of individuals, parents, and religious groups."

Thus we have seen in this chapter and the previous one the contrasting legal principles on which the educational systems of the two Germanys are based. Legal principles, however, are not meant to be completely abstract. They are not intended to create a reality of their own, however much they may seem at times to do just that; they are meant to influence human behavior, the ways in which people think and act. If this human dimension has been somewhat neglected in these two chapters, it is so that the stage can be properly set. One must understand the contrasting legal values of the two Germanys before proceeding to the dramas that are played each day in the schools of the two states.

NOTES

Epigraph to Chapter 4 is from Kurt Tucholsky. GDR author Reiner Kunze (born 1933), who has been living in the Federal Republic since 1977, has proposed to use this text for an opposition leaflet. In *Die Wunderbaren Jahre* (Frankfurt, 1976), p. 53f.

1. Norbert Haase, Lothar Reese, and Peter Wensierski, eds., *VEB Nachwuchs: Jugend in der DDR* (Reinbek, 1983), p. 168f.
2. Bundesverfassungsgericht, ed., *Entscheidungen des Bundesverfassungsgerichts (BVerfGE)*, 34 (Tuebingen, 1973), p. 181f.
3. Ibid., p. 182.
4. Ibid., p. 183f.
5. Ibid., p. 192.
6. Bruno Schmidt-Bleibtreu and Franz Klein, *Kommentar zum Grundgesetz fuer die Bundesrepublik Deutschland*, 3rd ed. (Neuwied, 1973).
7. The German word *Mensch* means "human being, male or female." *Mann* is used only for males.
8. Schmidt-Bleibtreu and Klein, *Kommentar zum Grundgesetz*, p. 191.
9. The *Frankfurter Allgemeine Zeitung* published von Hayek's essay, "The Ethics of Property and the Development of Cultures," on July 30, 1983.
10. Juergen Raschert, "Bildungspolitik im kooperativen Foederalismus," *Bildung in der Bundesrepublik Deutschland*, vol. 1, edited by Max-Planck-Institut fuer Bildungsforschung (Reinbek, 1980), p. 200ff.
11. Ibid., pp. 203–12.
12. Ibid., p. 130.
13. Ibid., p. 142.
14. January 3, 1983.
15. *BVerfGE* 47 (1981), p. 78.
16. Ibid., p. 74ff.
17. *BVerfGE* 41 (1975), pp. 29ff, 65ff, 89ff.

18. See note 16.
19. D. Margies, "Schule im Rechtsstaat," K. Roeser, "Rechte und Pflichten des Schuelers — Rechte und Pflichten des Lehrers," *Handbuch Schule und Unterricht,* vol. 3, edited by Walter Twellman (Duesseldorf, 1981), pp. 191–228.
20. Bundesminister fuer Bildung und Wissenschaft, ed., *Grund- und Strukturdaten* (Bonn, 1982–83), p. 112.
21. See Chapter 12 in *Between Elite and Mass Education,* pp. 263–91.
22. *BVerfGE* 33 (1973), p. 303ff.
23. *DVBL,* June 1, 1983, p. 597.
24. Ibid.

5

GOALS OF EDUCATION IN EAST AND WEST

Educational goals and guiding values help to build consensus in a
state founded on a constitution. They are indispensable and form a
part of its cultural identity. . . . Freedom and pluralism, human
dignity and democracy only become possible and reliable by way
of educational goals. . . .

Peter Haeberle

All I can say is that the old student truism is still valid: *Non
vitae sed scholae discimus.*

A student's opinion

SOME MAJOR PHILOSOPHIC TRADITIONS

The dramatic contrast presented above, between the lofty ideas of a
professor and the down-to-earth opinion of a student, could have been
found in either of the two German states; indeed, in any modern state. On
one hand, scholars philosophize about the final aims of education; on the
other, students puncture the pomposity of such high ideals and introduce
a little levity or irony to such discussions.

As is well known, the Germans have a tradition of philosophizing
ponderously about all human activity. With respect to education this is no
less so. Some of the leading German philosophers of the nineteenth
century also addressed themselves to questions such as the following:
Should the aims of education be derived from the needs of the individual

or from allegedly more objective norms such as eternal moral values or the needs of the state or the community?

In his answer to this dilemma, Johann Friedrich Herbart (1776-1841), the great philosopher of education, claimed that a theory of education had to be derived from absolute moral values. For Herbart, such concepts as morality, justice, equity, goodness, and "inner freedom," were clearcut and formed a base on which to build educational principles. He defined as the two main goals of education the harmonious development of all abilities and strength of moral character (*Charakterstaerke der Sittlichkeit*). Education would provide the individual with a "horizon of ideas," which Herbart thought was the "main seat of character formation." Moral behavior was seen as a direct consequence of instruction. One recent German educator[1] has characterized this Herbartian mode of thinking as "forming people." Education, thereby, basically becomes a process of "building" people in accordance with preconceived ethical ideas.

On the other hand, Herbart's contemporary, Friedrich Schleiermacher (1768–1834), doubted the possibility of deducing an educational philosophy from an absolute ethical system. As Schleiermacher wrote: "We cannot rely on such an ethical system, as there is none that is universally acknowledged."[2] This lack of a well-defined and well-ordered hierarchy of moral values not only complicated the problem of forming a set of educational goals, it made education itself an entirely different process from what Herbart conceived. It negated the notion of forming a particular type of person through education, by employing particular means or techniques to reach predictable goals.

Yet, Schleiermacher did not accept Rousseau's idea of "natural growth," which was so popular at the time. Instead, he posited a dialectical approach: that the aims of education were not defined externally by ethics, religion, or politics, nor were they defined internally by the structure or nature of the personality. Instead, Schleiermacher maintained that the process of education itself would define its goals, through the interaction of the everchanging individual personality with a society whose values and standards were in flux. It was the task of each generation to preserve what was good and to improve what was imperfect. According to Schleiermacher, education is constantly changing; it has many dimensions that seem to contradict each other, but in reality they do not. General education, for example, does not mean the rejection of specialized education from the curriculum; nor does education for the present mean precluding education for the future. Education involves a constant searching and striving for the good, which can never be completely defined; it involves the constant formulation and reformulation of syntheses.

Clearly, Schleiermacher's dialectical vision of education as a process contrasts dramatically with both Herbart's ideals of external character formation and Rousseau's notion of "letting grow." Indeed, Schleiermacher stands as the founder of a German school of pedagogy that has taught educators to integrate guidance with self-growth.[3]

Thus we see that contemporary educational dilemmas have deep-seated philosophical roots; that even such dilemmas as we ascribe to East-West ideological differences can be traced to the distant past. For example, Herbart's belief in an objective and universal moral order that can guide educators in "forming" people, finds its echo in modern dogmatic political systems such as that of the GDR. On the other hand, Schleiermacher's advocacy of taking a multiplicity of values — the demands of society as well as the respect for the individual — into account when building an educational system, finds its counterpart in the pluralism of modern Western democracies.

WEST GERMANY: CONTROVERSIAL ISSUES

> Since 1945 the development of our educational system can be seen as the dissolution of the old idea of "Bildung". . . . The landmarks of this educational planning, which were adopted from the USA, are the laws of the market and efficiency. Profit considerations have replaced substantive concepts of education which were derived from basic general truths. Educational planning in this sense, however, means in practice the elimination of everything that previously was understood as "Bildung" in European culture. The result of this has been the total destruction of the inherited concept of education.[4]

Although this statement at first might appear to be the ideological criticism of an East German Marxist, it is instead the harsh opinion of a very conservative West German. Such critical views can be found in the educational discourse of every Western state, often including the decidedly negative judgment of U.S. influence. Indeed, in the United States itself such sentiments have been expressed in the writings of Hyman Rickover and Mortimer Adler, among others. Critics of West German education are undoubtedly correct in this: any consensus about the "true" basis of education has been lost.

No single philosophy of education can any longer encompass the multiplicity of aims found in the educational literature of the Federal Republic. Nor could any simple description suffice to represent the complexity of West German schools. Perhaps only the broad, general language of the *Grundgesetz* (Constitution) can wholly embrace the full sweep of West German education. In describing "inalienable human rights," for example, Article 1 describes respect for the "dignity of man" as the goal and duty of the state. The following articles define fundamental rights such as the right of "free development of the person" (Article 2), "equality before the law" (Article 3), freedom of belief, opinion, and so on (Articles 4 and 5), and the "free choice of occupation, working place, and training institution" (Article 12). But can one really call such broad constitutional guarantees anything more than a framework, a broad set of ideals rather than a concrete set of aims? If anything, such ideals promote constant disagreement as to meaning rather than establishing a set of imperatives for education.

And this is what conservative critics like Guenther and others resent (see above). But are they right? Haven't "progressive" reformers also tackled the problem of identifying worthwhile goals for education today? For example, one leading West German educator, Hartmut von Hentig, has assayed to compile a list of important educational objectives.[5] Von Hentig's list comprises 13 goals, among which are included: education for consumerism, education for appreciation and critical use of modern technology, and education to assist in development of social-psychological skills. Although not all of von Hentig's "goals" are so untraditional, they are all directed toward preparing students for life in a modern, democratic society, and have therefore drawn intense criticism from traditionalists since their publication in 1969.

Three areas, especially, have provided the fulcrum for lively debate. These are, first, von Hentig's emphasis on preparing students for life in a rapidly changing society (his emphasis on change); second, his stress on the necessity of specialization; and third, his emphasis on social goals, especially the integration of all social classes.

With regard to the first of these, life in a constantly changing world, von Hentig wrote, "The student must be acquainted with the processes of *change* in our present time. From the beginning the school must permit pupils to experience the conditions under which *facts* may be *changed by ourselves*."[6] Von Hentig argues the amount of time it takes to acquire knowledge and skills cannot keep pace with the amount of time it takes for these to change. To avoid loss of control over their environment, students must learn how to learn and gain knowledge of the conditions of change in every realm (for example, technology, politics, science, philosophy, economics). Students must learn to be actors instead of objects. This requires, writes von Hentig, that schools abandon their traditional curricula and teaching methods. A new breed of curriculum specialists will be needed who can build a curriculum for as yet unanticipated tasks. Teachers will be required who can bring contemporary problems into their classrooms. Students will engage in problem-solving rather than in memorization, learn to define problems, choose subjects, and form learning groups; they must be prepared to assume responsibilities and to maintain their identities in a changing world.

Above all, this means learning to live in a world dominated by science and technology. In order to understand this world, in order to avoid being duped or misled, students must learn to understand and appreciate the scientific method that has made the modern world possible. Schools must begin to teach the scientific method as early as possible in its most elementary forms and proceed from there to more sophisticated study. The largest possible number of students must learn to appreciate the importance of such scientific concepts as the hypothesis, quantification, verification and/or falsification, data processing, communication of data, and replication of results. This would result in an ever larger proportion of young people attending institutions of higher education. And it would also mean, as proponents of the comprehensive school have been quick to note, abandonment of the traditional tripartite school system in favor of a comprehensive system.

These so-called progressive goals have tended to dominate the educational dialogue of the Federal Republic in recent years. In summary, the progressive agenda includes: preparation for life in a constantly changing world; social involvement; political responsibility; and an appreciation and understanding of modern science. Most important, it would also include structural changes so that advanced secondary and higher education would no longer be the domain of a small group of elite citizens, but the property of virtually all members of the younger generation. It is this program that has inspired reform-minded educators and politicians, but which has, at the same time, aroused the ire of those committed to more traditional educational verities.

In January 1978, for example, a group of such traditionalists gathered in Bonn under the banner, *Courage for Education*. In response to the demands being made by reformers, the Bonn Forum adopted a program of "Nine Theses" which ostensibly refuted all of the reform proposals of their opponents. Each of the theses or refutations begins grandly and boldly in language reminiscent of the Council of Trent's (1545-61) rejection of the errors of Protestantism in the sixteenth century. "We object to the error of . . ." (*Wir wenden uns gegen den Irrtum . . .*), they all begin.[7]

These theses not only denounced the educational ideas of the reformers, but many of their basic assumptions as well. For example, the conservatives rejected the notion that schools might mitigate the stresses and strains of living in a society that was as yet unknown. According to the Bonn Forum, the burdens of the human condition (*herkunftsbedingte Lebensverhaeltnisse*) were more enduring than wishful pedagogical thinking, and could not be easily overcome by initiating school reforms. Equally refuted was the notion of solving social problems through the schools. The schools should not be expected to initiate reforms "which society does not want to initiate through its political institutions." Even the goals of education that John Dewey had proclaimed and popularized more than half a century earlier were rejected: that the school in the interest of serving a better society should see "that each individual gets an opportunity to escape from the limitations of the social group in which he was born."[8]

The Bonn Forum held progressives responsible for many of the neurotic and selfish children the schools had already produced. The stress on seeking personal happiness (*Gluecksansprueche zu stellen*) had largely resulted in frustration and unhappiness. It had also resulted in neglect of the "virtues of diligence, discipline, and order," which were necessary for humanity. The Forum particularly objected to placing the political process and the use of the scientific method in the schools, when the pupils were not yet able to appreciate such matters. "We object to the error that the school must teach children to 'look after their own interests.'" "Before they can begin to look after their own interests, they [pupils] must be introduced to the realities of life out of which personal interests are generated," reads the refutation.

Thus, with the lines drawn, the debate on these issues often became acrimonious. In retaliation to the conservative charges, the progressives accused their detractors of wanting to "incapacitate the coming generation." Mocking the banner of the Forum, they asserted that the true "courage for education" was to be found in those who have the "courage for reform of society and schools."[9]

Nor has this controversy remained a purely academic one. Several of the *Laender* have instituted schools founded on progressive principles.

North Rhine-Westphalia, for example, has founded the *Kollegschule,* which uses a "scientific orientation" as the basis for all instruction, whether for future workers or professionals. In addition, the government of the state of Hesse has introduced a curricular concept of social studies, which stresses contemporary political and social conflicts, despite determined resistance on the part of conservative parent organizations, which have charged the Minister of Education with exacerbating social class conflicts. As with many such disputes in the Federal Republic, this one finally reached the law courts: on December 30, 1981, the Supreme Court of Hesse ruled in favor of the parents' groups, which had demanded more history in the social studies curriculum. Even new textbooks had to be introduced. A similar decision by the Standing Conference of the Ministers of Education mandated more traditional history courses in the advanced levels of the *Gymnasien,* as opposed to courses in politics and sociology.

Another heated controversy that has sprung from this debate has centered on the issue of general education versus specialization. Unlike most other Western states, Germany does not have a tradition of electives and individual choices in the schools. Rather, the idea of the "ordo docendi" has survived, which took the form of a unified, concentrated, and standardized curriculum for all students. This was a general course of studies and even had its origins in the study of the seven liberal arts (*artes septem liberales*).

Ironically, on this issue the educational conservatives in the Federal Republic share views that are in many respects similar to those of the Marxist educators in the GDR. The East Germans have instituted an *einheitliches* (unified) curriculum which stresses a well-rounded, harmonious education for everyone. Of course, the content of a general curriculum in the GDR differs markedly from that of one in the Federal Republic. In fact, the Federal Republic, which for many years after its founding was committed to a unified, standard curriculum, differentiated this curriculum according to schools and level of intellectual attainment.

Allgemeinbildung (general education), as it was called, took its simplest form in the *Volksschule,* which was "for the people." A more demanding variation existed in the *Realschule,* and a yet more demanding version or "mature" form was mandated in the *Gymnasium* for the academic elite of the nation.

"Maturity" (*Maturitaet*) is a term that one finds frequently in German educational literature, referring to the completion of a course of "general studies." Even the examination that young Germans must pass before being admitted to university study has at times been known as a "Maturity

Exam" (*Maturitaetsexamen*), thus signifying successful completion of general education. A leading German educational philosopher has defined the term as follows:

> Maturity is no quantitative sum; subjects are not containers for individual disciplines. They are courses which present an introduction to particular intellectual forms [*Geistesformen*] whose interplay contains a unified and homogeneous preparation for scholarly studies. As basic introductions they form a closed circle of "liberal arts" — *artium liberalium* — a complete study of a fundamental kind. Readiness for more specialized study and for cooperation with other research scholars can only spring from this base.[10]

Such ideals of unity and order in general education have rarely been challenged in the past. If one of the founders of this concept, Wilhelm von Humboldt (1767–1835), described education in terms of its "universality and totality," other more recent proponents have used words like "completeness" and "unity" to mean the same thing. Even the short eight-year course of the old People's School (*Volksschule*) was seen as such a "totality," a "humanistic core." Many great German scientists such as Einstein (1879–1955) have supported a general education based on an ideal of unity and order as well. And last, but certainly not least, the leading figures of German classical literature praised that world of order that transcended the apparent chaos of daily life. In the last stanza of Goethe's "Dauer im Wechsel," he wrote:

> Danke, dass die Gunst der Musen
> Unvergaengliches verheisst:
> Den Gehalt in deinem Busen
> Und die Form in deinem Geist.
>
> (Thanks! The Muses' gracious giving
> Make the imperishable thing
> In thy breast the substance living
> In thy soul the Form divine.)

Such deeply rooted ideas could not be easily uprooted or modified. The unified, humanistic tradition withstood challenge after challenge by its "barbarian" detractors. For instance, in 1959 the *Deutsche Ausschuss*, an official educational advisory committee at the federal level, argued that the ideal of a unified and homogeneous system of knowledge had already ceased to exist.[11] To delude oneself into thinking otherwise was to encourage further fragmentation of knowledge in the schools. Indeed, the importance of new subjects such as political science, economics, health education, and driver education could not be ignored and were relevant to any overall educational goals. Then, in the 1960s, the humanistic ideal came under further attack by those committed to *produktive Einseitigkeit,* a term that has a meaning similar to the English ideal "study in depth." Nevertheless, the traditional notion still held sway in 1970 when another federal committee, the famous *Deutsche Bildungsrat,* launched its criticism. In its "Structural Plan for the German Educational System," it propagated the idea of education as a matter of personal choice and responsibility. "Courses offered must be manifold in order to give the student an opportunity to form his/her individual curriculum," the *Bildungsrat* proposed.[12] Such issues as individual learning differences, motivation, interests, and goals could then be taken into consideration. The *Bildungsrat* concluded that education was much more a personal matter of ability and responsible choice than a homogeneous curriculum valid for all.

In 1972 the Standing Conference of Ministers of Education put its powerful support behind the idea of education as a matter of personal choice. As a result, the various *Laender* soon moved in this direction, abandoning the traditional, standard curriculum in favor of a growing catalogue of elective subjects on the upper secondary level.

But the controversy is far from over, the issue far from definitively settled. Just as the struggle continues in Britain for more general education in the highly specialized Sixth Form (Upper Secondary), and *The Paideia Proposal* of Mortimer Adler gains adherents in the United States for a basic curriculum, so too in West Germany does the public debate continue over whether there should be a unified curriculum for all students. In fact, a number of conservative factions in Hesse won a significant victory when the Supreme Court ruled in their favor by declaring that the Hessian school law, which provided excessive electives in upper secondary levels of the *Gymnasium* (grades eleven to thirteen), was unconstitutional; the Constitution of Hesse guarantees a broad, general education for all students.

However much, then, this debate continues in all Western states over individualized and specialized education as opposed to general education, it is still especially vehement in West Germany. The idea of *Allgemeinbildung* is so deeply imbedded in the consciousness of educators and the curricular structure of schools as to make reforms especially difficult. Interestingly, the proponents of individual choice and a pluralistic curriculum often see themselves as the guardians of German democracy, as opposed to those who still hark back to an authoritarian age.

The social goals of West German education have proved no less rancorous than the dispute over general education. The questions are as follows:

- Should the schools continue to educate an academic elite, largely drawn from upper- and upper-middle-class children, to take leading positions in society, or
- Should the schools integrate the children of all social classes, providing equal opportunity for all, irrespective of social and economic background?

These questions then raise a host of others, regarding the role of schools in determining who gets trained for what job or occupation and how far the schools should be responsible for integrating and stabilizing a society that has grown increasingly heterogeneous and factious.

Although discussion of such issues is not new to German educational circles, it has become especially volatile in recent years. In the late nineteenth century and in the early Weimar years, the Social Democrats had vigorously supported the idea of a "unified school" (*Einheitsschule*) which would serve to integrate all social classes. Yet, following the German defeat in 1945, the restoration of a three-class school system was not seriously questioned. Arthus Hearnden, an English comparative historian of this period, has found this lack of discourse rather puzzling. In 1973 he wrote, "But it did not reflect any profound consideration of the implications of restoring the tripartite system unaltered."[13]

Yet, the reasons for the restoration and continuation of the traditional system between 1945 and 1965 are not difficult to find. In the second chapter we discussed how the lack of a unified reform program among the Western Allies permitted the unruly western twin to restore much of the old tripartite educational system. And once established, there was little impetus for change. Postwar Germany lacked the racial and ethnic problems which, in countries like the United States, created a demand for educational change. Also, the successful reconstruction of the economy under Chancellor Adenauer and Secretary of Economic Affairs Ludwig Erhard not only made most West Germans self-satisfied, it also made it possible to absorb 10 million refugees from East Germany into the economy. West German exports gained an outstanding reputation in foreign markets for their high quality, and much of this was attributed to the excellence of traditional German craft and vocational training.

Many educational thinkers marched in step with success and supported this modern version of Plato's class system. Heinrich Weinstock, for example, writing in 1955, used the image of a machine to demonstrate the relationship between schooling, class structure, and the successful functioning of a society.[14] The machine, he argued, required a small group of inventors and managers, a large group of workers, and an intermediate group of people trained to repair it and improve its operation. In the same way, an industrial society needed a small intellectual elite, a somewhat larger middle class, and a large mass of workers. Fortunately, nature had distributed intelligence appropriately; thus West German schooling was in perfect harmony with natural law, social reality, and economic necessity.

As it might be expected, the fear of an economic crisis provided the principal motive for demands for educational change in the 1960s. With rapid changes in the world's economy, the so-called educational catastrophe suddenly became a byword for German educators and politicians. Of course, this was joined to discussions about social justice and social and political solidarity and education as the "right of all citizens." Empirical studies showing the undereducation of several significant groups in West German society added fuel to the growing conflagration. For example, children from lower-middle-class and lower-class backgrounds made up 50 percent of their age cohort, but were only 6 percent of those attending grade thirteen in the *Gymnasien* of the country. Girls, rural children, and Catholic children were also shown to be seriously underrepresented in the higher levels of the educational system. The "poor, working class, Catholic girls from a rural village" became the symbol of educational deprivation.[15]

In the early 1960s the "educational crisis" remained largely a matter of discussion and debate in academic circles, but by the mid-1960s growing student unrest and an economic recession propelled the issue into the popular arena. In addition, government domination by the conservative Christian Democrats finally came to an end in 1969 and was followed by a coalition rule by Social Democrats and Liberals, who were much more amenable to social change. In particular, it was the *Deutscher Bildungsrat,* the official advisory committee on educational affairs in those days, that lent its support to making education more accessible to all citizens. In its 1970 report this committee stated unequivocally that the right to a school education not only exists when each child has equality of educational opportunity, but "only when each child is supported in such a manner as to permit him/her to avail himself/herself of this opportunity."[16]

The *Bildungsrat* supported its recommendations with more than 50 research studies and reports, among which one of the most significant and prestigious was the almost 600-page volume entitled *Begabung und Lernen* (Ability and Learning). Edited by H. Roth,[17] this work quickly became an important source of reference for everyone engaged in the struggle to end social deprivation in the schools. The volume contained a wealth of research pertaining to schooling and genetic heritage, social environment, course organization, and teaching methods. Interestingly, it relied heavily on the research findings of prominent British and U.S. psychologists and sociologists; the work of people like Basil Bernstein in sociolinguistics, Carl Bereiter in teaching the disadvantaged, John William Atkinson in achievement motivation, Jacob W. Getzels in preschool education, David Clarence McClelland in motivation, and Harry A. Passow in ability grouping, as well as others. In essence, the Federal Republic now joined an informal "North Atlantic Treaty Organization for Reform in Education" as its youngest member.

The advocates of reform soon adopted many of the concepts and even the terminology of other Western reformers. But resistance did not disappear. As in practically all the states of Western Europe, conservative political parties, organizations of elite secondary school teachers, and many university professors built ramparts of resistance and even went on the attack as well. For example, the Association of Gymnasium Teachers quoted research results that "proved" that only 5 percent of any age group was capable of undertaking higher education. Many *Gymnasium* teachers also rejected the idea that the greater integration of all social classes in a comprehensive school would lead to greater social understanding and tolerance. Other conservatives more pointedly defended an elite system of education and its selectivity. "It's a simple truth," wrote Gerd Tellenbach, "that a thousand must endeavor to master the piano in order to allow one to become a perfect pianist."[18] Wilhelm Flitner added that secondary schools are for the education of an elite on which "the great continental nations are dependent."[19] And then there was the previously mentioned Bonn Forum, which attacked as erroneous the idea of "the schools undertaking social reforms which society does not want to introduce through its political system."

However, a number of articles and books that appeared in the United States in the 1970s were also quickly pressed into service by those who opposed education as a means of social integration, most notably Christopher Jenck's book, *Inequality* (1972), and Arthur R. Jensen's work on heredity and intelligence.[20]

These then are some of the major educational controversies in this fledgling state. Although the Federal Republic is a new Western-style democracy, its culture and traditions are among the most venerable in Europe. One of its strongest traditions was that of "authority"; it has not therefore found pluralism and democracy easy to accept, especially perhaps in the area of education. Educational disputes over such issues as the role that cultural traditions should play in the curriculum, *Allgemeinbildung* versus electives, and social integration versus elite training, have been particularly acrimonious. There have been numerous other controversies as well (for example, knowledge versus creativity, cognitive versus affective versus pragmatic goals, among others).

Lack of consensus on these issues, however understandable, can be difficult to accept. This is undoubtedly the fate of pluralistic societies. In grappling with this problem, John Dewey wrote:

> It is well to remind ourselves that education as such has no aims. Only persons, parents, and teachers, etc., have aims, not an abstract idea like education. And consequently their purposes are indefinitely varied, differing with different children, changing as children grow and with the growth of experience on the part of the one who teaches.[21]

This is reminiscent of Schleiermacher (see above) and defines education not as a means to an end, but as a goal in itself. Education in a democracy, according to Dewey, should provide a preparation for further intellectual, emotional, and social growth. "The purpose of school education," Dewey wrote, "is to insure the continuation of education by organizing the powers that insure growth."[22]

In West Germany, a group of curriculum theorists have tried to reify these ideas of Schleiermacher, Dewey, and others. Among them are Herwig Blankertz, Wolfgang Klafki, Saul Robinsohn, and Erich Weniger. They have used the German term *Bildung* to define that interaction between process and aim, individual and culture, that seems to express Dewey's notion of education. It was especially Erich Weniger who proposed a pattern of cooperation that would involve all social groups in the constant democratic process of defining and redefining the aims and content of education.[23]

This process of maintaining a constant dialogue on education and translating the results of this process into planning and action is always tenuous and frequently threatened. While many teachers and educators, prior to 1965, deplored the absence of public discussion of education, they have come to realize since the mid-1960s the hazards of popular debate as well. At times this has led to extremes of polarization and politicization. Yet, in general, since the war West Germans, like the citizens of other Western democracies, have shunned the extremes; a slow development along the middle of the road appears the most attractive way to the large majority.

EAST GERMANY: COMMUNISM STRAIGHT AHEAD

The structural conservatism of West German schools has not only brought them criticism from Western educators, it has also given East German ideologists an excellent target on which to focus. GDR critics like Helmut Klein have continuously denounced West German education as capitalistic, imperialistic, and bourgeois, the principal terms of opprobrium in the Marxist-Leninist rhetorical armory.[24] Even the recent controversies about education that have developed in the Federal Republic are not described as the outgrowths of a democratic and pluralistic society, but are rather depicted as manifestations of the class struggle. In this respect educational thought in the GDR is in perfect harmony with that of the Soviet Union.

By contrast with the Federal Republic, the educational goals of the GDR are seen as the logical reflection of material conditions. This derives directly from Soviet and Marxist-Leninist theory, which stresses the deterministic nature of ideas. As Lenin expressed it, "In reality the goals of man are produced by the objective world and presuppose it. . . . Yet it *appears* to man that his goals are derived from outside the [objective] world and are independent of this world ('freedom')."[25]

Free will is therefore largely regarded as an illusion, and the problem of defining and clarifying goals should really be only a technical problem. One need only translate objective factors such as economic and social development into norms for education in order to define its means and its goals.

The vocabulary of communist education does not at first appear to reflect this lack of idealism. One of its most explicit and frequently repeated aims, for example, is to develop "the well-rounded, educated socialist/communist personality." Or to develop a high degree of "versatility" and "harmony" in every socialist/communist comrade. These are ideals that have appeared in educational thought since ancient times and have particularly been in German educational lexicons since the

Enlightenment; neo-humanist and neoclassical thinkers in the nineteenth century have especially stressed such notions.

Undoubtedly, Marx was influenced by this tradition, but he reinterpreted these ideas in terms of the proletariat. Workers had been denied full participation in the capitalist economy. They were really only partial people with a partial function (*Teilfunktionen*) in society. What Marx foresaw was the leading role of the proletariat in the socialist society of the future, and this demanded that they become "totally developed individuals" who would be capable of mastering all of the functions of production. To produce such an individual would be the function of "polytechnic schools."[26]

This Marxian ideal of full and well-rounded development of every member of society has found its way, with some variations, into the educational theories of every Marxist state. As Helmut Klein of the GDR notes, "This basic idea, that in a socialist state everything must be done to promote the well-rounded and harmonious development of the people, occurs repeatedly as the highest political principle of communist and workers' parties."[27]

As this ideal is a historical one, however, dependent on the particular stage of social and economic development of a society as well as the consciousness of the workers, it requires constant redefinition and clarification. Yet, controversies are rare and, if they occur, seldom make it to any public forum in the GDR. "Public discussion is impossible," writes GDR refugee Martin Ahren.[28] Most decisions are made in the confines of party caucus rooms and meeting halls. Controversial educational questions are hardly ever a matter of public debate.

What then does the official aim ("the development of the well-rounded, harmonious socialist personality") of all education in the GDR actually mean? In his *Theory of Socialist General Education,* Gerhart Neuner elucidates: "for the socialist concept of education . . . ideological education, the development of socialist consciousness and behavior, must be at the center of the well-rounded development of socialist personalities."[29] This means the study of Marxism and Leninism on every level of education, in schools, youth organizations, universities, and institutions for adult education; acknowledging the leading role of the working class and the revolutionary political party (the SED) that represents it; and active participation in socialist/communist public and private life, at work, at home, and through political organs. The convictions of Marxism-Leninism must permeate every aspect of the "well-rounded, harmonious personality."

This general goal must, however, be defined more specifically, both in ideological as well as curricular and cognitive terms in order to be useful. With respect to ideology, the following, more specific aims have been adduced:

- a clear understanding of the nature of capitalism today, including its "inhuman quality and lack of perspective";
- acceptance of the conviction of the "inevitable victory of socialism/communism" and the "decline of capitalism";
- "insight into the nature of imperialism," including an understanding of the worldwide class struggle between socialism and capitalism;
- "an ability to judge all contemporary questions from the standpoint of socialism."[30]

In terms of the curriculum, "general education" in the GDR means "the imparting and acquisition of the fundamentals of science and technology, the mother tongue and foreign languages, the arts, and body culture (*Koerperkultur*)." In order to make best use of these subjects, the fully developed "socialist personality" will be equipped with "spiritual and cultural interests," "physical abilities," "creative capacities," and an "aesthetic relationship to social reality."

However personal this ambitious agenda of goals may seem, it is clear that societal needs should predominate over individual ambitions and plans. Even where individual achievement is encouraged in study and work, the ultimate GDR goals of ideological unity, achieving a planned economy, and maintaining military preparedness must always be kept foremost in mind. As defined in the official educational program of the GDR, these goals are:

- "being capable and ready to achieve high performance in all societal fields," including the development of "communist work morale" as the center of "socialist morality";
- "having the ability and willingness to apply all one's capabilities for the protection and defense of the socialist motherland, and the defense of the socialist community of states";
- "gaining mastery of scientific and technological progress, thereby increasing the economic productivity of the state";
- "participating in collectives, thereby developing organization and discipline."[31]

It was left to the great Soviet pedagogue, Anton S. Makarenko (1888–1939), who is greatly revered in the GDR today, to define the ultimate goal of socialist/communist pedagogy and the way these various elements can be combined to achieve it:

> In every collective, discipline must stand above the interests of the individual members. . . . Man behaves that way because he is convinced that the problem which he tackles is useful and necessary for the whole collective, for the entire (Soviet) society, for the state. . . . The essential part that must be emphasized is the political meaning of discipline.[32]

Obviously these educational goals are derived directly from the socialist/communist value system. The citizens of the GDR, young and old, are asked to pledge themselves, at certain important steps in their lives, to accept these values and turn them into personal goals of learning and behavior. These values also provide a clear guide for curricular decisions. This is especially obvious with respect to "ideological subjects" such as history, geography, social studies, language, and literature. One look at GDR student textbooks of these subjects suffices to reveal the underlying Marxist-Leninist concepts. It is equally true with regard to the natural sciences, sports, and military education. Then, of course, there is "polytechnic education" which is an educational ideal that is peculiar to Marxist states.

As we have already noted, it was Karl Marx himself who first declared that education in a socialist state should be "polytechnic," that it should contain a strong element of technological education, including theoretical as well as practical elements, and including productive work in factories in order to achieve that most important of all goals, the "absolute *Disponibilitaet* [availability] of man for the changing necessities of work."[33]

In the early years of the Soviet state, P. P. Blonskij (1884–1941), one of the leading educational philosophers of this era (who later fell from favor), devised the first detailed theory of polytechnic education. Blonskij's definition is still quite illuminating. He enthusiastically praised industrialism as "the greatest victory of mankind over nature." The aim of industrial education, he wrote, "is the development of the ability to produce objects which are useful for mankind. The essence of industrial education is the mastery of work tools and techniques. . . . The meaning of industrial education is the education of a strong person who owns the tools for the mastery over nature and who submits nature to the use and the needs of mankind."[34]

According to Blonskij, industrial education should not be one-sided, but "polytechnic-scientific-philosophical." The factory becomes the great organizer of cooperation and collective life. "The state of the future will take the form of an economic, industrial state whose social structure is constructed on the basis of production units and whose government is an elected economic administration that organizes societal production."[35] In fact, industry and polytechnic education will make the political government superfluous. Blonskij planned a school system in which work in the factories and in mechanized agriculture would play an important and ever-increasing role in the lives of growing children. Some Soviet educators like Sulgin went further than Blonskij in the late 1920s and even proposed that polytechnic education in factories replace schools altogether.

The enthusiasm of Blonskij and others notwithstanding, the history of polytechnic education in the Soviet Union as well as other socialist/communist states has been marked by great fluctuations of commitment; this has also been true in the GDR. However, for the last 25 years particularly, the GDR has sought to maintain a strong emphasis on polytechnic education in schools and productive units. This has been defined in two parallel ways: as a principle of instruction (that is, a stress on industrial aspects of subjects being taught) and as a particular subject or group of subjects (for example, Polytechnic Instruction, An Introduction to Socialist Production, Technical Drawing, and Productive Labor). Students are sent to work in factories or agricultural cooperatives once a week. In the workplaces, special "polytechnic cabinets" have been established to facilitate practical instruction in the use of machines and tools.

Although the role assigned to polytechnic education in the overall forming of the "socialist personality" has varied somewhat according to circumstances, the following goals have remained relatively constant. However neutral these objectives may seem ideologically, they too are permeated with moral and ideological purposes. The objectives are:

- introduction to the use of machines, instruments, and tools;
- introduction to the scientific bases and processes of industrial production;
- knowledge and application of technical thinking;

- creative use of technology for the solution of problems of production in various fields;
- understanding the economic base of modern industry;
- understanding personal abilities and skills;
- improving social behavior through cooperation in factories and cooperatives;
- vocational training as a means of preparation for vocational study and choice.[36]

Of course, the moral and social values of work education have been discussed in German pedagogical circles for more than 100 years. The great Bavarian educator, Georg Kerschensteiner (1854-1932), had numbered punctuality, diligence, conscientiousness, precision, discipline, and solidarity among the virtues to be gleaned from work education in the first years of this century. Yet, GDR educators make it very clear that even such positive outcomes must also be linked to ideological considerations.

A primary goal, therefore, of polytechnic education in the GDR is to introduce students to "societally useful" production, to teach them to use their skills, talents, and creativity for the building of a socialist industrial society. Polytechnic education is therefore defined as "socialist education," not just "work education." It is regarded as the most effective means of developing ideological convictions and a devotion to the goal of communism with its socialized production and rule by "the Party of the working class." Conversely, when properly employed in the curriculum, it helps future workers to develop necessarily critical attitudes towards "capitalists and imperialists." Some of the ideological objectives of polytechnic education are:

- "education for love of work, for socialism as an expression of the love of the younger generation for their socialist fatherland";
- development of "convictions about the meaning of material production in societal and personal life";
- "education for respect and love of the working class and development of a feeling of solidarity of the younger generation with the working class and the party of the working class";
- acquisition of "political-ideological convictions about the truth and beauty of the revolutionary struggle of the working class for socialism/communism. . . ."[37]

This commitment to the efficacy of polytechnic education as a means of inculcating ideology also derives directly from Karl Marx. Familiarity with economic and industrial processes not only will help to increase production, but will also assist in the building of a political superstructure. The means of accomplishing this goal will be discussed in greater detail in Chapter 7; however, a discussion of GDR educational goals would not be complete without a discussion of the principle of "equality in education."

In Article 25 of the GDR Constitution,[38] one reads:

> (1) Every citizen of the German Democratic Republic has an equal right to education [*Recht auf Bildung*]. Educational institutions are open to everyone. The uniform socialist system of education guarantees every citizen a socialist education and continuing education. (2) The German Democratic Republic protects the progress of the people toward a socialist community of well-rounded and harmoniously developed persons, who are inspired with the spirit of socialist patriotism and internationalism and who are equipped with both an advanced general and specialist education.

On the basis of these constitutional provisions, leading educators of the GDR proudly claim that equality in education at a high level is firmly established in their country.

Clearly, equality is one of the most important principles in socialist/communist ideology. Indeed, it is valued more than so-called individual freedoms to which Western, non-Communist states ardently subscribe. According to Marxist theory, schools in Western "imperialist" states serve only the interests of the ruling bourgeoisie and therefore can never support equality. In the GDR, however, "under the leadership of progressive forces of the people, with communists and genuine anti-fascists in the forefront, and with the solidarity of the Soviet occupation forces . . . a fierce class struggle against reactionary elements was won and, step by step, previous educational privileges were eliminated and private schools were abolished."[39]

In order to achieve classless education, a ten-year comprehensive, compulsory, and tuition-free General Polytechnic High School was founded. Its aim was to provide a higher level of general education for everyone. The authoritative *Akademie der Paedagogischen Wissenschaften* even boldly claimed that this institution genuinely embodied the educational ideas of Comenius, Rousseau, Pestalozzi, and Froebel, by no means a modest pedagogical panoply.

In its early days, prior to 1960, the GDR was notably successful in replacing rural village schools with more centralized Polytechnic High Schools, in much the same manner that unified schools replaced one-room schools in the United States. To a large extent this eliminated the educational disadvantages that had always been the lot of people living in sparsely populated, agricultural areas.

Traditional educational discrimination against girls has also been eliminated in the GDR. Under the provisions of the 1965 Law for a Uniform Socialist Education, girls have been guaranteed the same educational opportunities as boys at every level. Yet equality of opportunity does not necessarily ensure equality of condition. In East Germany, however, women have taken advantage of these educational opportunities and now constitute fully one-half of all students in upper secondary schools and universities. In part, this has resulted from economic necessity, in part from ideological considerations, but for whatever reason, the results have been dramatic.

With respect to social discrimination, which traditionally has meant that the children of professional people, bureaucrats, and businesspeople virtually monopolized higher levels of education, the changes have been even more striking. The government has adopted measures that amount to "reverse discrimination" and favor young people from working-class backgrounds; they are guaranteed a large number of places in advanced levels of education and are provided with financial support. As a result, 50 to 60 percent of upper secondary and university students now come from working-class backgrounds. Of course, children of leading SED members are "working class" per se.

All of these changes presuppose a high degree of centralized control on the part of a government that has totally nationalized every aspect of education. From the cradle to the last years of the university, young people are cared for, guided, and instructed; they are part of a gigantic preplanned societal apparatus that is geared toward that unquestionable goal of GDR school education: the "well-rounded, harmoniously developed socialist/communist personality."

NOTES

The first epigraph to Chapter 5 is from *Erziehungsziele und Orientierungswerte im Verfassungsstaat* (Freiburg/Muenchen, 1981), p. 13. "It's for school not for life that we learn," the reversal of a Latin dictum.

The second epigraph to Chapter 5 is from Theodor Eggers, *Schulhaus-Geruch* (Muenchen, 1979), p. 72.

1. Otto Friedrich Bollnow, *Existenzphilosophie und Paedagogik* (Stuttgart, 1959).
2. Friedrich Schleiermacher, *Paedagogische Schriften,* edited by Erich Weniger and Theodor Schulze (Duesseldorf/Muenchen, 1966).
3. Wilhelm Dilthey (1833–1911), Herman Nohl (1879–1960), Theodor Litt (1880–1962), Eduard Spranger (1882–1963), and others.
4. Henning Guenther, Clemens Willeke, and Rudolf Willeke, *Grundlegung einer bejahenden Erziehung* (Muenchen, 1977), p. 97.
5. Hartmut von Hentig, "Allgemeine Lernziele der Gesamtschule" in Deutscher Bildungsrat, *Lernziele der Gesamtschule* (Stuttgart, 1969), pp. 13–43.
6. Ibid., p. 18.
7. See Dietrich Benner et al., *Entgegnungen zum Bonner Forum "Mut zur Erziehung"* (Muenchen, 1978), p. viiif.
8. John Dewey, *Democracy and Education* (New York, 1916), p. 24.
9. Benner et al., *Entgegnungen,* p. 24f.
10. Wilhelm Flitner, *Die gymnasiale Oberstufe* (Heidelberg, 1961), p. 27.
11. Deutscher Ausschuss fuer das Erziehungs- und Bildungswesen, *Rahmenplan zur Umgestaltung und Vereinheitlichung des allgemeinbildenden oeffentlichen Schulwesens* (Stuttgart, 1959).
12. Deutscher Bildungsrat, *Strukturplan fuer das Bildungswesen* (Stuttgart, 1970), p. 36.
13. Arthur Hearnden, *Education in the Two Germanies* (Oxford, 1974), p. 71.
14. Heinrich Weinstock, *Realer Humanismus* (Heidelberg, 1955).
15. An excellent short report about research and findings in this area was included in the famous university extension radio course, *Erziehungswissenschaft,* by Wolfgang Klafki and his colleagues (Frankfurt, 1970), which since 1969 has reached large numbers of listeners and readers.
16. Deutscher Bildungsrat, *Strukturplan,* p. 30.
17. Ibid.
18. "Hochschule und Hochschulreife" (1958), reprinted in R. Lennert, *Das Problem der gymnasialen Oberstufe* (Bad Heilbrunn, 1971), pp. 39–47.
19. Flitner, *Gymnasiale Oberstufe,* p. 35.
20. Arthur R. Jensen, "Social Class, Race, and Genetics," *American Educ. Res. J.* 9 (1968): 1–42.
21. Dewey, *Democracy and Education,* p. 125.
22. Ibid., p. 61.
23. Erich Weniger, *Didaktik als Bildungslehre* (Weinheim, 1952).
24. Helmut Klein, *Bildung in der DDR* (Reinbek, 1974), p. 11ff.
25. V(ladimir) I. Lenin, *Werke,* vol. 38 (Berlin, 1964), p. 179.
26. *Das Kapital,* vol. 1 (Hamburg, 1867).
27. Klein, *Bildung in der DDR,* p. 25.
28. *Die Zeit,* May 3, 1985, p. 39.

29.   Gerhart Neuner, *Zur Theorie der sozialistischen Allgemeinbildung* (Berlin, 1973), p. 35f.

30.   Akademie der Paedagogischen Wissenschaften der DDR, ed., *Das Bildungswesen der Deutschen Demokratischen Republik*, 2d ed. (Berlin, 1983), p. 13ff.

31.   Ibid., pp. 13–18.

32.   Anton S. Makarenko, *Werke V* (Berlin, 1964), p. 40f.

33.   Karl Marx and Friedrich Engels, *Werke 23* (Berlin, 1972), p. 509ff.

34.   Pavel Petrovich Blonskij, *Trudovaja Skola* (Moskva, 1919), Chapter 1, p. 1.

35.   Ibid.; *Die Arbeitsschule* (Paderborn, 1973), p. 26.

36.   Heinz Frankiewicz, *Technik und Bildung in der Schule der DDR* (Berlin, 1968); Klein, *Bildung in der DDR;* Dirk Bode, *Polytechnischer Unterricht in der DDR* (Frankfurt/New York, 1978).

37.   Juergen Polzin, "Ueber Ziel, Inhalt und Methoden der sozialistischen Arbeitserziehung," *Paedagogik* 22 (1967): 31–42; Bode, *Polytechnischer Unterricht*, p. 162f.

38.   October 7, 1974.

39.   *Das Bildungswesen der DDR*, p. 847.

6

WHO RUNS THE SCHOOLS?

In all official matters the school teacher owes the pastor strict
obedience.

Old German school regulation; Merseburg, 1832

To the casual observer watching children playing in their schoolyards
during recess, it might appear that school life is essentially the same
anywhere in the industrialized world. Certainly this would seem true in
the two Germanys, where language and cultural backgrounds are similar.
Such an observer might truly wonder whether all of our discussion about
the aims and objectives of education really matters, or whether the great
ideological gulf that exists between these two states counts for much. Do
not children grow and get older in the same way on both sides of the
Wall?

Should our casual observer begin to examine the school days of
children in East and West Germany more closely, however, glaring
differences would be apparent. The divergence in values of the two
societies gives an entirely different tenor to school life in each. This
would be startlingly apparent in classrooms, equally so in school
assembly halls, and readily perceptible in lunch rooms, school buses,
workshops, and even in schoolyards and extracurricular activities. In
both Germanys the organization of education is deemed critically
important, and yet the means by which schools are organized are as
different as the two states. The question is, who or what has the *power*
and *obligation* to plan, organize, finance, administer, and regulate all of
those processes that we call "formal education" or "schooling"?

Of course both Germanys are heirs to the same traditions (for example, the kind of school regulation with which this chapter began). The administrative changes stemming from that great age of Prussian reform (1808–10) set standards that would be followed with minor divergences until 1933. The Prussian Minister von Stein suggested a distinction between external and internal matters of schooling, which became part of the German school tradition; even the Weimar Constitution of 1919 endorsed this distribution of powers. External matters, which became the responsibility of local school authorities, included: the construction and maintenance of school buildings; transportation; teaching aids and supplies; and administrative expenses. Internal affairs, the lot of the state, covered virtually every aspect of actual instruction (that is, educational goals, content of instruction, teacher education and methodology, etc.). Thus, if the heart of community self-government is control of schooling, as is sometimes averred, German local authority was decidedly weak. A truism best describes the situation: "The Community constructs the school building, but the State is master of the house."[1]

This tradition has, however, found a different echo in each of the German twins today. In the GDR, for example, we have seen the predominant role played in all educational matters by the "revolutionary process" and the Marxist-Leninist Party, the SED, which exercises "leadership of the working class." School education is clearly the monopoly of the *state,* and the ruling principle is that of "democratic centralism." Actual power is in the hands of the Council of Ministers and the Politburo of the SED. The 1965 Education Act describes these powers in great detail: the central government plans, regulates, and controls all levels and branches of education from the cradle through the university. It would be unthinkable, for example, that a university might go to court and succeed in defending its autonomy against the government and/or the legislature, as often happens in West Germany.

This centralized concentration of power, however, does not mean that lower levels of government fail to participate at all in education. Article 21 of the GDR Constitution clearly provides for citizen participation in such matters as education. It reads:

Every citizen of the German Democratic Republic has the right to take part fully in the shaping of the political, economic, social, and cultural life of the socialist society and the socialist state. The ruling principle is: "Cooperate in working, planning and governing!" [*Arbeite mit, plane mit, regiere mit!*]

But, whereas such a provision in the West German constitution would give rise to continuous conflict between local and state authorities and virtually limitless possibilities for litigation, no such problem occurs in the GDR. According to official socialist/communist ideas of democracy, the total involvement of citizens at all levels is only in support of government and Party plans. Legal ambiguities in such matters just do not arise.

Local levels of government, somewhat similar to the county or township in the United States, do, however, play the traditional role of providing a heated school with all of its equipment. As described in the Education Act, local governments shall provide the "material preconditions for a regular process of education and instruction in schools and preschools" (Article 77, Paragraph 8).[2]

Insofar as local units of government exercise any powers that appear to go beyond custodial matters, it is to implement planning, which has been done in councils of state and SED. For example, various political and economic goals are determined by planners in East Berlin, and it is the duty of local officials to see that these are achieved. The fulfillment of such goals may be similar to the fulfillment of production goals in the factory or on the farm, but it also may involve ideological supervision as well. Article 77, Paragraph 4 of the School Act, for example, provides for local oversight of principals with respect to both their professional competence as well as their political-ideological level of consciousness.

Another area in which central planning leads to implementation at the local level is that of vocational guidance. In a country where economic planning is deemed so vitally important, the selection and training of workers and professionals for various positions is seen as equally significant. It is the task of local educational authorities to fulfill established recruitment plans, which will ultimately lead to the fulfillment of production goals (Article 77, Paragraph 7). A planned economy requires obedient cooperation at every level.

Parents are expected to play a role similar to that of local school authorities. They are not expected to act as an independent interest group, but as an additional supporting limb of the revolutionary state and Party. In a document describing the creation of the Parent Advisory Board, this function is clearly delineated: "By the end of 1955, when our young republic and the political-moral unity of our people had become sufficiently strong, a new Parent Advisory Board Regulation could state that the Parent Advisory Board assists the school in imparting school policy as determined by the government." Even parental motives are carefully predefined: "a deep love of the child, firm confidence in our State, and the will to prepare the child for life in the socialist society."[3]

Parent Advisory Boards are constituted only at the local level for particular classes or grades in the school. The functions of these Boards are clearly defined — to guide parents

- toward active support of the instructional and educational work of the schools
- toward the socialist education of the children in their family
- toward support of meaningful and stimulating activities with the Free German Youth and the Pioneer Organization "Ernst Thaelmann"
- toward cooperation with other societal forces engaged in education.[4]

Parent Boards are not expected to participate in planning or organizing any essential particulars of education. They are supposed to provide logistical support, to oversee matters of hygiene and school meals. They are especially bidden "to make the goals and contents of socialist education known to all parents."[5]

As parents tend to be concerned with the future of their children, the School Regulations do recognize a vocational and professional guidance role for parents. But even in this area of concern, parents are told to perform this function "in cooperation with the state institutions in charge."[6] Conversely, the homeroom teachers and administrators of the General Polytechnic High Schools are told to work with parents only in this mutual area of concern.[7]

Thus, parents are supposed to provide support for schools, not an alternative source of authority. Their role in shaping attitudes and behavior in the GDR is not lightly regarded; they are the targets of a good deal of propaganda. But schools and parents constitute only two segments of the educational tripod in East Germany; the third sturdy limb is provided by the youth organization, the FDJ. It is this support which is the most unusual one for the Western reader.

The FDJ (*Free German Youth*) has no equivalent in the West. It has both an official status and an eductional function that make it far more important than any extracurricular organization in West Germany. The FDJ has its counterparts, however, in virtually every Eastern state, most directly perhaps with *Komsomol* in the Soviet Union. Yet, as with Marxism itself, the East Germans have no difficulty in finding authentic German origins for the FDJ. The German Youth Movement has had a history that runs the entire course of the twentieth century. Various communist and socialist youth groups attracted many thousands of members in the 1920s before all such youth organizations were banned or forcibly integrated into the Hitler Youth following 1933.

Currently in the GDR, the Free German Youth holds official status in the educational system. A full-time functionary of the FDJ is attached to all regular schools and is supposed to possess "such working class moral qualities as loyalty to socialism, steadfastness, courage, high initiative, creativity, and modesty." In addition:

> In the spirit of socialist patriotism and proletarian internationalism he feels closely connected with the Soviet Union and other paternal socialist countries. . . . He is filled with inextinguishable hatred for the enemies of socialism and is always prepared to employ all his power against the [working] class enemy.[8]

This paragon of socialist virtues has been given the unwieldy title of "leader of the pioneers of friendship" (*Freundschaftspionierleiter*). His function is not only to oversee all youth activities, but to work as the political consultant to the principal, teachers, parents, and local productive units (see below). He exercises more direct supervision of the FDJ itself, but also may teach as many as six hours a week.

Clearly the *Freundschaftspionierleiter* helps to maintain ideological purity in the schools as well as in the FDJ. This twofold system of control — school principal and FDJ leader — finds its counterparts throughout the structure of the GDR. To the outside observer, the system appears watertight. In this instance both the principal and the FDJ leader are normally party members; nevertheless, the success of this structure in maintaining and perpetuating doctrinal purity is still open to question.

And yet there is still one additional organization engaged in helping to run the schools: the Productive Unit. Productive Units, which are normally socialized factories and farms, have been assigned responsibility for the communistic education of the future workers. In practice this often means that a representative of a "sponsoring productive unit" (*Patenbetrieb*) sits on the school council. The Productive Units, in turn, play an active role in the polytechnic education of the pupils by negotiating work contracts with the school principal or even individual classes. Thus factories and collective farms, as well as the FDJ, play an active role in the schools of East Germany (see Chapter 7). As the official *Deutsche Lehrerzeitung* (Teacher's News) reported: "Our 'Paten' are eager to influence the education of every single student."[9] On one hand, therefore, the schools of the GDR are more heavily supervised and ideologically controlled than in the West; on the other, they are more carefully integrated into the social and economic life of the state.

How then does this centralized power structure actually operate? What are the possibilities for local initiatives and innovations? Let us observe the system actually in operation. The 1965 law on the *Einheitliche* Socialist System of Education was launched by the Sixth Party Congress of the SED in its Program for the "Complete Erection of Socialism" of 1963. This Congress in turn was well prepared by the Central Committee of the SED at its seventeenth session. Only a few weeks after the SED Party Congress had proclaimed its Program, as planned by the Central Committee, the Council of Ministers of the GDR appointed a "State Commission for the Elaboration of Principles for the Organization of the Unified Socialist Education System." It was chaired by one of the Deputy Prime Ministers. Their "Principles for the Organization of the Unified Socialist Education System" of 1964 were then propagated by the state-censored media and "discussed" in meetings and conferences of the FDJ, the Union, Party organizations, local governments, production units, and parents. The final act of legislation of the 1965 law in the *Volkskammer* (Legislature) was, as is usual, merely a matter of acclamation of a law that had been planned by the powerful Party and Government Centers. Its realization in the following years could be brought about smoothly under the powerful direction of Party and government agents on all levels, unhampered by opposition of other political parties, of reluctant teachers or parents, industry and commerce, rebellious students, or even the courts.[10]

The West German twin has inherited the same division of powers with respect to the schools as its eastern sibling; the local communities are expected to build and care for the schools and their equipment while the state serves as "master of the house," with the exception that, instead of one state with centralized power, there are eleven *Laender* (including West Berlin) exercising primary powers. And we have also seen that in West Germany, as in all pluralistic democracies, state powers are limited and challenged by a variety of individuals and groups.

To be sure, each of the *Laender* establishes, administers, and supervises a public school system, and each *Land* determines the structure of schools, the aims and content of the curriculum, school admission policies, the qualifications and licensing procedures for teachers, and the make-up and administering of examinations (see Chapter 5). The *Laender* even exercise a substantial amount of control over private schools. In practice, however, the power structure is not so clear-cut as it may appear. Figure 1 may more accurately depict some of the prevailing and countervailing forces at work in forming the West German school system.[11]

In general, this complex power structure has tended to reduce innovations and make the system conservative in nature. First, the federative structure of West Germany has increasingly acted to reduce disparities between *Laender* rather than to increase them. Given the relatively small size of the country and the mobility of the population, there is a general agreement that interests of the West Germans are best served by avoiding dramatic educational incongruities. To achieve this aim, a voluntary organization of all ministers of education was established. The Standing Conference of Ministers of Education and Culture meets regularly to discuss all major changes within the school system. Any official recommendations issuing from this group require unanimous agreement. This means that, while certain minor innovations

FIGURE 1
The West German School System

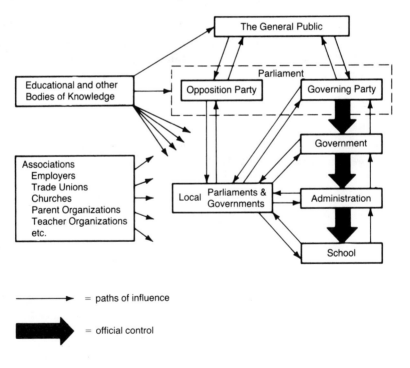

and efforts to standardize such matters as the school calendars have been successful, other more dramatic changes in the schools have been thwarted. The haphazard manner in which the Comprehensive School (*Gesamtschule*) has been introduced in the various *Laender* exemplifies the problem as well as the difficulties of trying to institutionalize a General Orientation Stage (grades six and seven). A minority of ministers of education can frustrate such innovations at the level of the Standing Conference, which in turn dissuades the various *Laender* from initiating new programs. All fear that their degrees and diplomas will be rejected or deprecated elsewhere in the Federal Republic.

A second impediment to innovation derives from the uneven division of powers between the *Laender* and local governments. For example, the introduction of an efficient counseling system (for example, guidance counseling, drug counseling, school social work, etc.) has suffered innumerable delays as a result of conflict between *Laender* and local governments over which should pay for such services. The *Laender* governments argue that counseling is one of those "material preconditions" of education, essentially an administrative cost, for which local organs of government are responsible. On the other hand, local governments aver that counseling services belong to the realm of the instructional and educational systems of the schools, for which the *Laender* are clearly responsible. Both levels essentially agree that West German schools, like those of most Western states, should provide counseling services, but neither have been willing to bear the necessary financial burden for these services.[12] Protracted economic recessions in the late 1970s and early 1980s have additionally intensified the reluctance of any governing group to undertake new programs.

Another traditional power center in West German education has been the entire teacher training apparatus — the professors of education, examination procedures, internships, and even the body of pedagogical literature itself. For the most part, educators tend to replicate themselves and the system they know, or launch ideal reform projects that are doomed to failure in the real world. Flexibility has certainly not been one of the hallmarks of West German pedagogy. For example, efforts to introduce a system of electives in the *Gymnasium,* which gained the support of the University Rector's Conference in 1972, have encountered heavy resistance among university faculty during the late 1970s and 1980s. Once it became clear that any reforms in the upper secondary levels would alter the nature of higher education as well, many university faculty began to oppose innovations in secondary schools.

In the area of vocational education, employers and trade unions have frequently clashed in their efforts to influence reforms. Their battleground has been the traditional German system of integrating apprenticeships with part-time vocational education. This system, which served Germany well earlier in this century and won high praise from foreign visitors for producing such a committed and highly trained work force, now appears somewhat antiquated. Graduates of the Main Schools (*Hauptschulen*) or Middle Schools (*Realschulen*) have normally been apprenticed in trades and businesses while continuing to attend school for at least one day a week. Trade unions and their various political allies (the Social Democratic Party and groups of "progressive educators") have argued that this system has now become a source of cheap labor and exploitation while often preparing people for dead-end jobs. Such a system does not take account of the vast social and technological changes that have occurred and which now require a great deal more formal education in science as well as civics. In addition, would-be reformers point out that this system tends to reduce the social mobility of the lower social classes. As a result, critics claim, thousands of young people in their mid-teens are without work, schooling, and a productive future.

As might be expected, a broad coalition of employers' associations and conservative politicians, largely Christian Democrats, have resisted such proposed reforms as an integrated upper secondary school (proposed by the *Deutsche Bildungsrat*[13] and experimentally instituted in several *Laender* under Social Democratic governance).[14] Even minimal innovations, such as a second school day per week for apprentices, have generally been stifled by this coalition.[15]

The general stagnation in the realm of vocational education has provided Marxist critics in both West Germany and the GDR with an easy target for their ideological arrows. According to such writers, the entire system clearly perpetuates the privileges of the ruling middle class and provides proof of the inhumane character of capitalism; apprentices and workers continue to be exploited and, if need be, discarded at will.[16]

Parental influence over education, as we have seen in the previous chapter, derives in part from constitutional guarantees that give parents the right to guide the personal development of their children without infringement by state and public schools. Throughout the Federal Republic, however, parents exercise a good deal more influence than just "defensive rights" in the education of their children. In each of the *Laender* the rights of parents to participate in the schooling of their children are guaranteed in a variety of ways. In some *Laender,* for example, parents may help in the selection of textbooks and curriculum planning through committees; in others, they may help select school principals or may be consulted about school legislation. The variety of provisions in the eleven *Laender* does not, however, permit easy generalization and description, yet one example can illustrate the powers given to parents in the education of their children.

In the state of North Rhine-Westphalia, for example, the School Participation Bill of 1977 guarantees parent membership on a large number of important school committees as well as in the all-important School Conference. In the latter, parents' delegates serve with those of teachers and students (for example, in full secondary schools, twelve teachers, six students, and six parents) to advise on a broad range of issues, including matters of content, methods of instruction, school finances, examinations, and so on. Yet, North Rhine-Westphalia is one of only two *Laender* (the other being Bavaria) that do not include parents' representatives directly on a state advisory committee (the School Conference is at the level of the particular school). In North Rhine-Westphalia it is felt that such a committee would ultimately give educated, upper-middle-class parents a disproportionate amount of power in school affairs, as these are the people most likely to have the time and inclination to serve on such a committee; this would further exclude working-class parents from influence in an area where their voice has been traditionally weak.

In Hesse, which has generally been regarded as one of the most socially progressive *Laender* of the Federal Republic (*Hessen voran!* — Hesse to the fore!), a measure providing for parental participation at the state level proves the point. What was introduced immediately following the war as a democratic measure has ironically given upper-middle-class parents the means to obstruct reforms designed to broaden educational opportunities for the less privileged. Thus, in spite of 35 years of continuous rule by reformist Social Democratic governments, the state of Hesse has been unable fully to reorganize the school system along more comprehensive lines (see above). Well-to-do parents simply resist the broadening of educational opportunities and are able to frustrate reforms, even where power is nominally held by the state government. Of course, such interest groups are unable to change the system either; they merely use the powers provided to parents to create unbreakable deadlocks.

One additional powerful interest group needs to be mentioned — the organization of *Gymnasium* teachers (*Philologenverband*). Like the Association of Agrégées in France, the *Gymnasium* teachers represent a highly privileged group that has enjoyed better education, higher salaries, and greater prestige than other groups of teachers. Not unexpectedly, therefore, the *Gymnasium* teachers have used their power and prestige to obstruct secondary school reforms that might alter their special status. Such reforms as the introduction of Comprehensive Schools or a General Orientation Stage have drawn their collective ire, because this would bring about a leveling of the five types of teachers in West German schools — *Gymnasium,* Middle School, Main School, Special School, and Vocational School teachers.

In summary then, it must be said that the West German school system has not proved very susceptible to reforms. Whereas more decentralized systems such as those of England and Wales with their Local Educational Authorities, as well as more centralized systems such as that of Sweden, have been capable of reorganization and expansion of educational opportunities, the West German schools have remained rather static. Even in *Laender* with reformist regimes and highly acclaimed plans for amalgamation of secondary schools, conservative interest groups have been able to thwart such efforts. In doing so, these interest groups have frequently been abetted by the courts, which have not developed to the point where a decision such as *Brown vs. Board of Education* (1954) would be possible. One can only speculate about what kind of crisis of social unrest would be needed before quality education for all children will be provided. Perhaps the four and a half million migrant workers whose children have largely been educationally deprived will eventually provide the necessary impetus.

Some hope might be gleaned from the publication of the liberal Ralf Dahrendorf's stinging critique of Germany's stagnation in the conservative *Rheinischer Merkur* of November 25, 1983:

> German inflexibility is especially bad. The Parliament has all but abdicated its initiative to the Executive Branch. The latter, in turn, has not only shackled itself to the bureaucracy, but to organized interest groups as well. As if this were not paralyzing enough, the process of reaching decisions involves so many stumbling blocks — committees, councils, ad hoc bodies — that no one will take the initiative other than with extreme caution. And behind all of this looms the heavy shadow of a judicial system which has actually, if not intentionally, become an institution of obstruction. There is so much that will not even be attempted due to anxious presentiments of the Courts.

NOTES

1. J. Staupe, "Strukturen der Schultraegerschaft und Schulfinanzierung," in Max-Planck-Institut fuer Bildungsforschung, ed., *Bildung in der Bundesrepublik Deutschland*, vol. 2 (Reinbek, 1980), p. 867ff. For an excellent discussion in English of German education prior to 1945 see Richard H. Samuel and Richard Hinton Thomas, *Education and Society in Modern Germany* (London, 1949).

2. Ministerium fuer Volksbildung, *Sozialistisches Bildungsrecht* (Berlin, 1973).

3. Ibid., p. 109f.

4. Ibid., p. 111.

5. Ibid.

6. Ibid.

7. Ibid.

8. Quoted from the official regulations of 1972, ibid., p. 274. See also Chapter 5, "The Youth State," in Hans Werner Schwarze, *The GDR Today: Life in the "Other" Germany*, translated by John M. Mitchell (London, 1973), pp. 72–90.

9. *Deutsche Lehrerzeitung (DLZ)* 10/85, March 8, 1985.

10. Cf. the official GDR *Geschichte der Erziehung,* 11th ed. (Berlin, 1973), p. 661ff.

11. U. Schwaenke, *Die Interdependenz von Bildungssystem und Gesellschaft* (Weinheim/Basel, 1980), p. 50.

12. Staupe, "Strukturen der Schultraegerschaft," p. 886ff.

13. Deutscher Bildungsrat, *Zur Neuordnung der Sekundarstufe II. Konzept fuer eine Verbindung von allgemeinem und beruflichem Lernen* (Stuttgart, 1974).

14. For example, Kultusminister des Landes Nordrhien-Westfalen, ed., *Schulversuch Kollegschule NW* (Koeln, 1976).

15. See Lothar Martin, "Benachteiligtenprojekt N — ein modernes Stans?" in *Westermanns Paedagogische Beitraege* (1986); see also Max-Planck-Institute for Human Development and Education, *Between Elite and Mass Education — Education in the Federal Republic of Germany* (Albany, 1983).

16. For example, Urs Jaeggi, *Kapital und Arbeit in der Bundesrepublik Deutschland* (Frankfurt, 1973), p. 296f.

7

DIFFERENT SCHOOLS FOR DIFFERENT TWINS

> After all, the public and state school is not the measure of all things: it is an existing instrument for the schooling of contemporary masses, which certainly opens opportunities for emancipation as well as dangers of manipulation.
>
> Rainer Winkel, a West German educator

THE TRADITIONAL PATTERN

> I will spoil all your careers for you.
>
> Direktor Wulicke of the Luebeck Realschule
> in Thomas Mann's *Buddenbrooks*

Both of the above statements will strike most modern readers as true. Not only do schools possess the power to either liberate or indoctrinate, they virtually determine the careers of their pupils and can even "spoil" them. These dicta, however valid elsewhere, have been especially so in Germany. The following account by a German educator (one of the authors of this work) illustrates this point:

When X was in fourth grade, at the age of ten, he very badly wanted to be among those who could enter the selective middle school (*Realschule*) of his town instead of remaining in the *Volksschule,* but his parents couldn't afford the tuition. Only children of wealthier families could go. There was, however, one chance; the town paid for one scholarship on the basis of achievement and need. Now he happened to have a good friend in the same class, who was just as bright and just as poor. They both would have deserved the scholarship, but only one of them could get it. For whatever reason — was it the letter that his father gave him one day for his homeroom teacher? — he was lucky which meant that his best friend was not. For him it was the beginning of a school career in the *Realschule* and *Gymnasium,* later in the University and into his profession as a scholar and University teacher, while his friend never had the chance to experience an academic education. Like 80 percent of his age group, he had to leave school at fourteen and become an apprentice, and that, for most people, meant a life-time as a worker or a modest clerk.

The school organization that the German twins inherited had a long and distinguished history. Its roots lay in the religious and private schools of the Middle Ages; it had been shaped by such legendary figures as Luther, Melanchton, Comenius, Francke, Pestalozzi, von Humboldt, and Herbart, who had often gained the friendly support of German noblemen, princes, and kings. Leading foreign educators such as Horace Mann from the United States, Matthew Arnold from England, and Victor Cousin from France visited the German states and wrote glowing accounts to inspire their countrymen to make similar progress. And, yet, tradition cuts both ways. In his well-known poem, "Xenien," Goethe expressed some of its disadvantages:

Amerika, du hast es besser
Als unser Kontinent, der alte,
Hast keine verfallenen Schloesser
Und keine Basalte.
Dich stoert nicht im Innern,
Zu lebendiger Zeit,
Unnuetzes Erinnern
Und vergeblicher Streit.[1]

(America, you're better off than
Our continent, the old.
You have no castles which are fallen
No basalt to behold.
You're not disturbed within your inmost being
Right up till today's daily life
By useless remembering
And unrewarding strife.)

Translation by Stephen Spender

The German educational tradition, however admirable in many ways, was nevertheless based on the rigid social structure of German society — the nobility, the educated "bourgeois" merchants, the craftsmen of the cities, and the common workers and peasants. These various social classes were served by particular schools suited to their "needs." Periodic efforts to provide a common school for the children of all classes date from the early nineteenth century; in the School Bill of 1819, for example, the Prussian school reformer, Johann Wilhelm Suevern, had hoped to found an elementary school that would be attended by "the youth of the whole of the people irrespective of class differences or future occupations." Although in the Weimar Republic integration of all pupils at the elementary level was eventually achieved, not even the Nazis could break down the tripartite vertical division of secondary schools.

Thus when the German twins were born east and west of the Elbe and the Werra, they fell heir to a wide variety of schools:

The Volksschule. As its name implies, this was the traditional school of the "common people." Most children attended this school for eight years (from ages six to fourteen) and received a basic education in German, math, history, geography, religion, music, sports, and natural science. Teachers were drawn largely from the common folk as well and had usually received a modest amount of education beyond the *Volksschule,* perhaps at a *Mittelschule;* their teacher training took place in special seminars. As late as 1952, 81 percent of all West German twelve-year-olds were in the *Volksschule* and were mostly destined for unskilled labor and apprenticeships.[2] When one considers that 2 to 3 percent of this cohort was in special schools for the mentally or physically handicapped, it becomes even more apparent how few children, perhaps 15 percent, received as much as ten years of schooling, few of them more.

The Mittelschule (or Realschule). Following the first four years of the comprehensive elementary school, the "better students" moved to a *Mittelschule,* or as it was sometimes called, a *Realschule,* which had a six-year curriculum and embraced grades five to ten. Most of those who attended this school were middle-class children who were destined for apprenticeships in more demanding trades, or who might go eventually to technical schools and prepare for careers as engineers or technicians. The "real" or "useful" subjects dominated the curriculum of this school (for example, math, science, and modern languages).

*The Gymnasium.*This was the traditional route to higher education and the professions. Students entered the *Gymnasium* after the first four years of elementary school and remained for nine years to complete the course. Traditionally, there were three types of *Gymnasien:*

1. The classical *Gymnasium,* which had a required curriculum of Latin, Greek, German, and math as major subjects and English (or French), history, geography, philosophy, physics, chemistry, biology, art, physical education, and music as required minor subjects;
2. The modern language *Gymnasium,* with Latin, English, French, German, and math as required majors and the same minors as 1;
3. The natural science *Gymnasium,* with Latin, English or French, German, math, and physics as required majors.

In the traditional system, however, the majority of German youths left either *Volksschule* or *Realschule* after eight or ten years of schooling and entered apprenticeships in factories, shops, and offices. Thereafter they were required to attend vocational schools for one day each week to gain a theoretical education to complement their practical training. Foreign visitors lavished praise on this mixed system of education for the masses as well as the *Gymnasium* and university education, which produced a highly trained intellectual and professional elite. Yet, at times, as Goethe noted, "castles," although famous, can be impediments to progress.

SCHOOLS IN THE POSTWAR FEDERAL REPUBLIC

Following World War II, the western zones of occupation, which eventually became the Federal Republic of Germany, reconstructed their system of education along traditional lines. Most western observers and occupying authorities opposed this policy, as they believed the traditional German system was somehow implicated in the rise of Nazism and its horrendous crimes. Yet, as believers in democratic values, they found it difficult to oppose the will of like-minded Germans, who had opposed Hitler, and now wanted to restore the once highly praised system of schools. Indeed, the real task for Germany and the West soon became the reconstruction of the West German economy and the creation of a bulwark against the Communist giant in the East. Also, as one of Konrad Adenauer's granddaughters noted, "Grandfather's interest in cultural policy was probably not strong enough.... Positive ventures in cultural and educational development were trampled down by the *Wirtschaftswunder* [economic miracle]."[3]

School reforms, such as the proposals to integrate the first six years of elementary education and the reconstruction of secondary education along comprehensive lines, were broached in vain. By 1960 the system, as shown in Figure 2, was well entrenched. The figures given next to the schools indicate what percentages of the total age cohort attended that school (for example, 77 percent of all eleven-year-olds attended the *Volksschule*).

It should be noted, however, that the West German tripartite system, shown below, was fairly typical of educational systems elsewhere. The highly selective *Gymnasium,* for example, corresponds to the English Grammar School and the French *lycée;* they were all exclusive and highly academic. Yet the question remains: How well adapted was this system to the needs of a modern industrial society with a commitment to democratic values?

To young North Americans who first found West German exchange students in their college and university classes in the 1950s and 1960s, it was obvious that these Germans had received an unusually fine academic education. Not only were the Germans, virtually all *Gymnasium* matriculants, able to follow lectures in English and take notes, they were proficient in one or two other languages as well. To their amazement, the Americans often found the Germans able to quote Shakespeare better than they could and discuss intelligently Wordsworth, Dostoevsky, and even Faulkner. In addition, the Germans were proficient in math and basic science and, while not well versed in Civil War battlefields, could certainly identify those on which Frederick the Great and Napoleon had fought.

In English, the word "gymnasium" had kept its original Greek meaning and described a place for athletics. The Germans, on the other hand, had adapted the term to describe their classically oriented, academic secondary school. Both in number of years pupils attended the *Gymnasium* (usually eight or nine) and in the curriculum to which they were submitted, it far exceeded the typical U.S. senior high school. In addition, the school was highly selective and enrolled only 4 to 6 percent of all eleven-year-olds, more than 50 percent of whom never completed the entire course. However selective and elitist this school might seem to an American, its restoration must be understood in the context of the immediate postwar years; many Germans felt the need to create a new elite to govern and administer their country following the Nazi debacle. Where better to do this than in the precincts of the *Gymnasium,* whose commitment, they felt, was to Western humanism?

In fact, it can be argued that other West German schools also served the needs of a defeated and destroyed nation exceedingly well. Had one traveled through the bombed-out ruins of Cologne or Kassel or seen the

FIGURE 2
Structure of the Public School System in West Germany in 1960

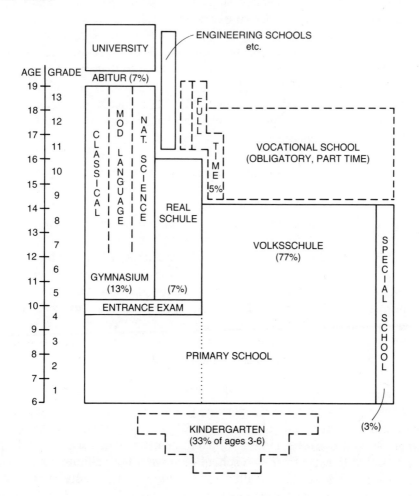

rubble of Munich and Frankfurt, it would have been readily apparent how many bricklayers, carpenters, plumbers, and mechanics were going to be required to reconstruct the country. The traditional German system with its elementary school, apprenticeships, and part-time vocational education had produced an abundance of excellent craftsmen. However deficient West German schools may have been in some respects, they were in a major way responsible for the postwar West German "economic miracle."

Yet, by the 1950s these schools already began to elicit criticism for their undemocratic methods as well as their class orientation. In 1950, for example, a West German educator, who had recently returned from a visit to the United States, warned his countrymen, "In our schools [Gymnasia] young people are treated as objects rather than as subjects; rather than learning to experience freedom, they are treated exactly as though they are living in an authoritarian state. Freedom, however, must be the basic experience of every democracy . . . if they are not being prepared to be active in society, it is a result of the organization of the school."[4]

Indeed, the first postwar national educational advisory committee rendered a similar judgment in 1959. In the introduction to its now famous *Rahmenplan* (Skeleton Plan) for the Reorganization and Unification of the Public School System, the *Deutsche Ausschuss fuer das Erziehungs- und Bildungswesen* asserted: "The German school system has not kept pace with the revolutions [*Umwaelzungen*] which have changed society and state during the last fifty years."

Yet despite this dramatic statement, the *Deutsche Ausschuss* made rather moderate proposals for reform. Essentially, the *Ausschuss* did not recommend changing the tripartite system of schools, but urged that changes be made that would promote greater social justice. For example, it proposed that greater numbers of pupils be matriculated at all secondary levels, that transfer from one school to another be facilitated, and that grades five and six, the so-called *Foerderstufe,* become fully integrated. As we have seen, this latter proposal, when eventually enacted in the state of Hesse, led to lengthy court battles (see Chapter 4). Other recommendations made by the *Ausschuss* were of a similar conservative nature.

Much more severe and far-reaching criticism would follow in the next decade. For example, Hansgert Peisert published a book in 1967 that showed the distinctly urban bias of German schools.[5] More than one-third of all German villages, 8,000 in number, according to Peisert, had no child attending a *Gymnasium* in 1961.

Wolfgang Klafki made a similar charge with respect to class bias. In the textbook that Klafki and his colleagues wrote to accompany a popular radio course, he pointed out that, although industrial and agricultural workers constituted 50 percent of the population of West Germany (1963–64), only 12 to 15 percent of working-class children attended *Gymnasia,* 7 percent passed the *Abitur,* and 5 percent became university students.[6]

The search for underrepresented groups in the *Gymnasia* soon revealed a sexual and religious bias as well. Only 40 percent of those beginning the *Gymnasium* were female, 26 percent finishing, and 17 percent receiving university degrees. In addition, researchers found that the Roman Catholics of West Germany, roughly half the population, were underrepresented in the secondary and higher schools of the country. All in all, a composite, fictional figure was born who became the notorious symbol of social deprivation in the German schools: a Catholic, working-class girl living in a rural area.

The West German "economic miracle" was not the only impediment to reform, however. The growing fear of communism also served as one of the principal buttresses to educational conservatism as well. The West Germans were not only conspicuously successful in the marketplace, but faced a divided portion of their own country which posed an immediate threat to their entire social and economic structure and their culture. Efforts to reform the tripartite system, therefore, provided ammunition for those who defended the traditional structure; they could discredit such efforts as the work of socialists or communists. As late as 1985 the respectable *Frankfurter Allgemeine* decried the desegregation of grades five and six as communistic.[7] Thus, as other West European states worked on plans to reform their schools, the West Germans remained obdurately committed to their course.

But the would-be reformers did not rest their entire case on the argument for "social justice." The sociologist Ralf Dahrendorf, for example, published a programmatic book in 1965 whose title, *Education Is the Right of Citizens,*[8] raised a whole range of critical questions. In addition, a collection of research studies was published in 1969 by the *Deutsche Bildungsrat,* entitled *Begabung und Lernen* (Ability and Learning), which attacked one of the mainstays of the tripartite defenders. Heretofore, a number of educators and psychologists such as Heinrich

Weinstock[9] had maintained that the German academic pyramid mirrored the distribution of natural abilities in a fairly accurate way; for example, that approximately 6 percent of the population possessed the intellectual abilities to achieve the elite status that a *Gymnasium* and university education conferred on them. The contributors to *Ability and Learning* challenged this assumption, however, and scientifically demonstrated that once some of the environmental and motivational impediments to learning were removed, almost undreamed-of growth could be achieved; intellectual ability was not nearly so narrowly distributed as previously claimed.

Criticism emerged from another quarter as well. Saul B. Robinsohn's book, *School Reform As Reform of the Curriculum,* impressed a large number of educators when it appeared in 1967 and virtually launched a curriculum movement, the upshot of which was the demand for curriculum reform in all three traditional secondary schools. The curriculum reformers demanded the introduction of more modern subjects and subject matter, as well as individualized courses in order to prepare young West Germans for what Robinsohn termed "mastery of future life situations in a world of change and democracy."[10]

What finally transformed this flurry of criticism and concern into a storm, however, was the possibility of impending economic disaster if school reforms were not made. Raimond Poignant's report submitted to the European Committee,[11] as well as Georg Picht's book, painted a gloomy economic picture of the future if manpower needs for academically trained people were not met, especially in technical fields.[12] It was this urgent criticism that especially gained a popular following through mass circulation magazines such as *Der Spiegel* and demonstrations of students calling for immediate reforms to meet the *Notstand* (state of emergency).

What then were some of the specific demands being made by these critics? What were the "trouble spots" of the traditional school system on which they focused attention?

1. Only one-third of German preschoolers were in kindergartens, much less than in France or the GDR, for example, and most of these kindergartens were operated by churches. In other words, two-thirds of West German children between ages three and six lacked the cognitive, emotional, and social stimulation that kindergartens provide, and even existing kindergartens needed improvements most urgently.

2. Slow learners faced overwhelming obstacles to success. The curriculum of virtually every school was formalized and had very little flexibility. For those who had difficulties with one subject, the only choice seemed to be retention in the same grade for another year. In 1970–71, for example, 110,000 pupils were held back for another year or were impelled to drop out.[13] Almost no means existed for dealing with reading and writing difficulties, a situation that bore hardest on those between six and ten years of age.

3. The most important selection point in the entire school system occurred at the end of the fourth school year, when pupils were ten or eleven years old. In 1960, for example, 13 percent were selected for entrance into the *Gymnasium* and 7 percent for the *Realschule*, while the remainder remained in the *Volksschule* (with a small percentage going to special schools for the handicapped). And, as we have seen, this selection was highly biased and varied significantly from one state to another (for example, 4.4 percent of young Saarlanders entered the *Realschule* and 25 percent of young Berliners). Not only were selection procedures highly unreliable, but a body of information had already been gathered in Britain and elsewhere that showed that selection at such an early age lacked validity.[14]

4. Little crossover from one secondary school to another was permitted. Pupils wishing to switch had to virtually start over; "Succeed or Drop Out" was the motto. Indeed, more than half the *Gymnasium* students and one-third of those in *Realschule* did drop out. A standard curriculum left almost no opportunity for maximizing one's strengths, and efforts to create a fifth- and sixth-grade "orientation stage" were generally thwarted.

5. A lack of elective subjects created an especially difficult situation in the upper levels of the *Gymnasium,* grades eleven to thirteen for ages sixteen to nineteen (many were even older due to being held back). This tended to destroy motivation, self-respect, personal involvement, and to inhibit the development of a sense of personal responsibility among students.[15]

6. The once highly vaunted vocational training, which combined apprenticeships with one day of schooling per week, was becoming outdated. Many newer vocations required a great deal more theoretical training than was being given. In addition, the demands of a democracy and modern citizenship required a much higher level of social and political awareness than previously; additional schooling was needed to

provide this. The traditional system allowed little opportunity for pupils to return to full-time education, if they chose to do so.

7. Only 7 percent of the age cohort passed the *Abitur* in 1960. This not only created a tremendous shortage of academically trained people, especially teachers, but further added to an already considerable wastage of human resources that resulted from the curriculum of the *Gymnasium*. A great deal of talent in such fields as engineering, business, and the social sciences merely went untapped.

These "trouble spots," of course, represent only the most severe problems that critics identified, but they helped to create the explosive situation in the late 1960s that culminated in student unrest and violence.

Under these circumstances school reformers clearly gained ground in the 1960s. For a while it even appeared that not only all political parties, but such traditionally conservative organizations as the *Philologenverband* (the Gymnasium Teacher's Union) were won to the ranks of the reform movement. And in 1970 the *Deutsche Bildungsrat,* which had succeeded the *Deutsche Ausschuss* as the official planning organ of the Federal Republic, proposed a far-reaching reform plan, its *Strukturplan fuer das deutsche Bildungswesen* (Structural Plan for the German Educational System). The thrust of this proposal was reorganization of West German education along horizontal rather than vertical lines, to shape it more closely to U.S. and Swedish models. For example, the *Bildungsrat* proposed a universal preschool or kindergarten for all children, aged three to five, an orientation stage for those who were about to enter secondary schools (ages ten and eleven), and an upper secondary school which would integrate *Gymnasium* and vocational students.[16]

Although these reform proposals were made in the early 1970s, the pace of change in a pluralistic democratic society, as we have seen, is painstakingly slow. The situation in the early 1980s had reached the stage as illustrated in Figure 3.

We can see from this figure (and the previous one) that German schools were in a state of transition. Clearly, there were a number of indicators of expansion of educational opportunity — a greater number of integrated levels existed than formerly, as well as an increasingly horizontal structure. Yet progress had been slow and became even slower in the 1980s as a result of a conservative government, a nagging economic recession, and an excess of highly trained people in the economy. This should not obscure, however, the striking changes that were occurring at virtually all levels of instruction.

FIGURE 3
Federal Republic of Germany: Public School System, Early 1980s

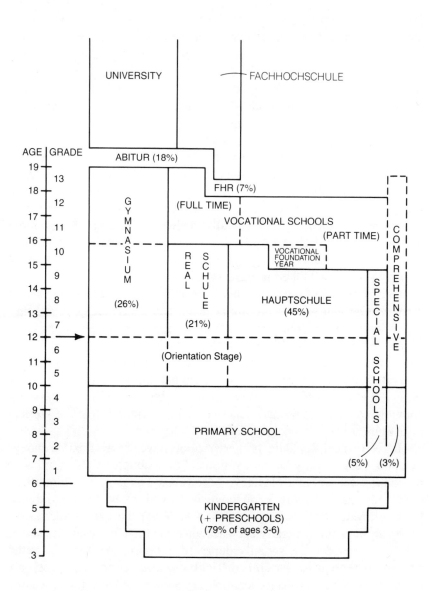

Kindergarten. There has been a dramatic increase in the number of kindergartens (which is defined in West Germany as an institution for three- to six-year-old children) as well as overall attendance. Between 1960 and 1980, the number of kindergartens virtually doubled, from 12,290 to 24,011, and the percentage of the age cohort attending has jumped from approximately one-third to 79 percent. As kindergartens have not been provided or mandated under the regular school laws of the Federal Republic, but under special youth welfare legislation, they have largely been supported and operated by local parishes rather than the *Laender.* In the past, this has given them an overwhelmingly middle-class character. This seems to be slowly changing, with community-operated kindergartens constituting 29 percent of the total in 1980 (yet with considerable variation from one *Land* to another).

In this same vein, qualitative improvements have been recommended and implemented in kindergartens. Under the influence of a number of educators and governmental commissions, kindergartens have been pressed to provide more stimulating social, emotional, and cognitive experiences, especially for socially deprived children. Many more handicapped children, rising from 13,680 in 1970 to 17,014 in 1980, have also been placed in kindergartens in order to prepare them to enter primary schools with their peers at age six.

Grundschule or "Primary School." Probably the least controversial of all West German schools are the primary schools (grades one to four). These schools are compulsory and fully comprehensive; even attendance at private primary schools is minimal and under state supervision. In fact, the current *Grundschule* Laws were influenced by the Weimar Constitution of 1919 when, following the national catastrophe of World War I, German reformers saw their fondest hope for a classless, compulsory, and free primary school based on Article 146 of the Weimar Constitution.[17]

In the Federal Republic, primary schools have proved flexible enough to embrace a variety of innovations. For example, rigid admission procedures for six-year-olds have been relaxed as more children attend kindergartens and more knowledge is gained about early childhood learning. More far-reaching proposals to lower the age of admission, however, have not generally been accepted. Yet much greater assistance has been provided for socially deprived children; teachers are better trained to recognize learning difficulties, and "support groups" are frequently created to enhance learning experiences and assist with reading difficulties, and other problems. In addition, as the transition to secondary schools following the fourth grade has become less selective, many of the pressures previously associated with this year have been reduced. No longer do teachers and pupils have to feel that future careers will be definitely decided at this tender time of life.

Some of the additional problems associated with the primary schools derive from regional or ethnic problems. For example, the West German schools have not been notably successful in establishing bicultural, bilingual, or multicultural programs for the children of foreign workers (*Gastarbeiter*). Many of these children have presented teachers with learning and behavioral problems with which the teachers are ill-prepared to deal. Teachers have also come under criticism for their lack of training in social learning. Many teachers are just not accustomed to cooperating with each other or with parents, or to using encouraging methods of teaching and learning, individually and in groups.[18]

Foerderstufe or "Orientation Stage." As has already been shown (Chapter 4), grades five and six, the so-called Orientation Stage, have become one of the principal battlegrounds in the West German educational system. The battle has been fought in the schools, in the courts, and in the political arena. And the reason for this volatility results from these two years being seen as the key to secondary education. Conservatives have fought to maintain a highly selective, tripartite system, while "progressive reformers" have opted for a comprehensive, socially integrated structure. Yet, by the 1970s a minimal level of agreement had been reached among the education ministers of the various *Laender*.

Based on a good deal of educational research as well as the negative experience Britain and other countries had encountered with the so-called 11+ examination and similar instruments of selection, the governments of the *Laender* agreed that the end of grade four was too early to determine the future lives of their citizens. Rigorous selection procedures that had been employed at this stage would be relaxed in favor of an "Orientation Stage" (grades five and six), in which pupils could experience a broad range of subjects and educational situations. The supporters of this reform hoped it would postpone by two years the age at which West German pupils would be channeled into secondary schools. In addition, a new comprehensive school, *Gesamtschule,* would be created to provide an alternative to the trio of traditional secondary schools.

According to the 1973 decision of the Federal *Laender* Commission for Educational Planning, "The Orientation Stage must be organized independently from other forms of school. A selection of students for admission shall not take place. In the Orientation Stage curricular offerings . . . shall be homogeneous."[19]

Yet, despite this injunction, the traditionalists were not yet ready to abandon the tripartite system, even at grades five and six. In all five *Laender* ruled by the Christian Democrats in 1973, a minority position was enacted that linked these two grades to the traditional schools — the *Hauptschule,* the *Realschule* and the *Gymnasium.* Thus, instead of forming a distinct Orientation Stage, these grades remained virtually preparatory years for schools to which they were tied. Although transferring from one school to another technically became easier, in fact this possibility was undermined by curricular differences such as making Latin the preeminent subject for those housed in a number of *Gymnasia.*

The best that can be said for the Orientation Stage today is that its ambiguous adoption is symbolic of the diversity in a pluralistic, democratic society. Marxist critics in the GDR have less favorable comments to make. In fact, even the West German Minister of Education and Science rendered a harsh judgment in 1978:

> A rapprochement concerning the various ideas of the *Laender* about how to organize the ways and means of transition following the Primary School cannot be achieved. Instead, all signs indicate that in this, as in other matters [e.g., the Comprehensive School vs. the tripartite system], the school systems will drift ever further apart and whatever agreements the *Laender* governments reach, they will have little influence on the course of events.[20]

The entire matter of an "orientation stage" has become so intertwined with political, social, and economic issues as to make it one of the stickiest questions on the West German educational scene. In Hesse, the Social Democratic government has fought a coalition of conservative forces for decades to insert this *Foerderstufe* into the school structure. In Berlin, under the direct influence of the Western occupying powers, the primary school was extended to include the fifth and sixth grades, while in Bremen and Lower Saxony, an Orientation Stage was installed by Social Democrats and has not been abolished by succeeding governments, even when they were Christian Democratic. In the most populous of the *Laender,* North Rhine-Westphalia, a popular referendum put a halt to efforts that were already in progress to install an integrated lower secondary school. A "probationary stage" (*Erprobungsstufe*) is part of the traditional tripartite systems, with the exception of 64 fully comprehensive schools (1985–86).

Thus, a variety of curricular reforms under various titles have been introduced at this stage in the school structures of the *Laender*. Each seems to embody the value system of a particular group or coalition. When the orientation stage is integrated into the traditional system, it frequently represents an effort to ward off more fundamental reforms. Terms such as "probationary stage" (see above) or "observation stage" (*Beobachtungsstufe*) are then used to describe this change. In *Laender* where concern for the social integration of children of all social and ethnic backgrounds is more sincere, a separate and distinct orientation stage has generally been the result or, in some instances, an extension of primary schooling for two additional years.

The struggle between various interest groups has resulted in confusion. Certainly, *Gymnasium* and *Realschule* teachers have contributed much to this situation by their persistent efforts to maintain their status. They have tried to continue serving a privileged constituency that is not eager to have its children socialized by mixing them with children from working-class or ethnically diverse backgrounds.

Perhaps the Federal Republic has confronted no greater test of its ability to accomplish social integration than that presented by the reorganization of grades five and six of its school system. The question of whether potent interest groups can frustrate needed school reforms gives some substance and credibility to attacks by GDR critics, who claim that the bourgeoisie in West Germany continues to dominate and exploit the working class.

Gesamtschule (Comprehensive School). Secondary education, as we have seen, has largely been social-class-specific in the German past. The first Comprehensive High Schools in the Federal Republic date from 1969, yet this should not belie the dream of reformers such as Comenius and von Humboldt, who envisioned the possibility of such schools centuries earlier.

The current effort to establish a Comprehensive School must be seen, however, in an international context. The U.S. high school, whose ascendancy dates from the period following the Civil War, was an oddity until the middle of this century; in no other country did a comprehensive secondary school become the prevailing institution at that level. Only following World War II have many other Western states begun to replace traditional class-segregated and selective schools with schools that integrate all children of the secondary age group. This has, for example, been occurring in Japan, Britain, and Scandinavia. And although the Federal Republic has been slow to follow this path, the arguments for doing so are essentially the same as in other pluralistic and democratic industrial states: that equality of educational opportunity be provided for all citizens, that more young people be permitted to develop their potential to the fullest, and that all students learn the skills of communication, cooperation, and citizenship that are needed in a modern society.[21]

As we have seen, the numerous impediments to educational reform in West Germany made any changes extraordinarily difficult to realize. Thus, the establishment of 266 Comprehensive Schools by 1981 appears rather impressive; however, this meant that only 3 or 4 percent of all those attending lower secondary levels (grades five to ten) were attending Comprehensive Schools.[22] As with other innovations, the overall picture is very uneven, with a larger percentage of young people in Comprehensive Schools in Berlin, Bremen, Hamburg, Hesse, and North Rhine-Westphalia than elsewhere. In addition, there are a variety of other means by which traditional schools are loosely integrated (by sharing facilities, personnel, administration, etc.). This adds perhaps 100 to 200 additional so-called additive Comprehensive Schools to the total.

The goals of Comprehensive Schools are essentially the same everywhere in West Germany:

1. To provide all young people with a sound, general education, critical skills, preparation for lifelong learning, and the practice of communicating with others, of whatever background and abilities.

2. To provide equality of educational opportunity for all pupils, whatever their social and economic backgrounds. This would mean abandoning early selection processes and providing special or remedial courses where necessary, to permit pupils to overcome personal problems and social deprivation.

3. To provide social and community education for all students, thereby breaking down traditional class barriers and hostilities. Trust and cooperation would thus replace competition and anxiety. Student self-government, sports, school projects, extracurricular activities, and core courses would provide opportunities for students to learn these skills.

4. To provide pupils with greater opportunities for self-development through the introduction of more elective subjects. This would also assist pupils in the development of a sense of initiative and personal responsibility. As they grow older, they are given greater volition in selecting the subjects they wish to study. For example, in North Rhine-Westphalia's Comprehensive Schools, required subjects constitute 83 percent of the grade six course load and only 33 percent in grade eight.[23]

The organizational pattern bears a strong resemblance to that of a large U.S. high school.

Controversies concerning the introduction of the Comprehensive School abound; many are merely old disputes carried on in new garb. Critics claim that the new secondary institution dilutes the curriculum and, in the name of promoting equal opportunity, lowers the general level of learning; the argument is one used universally. The role of the Comprehensive School in the overall educational picture is somewhat worsened by the fact that the new school must usually compete with the traditional ones; the tripartite system has not been abolished on the introduction of a Comprehensive School. Middle-class parents, therefore, frequently choose to send their children to the Comprehensive School only when they are doing poorly in the *Gymnasium* or the *Realschule*. In Britain, Comprehensive Schools have for many years suffered from this same process of "creaming."

Efforts to evaluate Comprehensive Schools affect additional heated controversies. Employers, for example, are uncertain of how to evaluate a Comprehensive School diploma. Researchers, on the other hand, are not sure of what to measure to determine whether these schools have succeeded or failed. To measure the Comprehensive School by the standards of more traditional schools does not appear just, yet the objectives of the Comprehensive School seem, in some cases, too indefinite to assess. Such factors as school atmosphere, personal growth, and social integration test the skills of even the most competent educational researchers. Personal bias in both reporting and interpreting this research has further clouded an already murky picture.[24]

Yet, in the final analysis, the issue is not really one of either personal preference or testing. Just as many North Americans who originally opposed school integration of whites and blacks have come to accept it on the grounds of human dignity, so too have many West Germans begun to accept the Comprehensive School. After all, the first article of the West German *Grundgesetz* (Constitution) reads: "Human dignity is inviolable." The Comprehensive School is growing — a "mighty midget."

Gymnasium. This has traditionally been the jewel of the German educational crown, the highly selective school that produced future university students and ultimately the intellectual and professional elite of the country. The *Gymnasium* was the German version of the French *lycée* and the British grammar school. Its influence in German life reached its apex around the turn of the century although, as we have seen, it is still, in its present form, a highly respected institution.

Traditionally, the curriculum of the *Gymnasium* was classical, and stressed the study of Latin and Greek. Under the influence of Kaiser Wilhelm II in 1900, various curricular reforms were introduced — the Kaiser had claimed that the *Gymnasium* produced good Greeks and Romans, but not good Germans — which ultimately resulted in the evolution of three kinds of *Gymnasien:* a classical *Gymnasium,* a modern language *Gymnasium,* and a math-science *Gymnasium.*

The high quality of *Gymnasium* education derived from three factors. First, the teachers formed an elite corps. Recruited from the ranks of outstanding former students, they attended universities and obtained degrees before undergoing a rigorous theoretical and practical teacher training course. It should be recalled that formerly very few teachers in other German schools had ever attended universities, but went instead to various teacher training schools. *Gymnasium* teachers, in keeping with their academic achievements, were entitled to all the status and perquisites of high civil servants, which amounted to significant honor and pay in Old Germany.

The pupils whom these teachers taught were also the products of a rigorous selection procedure. This constituted the second of the three elements that gave the *Gymnasium* its special ethos. Selection for the nine-year course occurred after the first four years of the Primary School, and was based on an entrance examination, teacher recommendations, and parental choice.

The third ingredient in the making of a *Gymnasium* was its curriculum. Originally based on the ideals of early nineteenth century neohumanistic reformers, such as von Humboldt, the *Gymnasium* curriculum was supposed to transmit the highest ideals of Western culture, to provide a "true, general, all-around, harmonious human education."[25] It included two or three foreign languages, German, and mathematics as core courses, and history, geography, physics, chemistry, biology, music, religion, sports, and art as well. Other more specialized subjects would be added, depending on the particular type of *Gymnasium.*

Although the ultimate goal of a *Gymnasium* education was the *Abitur* (leaving examination), a university education, and elite status in German society, the path was a rocky one. Despite rigorous selection procedures, failure has been a common experience for many *Gymnasium* students. In 1971, for example, 113,000 *Gymnasium* students of a total of 1,100,000 (more than one in ten) were held back.[26] Only 40 to 50 percent of those admitted ever reached the point where they could take the *Abitur*. This time-honored examination was the most important event in any academic school career and led, when successfully completed, to securing a "Maturity" diploma and admission to university.

Of course, criticism of the *Gymnasium* grew more vociferous in the 1960s. Statistics clearly showed that the schools tended to perpetuate social status rather than providing an opportunity for social mobility. If anything, the small percentage of children from working-class backgrounds who were admitted to the *Gymnasium* in grade five was declining rather than increasing, while in the upper grades, those whose origins were in the upper class increased from 29 to 42 percent of the total.[27] The curriculum also came under intense fire for stifling the development of "individuality," personal interests, and responsibility; such criticism found echoes at that time in virtually every Western state. So, too, did other bywords, such as "undemocratic."

In response to such criticism the *Gymnasium* has changed dramatically since the late 1960s both in the social composition of its clientele and in its curricular offerings. Indeed, some traditionalists mockingly refer to it now as the real German Comprehensive School. Yet, these changes must be seen in relative terms. Although the *Gymnasium* now admits a much larger spectrum of social and ethnic students, middle- and upper-class children are still overrepresented in its classrooms. Abolition of an entrance exam at age ten and the introduction of a two-year orientation stage or at least probationary stage (see above) have made admission procedures somewhat less rigorously selective. Also, various curricular adjustments have eased the transfer of students from one secondary school to another. Many students from the *Realschule* and even some from the *Hauptschule* who were formerly denied any opportunity of taking the *Abitur* now do so with the help of some *Gymnasium* classes. In addition, there are those evening *Gymnasia* and *Kollegs* which open the possibility of the *Abitur* for people already embarked on and embedded in nonacademic careers; more than 30,000 West Germans were availing themselves of this possibility in 1980.

Yet such changes in the Federal Republic seem to occur at a slow if not slothful pace. Five percent of the age cohort passed the *Abitur* in the early 1950s, which increased to only 7.5 percent by 1960, and 16.8 percent by 1981. The number of girls to be found in *Gymnasium* classes has increased markedly, from 41 percent in 1960 to 51 percent in 1981. The children of foreign workers (*Gastarbeiter*) continue, however, to be seriously underrepresented; only 41,000 of 635,000 were *Gymnasium* matriculants in 1980. How many (or rather, how few) of them will be handed the *Abitur* certificate?

Clearly, the *Gymnasium* is in a state of transition. No longer the elite middle-class school of former days, it has not yet been fully redefined. In some suburban areas, a *Gymnasium* may now enroll 50 percent of the age cohort among teen-agers; this hardly entitles it to its former praise or criticism as being too selective. Whereas it was formerly widely maintained that only 5 or 6 percent of the population could profitably be prepared for higher education, more than 20 percent is being matriculated in the *Gymnasium* in the mid-1980s. How much of this is a result of a dilution of the curriculum and examinations has been the subject of heated debates. The value of the *Abitur* has certainly declined in several respects. As a result of declining birth rates and lengthy economic stagnation, it no longer automatically confers a lifelong career on those who pass it. The shortage of academically educated people that existed in the late 1960s gave way in the late 1970s to a surplus of university-educated people, a situation that has threatened to become chronic.

Realschule. The role of the six-year *Realschule* in the West German system has had several justifications. At first glance, it might appear that its role is to educate those who are not quite as intellectually gifted as those who enroll in the *Gymnasium*. Intelligence tests might seem to confirm this, as shown in Figure 4.

FIGURE 4
Intelligence Test Results, West Germany, Late 1960s

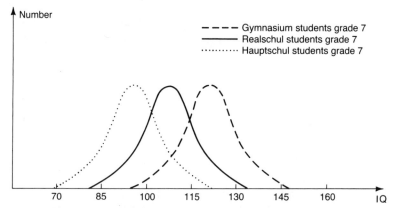

Source: Research done in the late 1960s. Cf. Ministerium Baden-Wuerttemberg, ed., *Bildungsberatung in der Praxis* (Villingen-Schwenningen, 1975).

Yet the considerable overlap between pupils attending these schools indicates that standard IQ exams do not fully explain the constituencies that these secondary schools serve. A better justification for the *Realschule* emerges when one examines its curriculum and history.

The *Realschule* grew in the nineteenth century apace with the growth of industry and commerce in Germany. It appealed to parents, almost entirely middle class, who wanted their sons to learn more "practical" subjects than those taught in the *Gymnasium,* subjects such as modern languages rather than classical ones, and more math and science. The *Realschule* offered an alternative to the *Gymnasium.*

The government and the army also came to appreciate the *Realschule,* as they developed a growing and almost insatiable demand for lieutenants, teachers, engineers, and medium-level administrators. In one official document after another, the importance of the *Realschule* was underlined. In the famous *Rahmenplan* of 1959, for example, the first great educational commission convened after the war, the *Deutsche Ausschuss,* argued for its preservation: "The contemporary economy and administration require this type of education. . . . The *Realschule* is . . . oriented toward usable knowledge, skills and abilities. . . . Scientific modes of thinking and acting determine our existence to such a degree that they must permeate the education and training of every social class."[28]

The number of pupils attending *Realschulen* has increased greatly, as have the number of schools, since the founding of the Federal Republic in 1949. In North Rhine-Westphalia the number of these schools increased from 139 in 1949 to 478 in 1976, and the number of pupils from 56,000 to 309,000 in the same period.[29] A similar pattern of expansion has occurred in most other *Laender* as well.

The increased popularity of *Realschulen* stems from several factors. First, the subjects that form its curriculum (math, science, and modern languages) have gained increasing status and popularity in the postwar decades. More parents and pupils have selected these as means to prepare for both higher education and future occupations. Second, the higher educational opportunities for those who complete the *Realschule* have vastly increased. Pupils may now prepare to enter higher professional schools (*Fachoberschulen*) and eventually pursue careers in engineering, forestry, social work, administration, and so on. In addition, transfer to the upper levels of the *Gymnasium* has been facilitated; pupils from the *Realschulen* may now more easily prepare to take the *Abitur* and eventually matriculate at universities.

Much more than the *Gymnasium,* the *Realschule* has proven to be an attractive educational alternative for working-class children. The elite aura of the *Gymnasium* as well as its less practical curriculum have probably dissuaded many working-class parents with bright children from sending their offspring to this school, while the opposite factors have probably attracted them to the *Realschule.* Primary school teachers have undoubtedly contributed to the growing popularity of the *Realschule* as well, for most of them are well aware of the desolate situation in that other alternative, the West German *Hauptschule,* or Main School.

Hauptschule. In the spring of 1984, an article appeared in the prestigious *Frankfurter Allgemeine Zeitung* entitled, "The *Hauptschule* is Bleeding to Death."[30] The report recounts how the parents of the city of Marburg, a middle-size university town, are considering measures to save the *Hauptschule* of the city, which now enrolls only 17 percent of its age cohort pupils. The situation in Marburg is similar to that in many urban areas. The *Hauptschule* receives those children who are left after all social and academic sifting is finished; this consists of the most backward and deprived West German children and most of the children of southern European laborers (*Gastarbeiter*).

This was not always so. The *Volksschule,* out of which the *Hauptschule* grew, has deep and distinguished roots in the German pedagogical past. The Reading and Writing and Math schools that flourished in medieval German towns and which attracted an upper-class clientele were the progenitors of the *Hauptschule.* The spiritual family tree of this school also includes such distinguished names as Martin Luther (1483–1546), Wolfgang Ratke (1571–1635), Jan Amos Comenius (1592–1670), and A. H. Francke (1663–1727). And in the nineteenth century when the *Volksschule* became one of Prussia's attractions for visiting educators, the names of Pestalozzi (1746–1827) and Herbart (1776–1841) were added to this list. In those days, the *Gymnasium* and the *Realschule* served only a very select few, while the *Volksschule,* predecessor of the *Hauptschule,* served the many and not merely the chaff.

As late as 1952, 81 percent of all twelve-year-olds in West Germany were still attending *Volksschulen.* Then the erosion began. As can be seen in Figure 5, the growth of both the *Gymnasium* and the *Realschule* has dramatically reduced the percentage of pupils attending the school of the "people," although it was given the proud name *Hauptschule.*

FIGURE 5
Twelve-Year-Old Students in Five Types of Secondary Schools

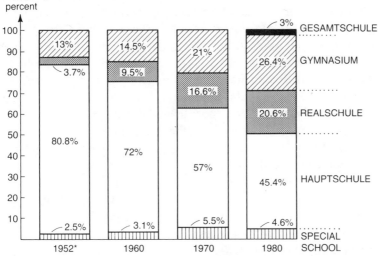

Sources: Der Bundesminister 1982–83; *Groothoff and Stallmann 1960, p. 1012; Kuhlmann 1969, p. 144f.

In fact, the decline of the *Hauptschule* is even more striking when one takes into account that almost 20 percent of those still attending this school are the children of foreign workers. In fact, urban *Hauptschulen* can be identified where more than a majority of the pupils come from this alien and frequently disadvantaged population.

Efforts to improve and thereby save the *Hauptschule* have been numerous and largely unsuccessful. The *Deutsche Ausschuss* of the late 1950s, whose words and deeds we have already frequently quoted (and described), had this to day about the *Hauptschule:* "The recovery of our educational system depends on whether we succeed in improving the efficiency of our *Volksschule* as a *Hauptschule* by raising its achievements and elevating its social prestige."[31]

Indeed, the old village *Volksschule* and schoolmaster were replaced by large, well-equipped schools and better-trained, better-paid teachers, but the decline was not reversed. Curiously, the cause of the *Hauptschule* has found some unlikely recruits in those who oppose the budding movement for Comprehensive Schools (*Gesamtschulen*). The failure of the *Hauptschule,* they believe, will open the way for its nemesis, the Comprehensive School.

Other efforts to resuscitate the *Hauptschule* have focused on curriculum reform and creating more opportunities for pupils who complete the *Hauptschule* and receive a certificate (*Hauptschulabschluss*). Formerly, this led to an apprenticeship and virtually nowhere else. Now, some of the better students receive a Preliminary Professional Certificate (*Fachoberschulreife*), which is recognized as equivalent to the *Realschule* diploma; and a very select few may even continue their education in the upper levels of the *Gymnasium.*

Thus, one final sifting reduces the residue again. Those who still remain are destined, for the most part, for unskilled jobs and casual employment. During difficult economic times, they may often become the unemployed. Of course, there is no school system in the world that does not have children with marginal intelligence, lack of motivation, social deprivation, and ignorance of the national language. The only question is whether it is best to remove the rest and leave all the "hopeless" cases in one institution, the *Hauptschule.*

Special Schools. In many respects, children with diagnostic problems fare better than many *Hauptschule* pupils; they receive special treatment based on their degree of handicap, whether it be deafness, blindness, or some other physical or mental disability. This disabled group constitutes between 4 and 5 percent of their age group.

At first glance it would appear that such children receive excellent care in the Federal Republic. They are grouped according to their particular disability and are taught by specially trained teachers, often using the latest equipment. Indeed, the teachers receive higher pay and prestige than the majority of their colleagues. Such specialized care would appear to be selective and segregated education at its best.

But where does even the best in special education lead — to a life alone rather than in the community? To leisure time spent in isolation in front of the television? To work in special "workshops for the disabled" rather than in integrated workplaces? This is the dilemma of special education. Excellent diagnostic tools and outstanding schools may well lead to a life in seclusion. Social integration and tolerance must be learned by the disabled as well as the nondisabled. The problem is well known to German educators and many would like to try to remedy it, but in a democratic and pluralistic society, the advice of experts is often ignored.

Berufschule (Vocational Education). The traditional path for young Germans who wished to learn a trade or a craft led through an apprenticeship and the *Berufschule.* Having completed the *Volksschule* in former times, most teen-agers left their school desks for a work bench, there to receive a practical training in what would normally become their life's work. At the same time they would continue to attend school one day each week to gain more theoretical knowledge.

This system of vocational education, however appealing it may have been at the turn of this century and however much it evoked nostalgia for an earlier time (perhaps the Middle Ages, when masters taught apprentices the secrets of their craft), has come under increasing criticism. The *Deutsche Bildungsrat,* for example, charged in its 1974 report that this system no longer fulfilled its function in a democratic society. If anything, it served the needs of "private enterprise" rather than the needs of individual students. Specifically, the Commission charged:

- Young people from a socially deprived social background have only a relatively small chance of achieving careers that are educationally more demanding.
- Current learning programs frequently do not correspond with the needs of occupations and society.
- Educational and psychological knowledge are neglected in a number of fields of vocational education and training.[32]

Critics seem to agree that in the case of the average fifteen- or sixteen-year-old, too much time is spent in the workplace (usually four days each week), and too little time in the public school. The private enterprises in which these young people spend their days are more concerned with making a profit, in most instances, than in providing training or an education. Furthermore, it is argued, in times of economic recession many apprentices receive virtually no training in usable skills at all.

The *Deutsche Bildungsrat* did not recommend abandoning this mixed system of on-the-job training and schooling, but did strongly recommend greater efforts at integrating and coordinating the practical with the theoretical. Much broader educational opportunities should be offered to vocationally oriented students, including the chance to resume an academic education. Within the framework of the vocational school, however, students should be given the opportunity to take courses that would help them with career planning, with coping with the problems of private and public life, and with preparation for life-long learning.

Such recommendations have been fiercely resisted by many businesspeople and business-oriented organizations in the Federal Republic. These opponents have staunchly defended the "dual system," with its practical orientation, as opposed to a more integrated and more government-controlled plan. Yet, despite this determined defense, the traditional system has gradually been altered. First, fewer young people have been participating in the older vocational education programs; more than one-third of all vocational school students are now attending full-time schools, as opposed to the small fraction who did previously. Second, a growing number of students now attend a Vocational Foundation Year (BGJ) before entering apprenticeships. The BGJ offers a broader perspective on occupational areas dealing with practical and theoretical aspects of such fields as metallurgy and electronics. And last, an increasing number of new, mostly full-time vocational schools called *Berufsfachschulen* have been created to provide training in many fields such as nursing, medical and dental technology, and bookkeeping. Thus, a diverse group of additional educational opportunities has been created that are almost too varied to describe in detail. Yet, mention must be made of the *Fachoberschule,* which since 1969 has prepared an increasing number of students (150,000 in 1981) for the *Fachhochschule,* which is the lower practical-oriented institution of higher learning. Experiments with complete integration of vocational and general education continue.[33]

However much businesspeople may resist some of these developments (and indeed have gone so far as not to recognize some of the newer programs), the overall thrust of vocational training is still strongly supportive of the existing capitalist system. Students who complete their vocational training are admitted to their chosen fields by examinations, which are administered by practitioners in the field who will ultimately be their employers as well. The forces of conservatism in West German education are indeed powerful.

How then does the overall system function? If your name is Fritz or Elke and you belong to the brightest 5 percent of German children your age, you are almost certain to receive 13 years of fairly good education and then attend a tuition-free university. Your educational path to this goal may be somewhat more varied than previously and take you even by way of a *Realschule* or even a *Hauptschule.* If your intellectual abilities are not so outstanding as those of Fritz and Elke, your education will depend a good deal on the educational aspirations of your parents. If your parents are well informed and hold high aspirations for your future, you will probably follow the same route as the brightest children; if not, you will in your mid-teens join the ranks of those who are apprenticed to learn a trade or who become skilled factory or office workers. Should you belong to a lower intelligence group and have parents who are uneducated and uninformed, you would probably end your full-time schooling at fifteen or sixteen and become part of a large semiskilled or unskilled labor pool; one day each week you would attend classes with others like yourself in the local vocational school. And if you name were Ahmet and your father worked in the VW plant, having migrated to West Germany from Anatolia ten years ago, you would probably end up in the third group of students, no matter how bright you were.

In Summary. Thus, we have seen that the school system(s) of the Federal Republic do not stem from any clear and coordinated vision, whether that of pedagogues or ideologues. By comparison, therefore, with the educational system of the GDR, that of West Germany seems chaotic. Clearly, the distant past has bequeathed many educational institutions and ideals to the present. Older social class distinctions, which were mirrored and perpetuated in the schools, still persist, especially in the secondary schools. Efforts to overcome these social prejudices have frequently been met by organized resistance on the part of some parents, teachers, religious groups, and political parties. The slow and vexatious struggle to introduce an "orientation stage" and a "comprehensive school" clearly illustrate the problem. Even the governments of the various *Laender* as well as the courts can be stymied in their efforts to reshape the schools. As we have seen, West Germany has had a series of national planning commissions, each of which has projected a plan for educational reform and improvement. First came the *Deutsche Ausschuss* (1953–65), which was followed by the *Deutsche Bildungsrat* (1965–75). The latter commission bolstered its *Strukturplan* with more than 50 volumes of findings and reports by experts in various educational fields. These volumes made laudable reading for those interested in education, but were frequently ignored in policymaking. Finally, the *Federal-Laender-Commission* (1970–82) was appointed and produced a *Bildungsgesamtplan* (Comprehensive Educational Plan) in 1973. These various plans, formulated in the hope of reforming West German education, have been only partially realized.

Popular malaise about education continues, not only in the Federal Republic, but virtually in every Western state. This malaise may often inhibit reforms as well as promote them. In 1984 perhaps as many as 1 million people demonstrated in Paris against greater government control of Roman Catholic and other private schools. Similarly, several hundred thousand citizens of North Rhine-Westphalia signed petitions opposing Comprehensive Schools in 1978.

Yet, however frustrated educators, politicians, and the public may be about the making of educational policy and its implementation, would they willingly trade their system for one in which the government and the Party made all decisions? In education, perhaps more than elsewhere, Winston Churchill's famous dictum may apply: that democracy is a poor form of government, but better than all the rest. Nevertheless, the vision of a line of well-dressed Rheinish citizens signing petitions in order to deny working-class and foreign children a decent and desegregated education is despiriting and depressing. Can a democracy truly survive its own paradoxes?

THE STRUCTURE OF EDUCATION IN THE SOCIALIST/COMMUNIST STATE

Fritz's and Elke's cousins in the GDR do not suffer from too great diversity of schools and curricula. Nor do they suffer from regional differences, a premature selection process, private control of vocational education, or constant conflicts between interest groups and political parties over educational policies. Their educational system, that of East Germany, is clearly determined by political and ideological considerations that place a high value on unity or *Einheit*. Two powerful agencies of control, the government and the Party, ensure that such unity exists at every level and that it will be double-checked.

Thus the educational system of the GDR reveals a logic, consistency, and homogeneity that cannot be matched in any Western state. Indeed, in this respect the GDR surpasses its eastern neighbors, Poland and Czechoslovakia, whose communism is reluctantly embraced, as well as the Soviet Union, whose immensity and diversity make homogeneity a virtually unachievable goal. East Germany is a small cohesive state firmly committed to its Marxist-Leninist ideology.

As might be expected, state and Party control of education does not commence when children enter primary school at age six or seven, but begins virtually at birth. The state medical and social systems provide assistance to mothers in the form of whatever diagnostic and social care may be needed to ensure healthy babies and normal development. Thereafter, free, publicly supported nurseries provide daily, weekly, and seasonal child care, both in order to permit mothers to return to productive labor as soon as possible, and because "the development of Communist morality already begins at the earliest age."[34]

The number of available day nurseries has grown steadily in East Germany until, by 1983, 63 percent of all children from age five months to three years were being cared for in these institutions. These were maintained by either local communities or local production units (*Betriebe*), and families were charged only a minimal fee to cover expenses for food. GDR educators claim that this system of day nurseries provides an optimum of health care and stimulation, and an appropriate setting for the emotional, social, and cognitive growth of all children. Thus, according to officials, class and cultural differences are minimized, and all children receive the best possible care.

Here, at the outset, we encounter a dramatic contrast between our estranged twins. In the GDR, authorities maintain that the day nursery is the most desirable place for a child to spend its early months and years, while in the Federal Republic, despite the growth of day care, the prevailing ideology still maintains that the family is the best setting for children under the age of three. Western experts claim that values such as trust and confidence are learned in the warm atmosphere of the home, to say nothing of individualism. In the East babies are quickly and desirably socialized with their peers under professional care in state institutions; the aim is to foster "socialist traits of character and qualities of will" (*sozialistische Charaktereigenschaften und Willensqualitaeten*),[35] rather than independence.

The same kinds of concern for preschool education can be seen in the kindergartens of the GDR as well. Virtually all children between the ages of three and six are enrolled in state-supported and operated preschool kindergartens. The importance of very early inculcation of a "socialist life style" is deeply appreciated by policymakers in East Germany. Kindergarten teachers are trained not only in such subjects as music, art, physical education, and German language, but also in the principles of Marxism and Leninism. The state is not only concerned at this age with cognitive, physical, and emotional development, but with future values and behavior as well. In describing the goals of kindergartens, the Academy of Educational Sciences makes such goals quite clear:

> Kindergartens . . . lay the initial foundation for the all-round development and education of children. The pedagogical work shall be done on the basis of an educational plan which is compulsory for all kindergartens. . . . Great attention shall be given to the development of thinking and the use of the mother tongue. . . . Collective life in the group offers favorable opportunities from very early on to shape an active relationship of children with their environment, to train them for a love of work, to enable them to

undertake duties and fulfill them responsibly.... In this way, children shall at a very early age adopt certain basic attitudes ... which are in accordance with their position and responsibility as citizens of the socialist society.[36]

Thus in the GDR we observe central planning and supervision of education at the preschool stage, while in the Federal Republic such education is left to the initiative of parents who, if they send their children to kindergartens, usually do so at those operated by Catholic or Protestant churches, or community or social welfare organizations. The goals of such West German kindergartens are vague or varied. In addition, such a haphazard system still denies many children any opportunity to attend kindergartens at all.

East German schools, unlike those of the West, represent a dramatic break with the German past and the traditional educational structure. Within 12 months of the surrender of the Nazis, in May 1946, the Soviets abolished the tripartite system in their zone of occupation. Under the provisions of the "Law for the Democratization of the German School," an eight-year comprehensive and nonselective *Grundschule* (basic school) was established for all children ages six to fourteen or fifteen.

As some GDR historians have pointed out, this *Grundschule* probably resembled what many Western reformers had wanted to introduce in their zones of occupation, but failed to achieve. Indeed, the Soviets are credited with more carefully fulfilling the provisions of the Potsdam Treaty which, under Article 7, stipulated that fascism and militarism were to be extirpated from German schools by the occupying powers. This was reiterated in Order 54 of the Allied Control Commission on June 25, 1947, which stated that all compulsory schools should be comprehensive and not be divided, as formerly, in a vertical fashion, but rather only in horizontal levels (for example, "primary" and "secondary" education, etc.).

The standard East German history of education vividly describes the "battle for democratization" of the schools in the Soviet zone of occupation. The struggle was eventually won due to the efforts of "the democratic public, particularly the organized working class," along with "the purposeful, energetic, and unselfish efforts of [Soviet] Education Officers and the ideological help which the SMA [Soviet Military Administration] provided for teachers by propaganda and the publication of the classic works of Marxism-Leninism. ..." Thus, "the old bourgeois school was completely extinguished in the course of a thorough-going revolutionary process" and "the educational privileges of the former ruling and property-owning classes were removed."[37]

The structure of the "German democratic school" that resulted from these efforts in 1946 can be seen in Figure 6. This system was developed further in 1958–59, and was finally reorganized in 1965 under the provisions of the "Law for the Unified Socialist System of Education."

Obviously, a diagram does not reveal more than the external structure of the system. Underlying educational principles, curricula, admission practices, and teaching methods are not capable of being represented in this way. Nevertheless, the tables clearly indicate how important a basic, unified and comprehensive eight-, then ten-year school has been; first a *Grundschule* from 1946 to 1959, then a General Polytechnic School following 1959. GDR educators and officials contrast their system with that of the Federal Republic, which they see as "safeguarding the educational privileges of the ruling monopoly bourgeoisie."[38]

Of course, the principle of comprehensiveness is not unique to East Germany. It means that all children of a given district attend the same school, regardless of their intellectual gifts or their social class background. In most Western societies this has been regarded as a desirable goal and, as such, has been virtually achieved in the United States and in the Scandinavian states and to a lesser extent in Britain and other societies. As we have seen, West German progress toward this goal has been rather slow.

Socialist/communist states have been particularly rigorous in the application of the principle of comprehensiveness. The establishment of an eight-year *Grundschule* in the Soviet zone in 1946 immediately destroyed the traditional *Gymnasium* and *Realschule* system. The *Gymnasium,* with its three branches (classical, modern language, and math/science), was retained for grades nine to twelve only. Then, in 1958, the compulsory comprehensive school was extended for two additional years, leaving only two years of secondary education, which were retained in an *Erweiterte Oberschule* (Academic High School). The rapidity with which the time-honored centerpieces of German education were replaced indicates how seriously the commitment to comprehensive education was taken in the GDR. Since 1958 the state has tolerated very few exceptions to ten years of compulsory attendance at the Polytechnic School.

In addition, the principle of total integration carries over into the school itself; grouping according to ability or interest is not allowed. The

FIGURE 6
GDR School System

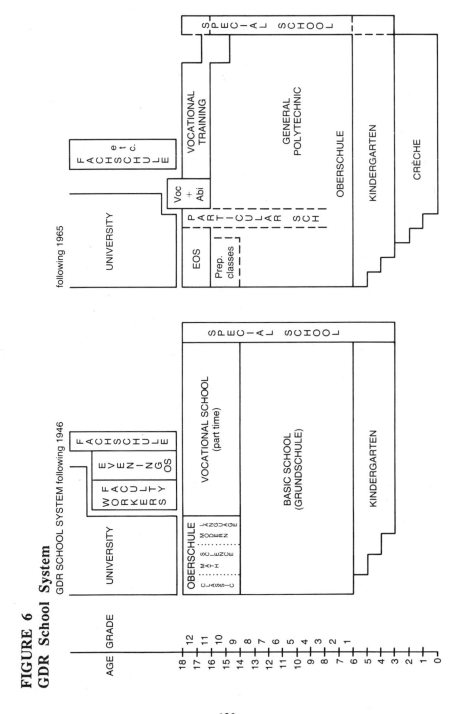

concept of "collective learning" subsumes individual differences and personal interests; it stresses mutual help and cooperation, the harmonious and all-around development of the entire group. The idea of an "intellectual elite" and "egoistic" personal goals are rejected by GDR pedagogy; coeducation of boys and girls is absolutely mandated. "The school class is a collective, the image (*Abbild*) of the socialist society; it is a community of learning and provides the necessary conditions for the development of socialist personalities."[39]

Other basic principles of socialist ideology are also applied rigorously to education in the GDR; absolute secularity, complete state control, and "democratic centralism" are three such principles. Parochial and private schools, for example, many of which are religiously maintained, are protected in West Germany by constitutional guarantees. In the East such schools are banned and regarded by the government as reactionary remnants of a bourgeois society. In a classless society all children must be given equal educational opportunities; none must be privileged. Furthermore, religion, the "opiate of the masses," must have its influence constantly reduced; the abolition of religious schools is an important step in that direction.

Of course, one impediment to equal education has always been the difference between urban and rural schooling. In the sparsely populated countrysides of all states, it has been impossible to provide rural people with the same educational opportunities as city people. The legendary one-room schoolhouse of the U.S. countryside provides testimony to the problem. Following 1945, efforts to amalgamate such schools were undertaken everywhere — the United States, the Federal Republic, and the GDR included. In no country has the policy of "liquidation of the one-room country school" been pursued more vigorously than in East Germany. The goal of having all children attending fully implemented Polytechnic Schools was virtually achieved.

In the GDR, official pedagogy holds that schools must reflect the objective conditions of society, its stage of development, and its social and economic needs, hence, the principle of planned proportional development. As the needs of society change, of course, so too must the schools. They must reflect historic development in all of its manifestations. Thus the eight-year *Grundschule* reflected the necessity of "concentrating all available resources in schools of general education for all." This "corresponded not only with the political needs of society, but also with the economic needs of the anti-fascist democratic order." "The educational level of all workers had to be raised."[40]

The establishment of the ten-year Polytechnic School, in the late 1950s and 1960s, then mirrored a more advanced stage of political maturity in the GDR. It also satisfied the requirements of a new "scientific-technical revolution." The government thus uses schools in a much more direct fashion than in the West for economic and social planning. The principles of "democratic centralism" and "planned proportional development" permit the leaders of the GDR to employ the schools as one of many tools in their work cabinet, others being the law, administration, Party control, the youth organization (FDJ), production units, and workers' organizations. An "objective" interpretation of social and economic necessities thus finds its way into every aspect of education: the structure of the school system, the curriculum, and the testing and qualifying of students for various jobs.

In Western, capitalist societies such extensive planning would be regarded as abhorrent and an infringement of fundamental rights. East German planners see their way as more humane in that individual interests and goals are harmonized with the needs of the "objective social order." They regard Western notions of "free choice" as a sham — young people are surreptitiously directed into jobs that ultimately maximize profits for the ruling bourgeoisie.

Yet the East German system of education is not so completely classless as it purports to be. Educators in the GDR would have observers believe that virtually no academic selection occurs until the completion of the Polytechnic School, when at age sixteen, some students are chosen for admission to the Academic Senior High School (EOS); however, a number of selective mechanisms are already at work within the Polytechnic Schools. For example, students who want to be admitted to the EOS must elect to study a second foreign language (Russian is obligatory as the first foreign language), often as early as grade seven. In addition, preparatory classes in grades nine and ten have been established for those who hope to continue in senior high school. While these classes were not required for admission, students competing for scarce places in grades eleven and twelve enhanced their chances for selection by enrolling in them. Western critics claim that such classes prove that equality of opportunity in the East was "more programmatic than real."[41] GDR educators must have agreed, because preparatory classes in the polytechnic schools are being abolished in the mid-1980s.

An additional means of maximizing one's opportunity for an academic career has been by means of so-called special schools or classes. Under the Education Law of 1965 (Paragraph 18), the Ministry of Education was authorized to establish a number of *Spezialschulen und Spezialklassen* for students to specialize in such fields as math, technology, science, foreign languages, arts, or sports. According to the Ministry of Education (1973), such schools and classes "serve the particular needs of the economy for the development of junior staff in the sciences, sports, and culture. The *Spezialschule* accepts students of high achievement and unusual abilities."[42]

Perhaps because these schools represent a departure from the principle of unified, comprehensive education, precise information about their number and size is difficult to obtain. They seem to operate in all parts of the GDR, and those that specialize in the study of Russian are better known than others. In an article in *Junge Welt,* the central organ of the youth organization, for example, one such school in Wickersdorf is described where there are four teachers from the USSR and where, in 21 years, 1,000 students have prepared for university matriculation in Russian studies.[43] Special instruction in Russian apparently begins as early as grade three, while specialized schools in music and the arts take students from grades five to seven. Math and science schools do not appear to accept students prior to grade seven.[44]

Through these special schools and classes, the GDR provides opportunities for especially talented or gifted young people. Although this seems to violate the principle of comprehensive education, it has undoubtedly enabled East Germany to gain remarkable achievements in such areas as the International Olympics. Students who complete the special schools normally earn the diploma that is an important prerequisite for university admission. In this way an elite of athletes, musicians, ballet dancers, mathematicians, scientists, and Russian language specialists is created, provided they are politically reliable.

Treatment of disabled children in the GDR reflects ideological considerations, as does all education. The Soviet concept of "defectology" has been fully accepted, which means that social and psychosocial origins of any handicaps are rejected in favor of a physical or psychic diagnosis. The pattern of intervention is directed at early diagnosis and special pedagogical treatment in separate facilities. In 1981, a system of 518 special schools cared for the needs of the blind, the deaf, the physically disabled, those with impaired eyesight and hearing, and those with learning disabilities and mental defects, some 61,400 in all (1981).[45] As productive work is regarded as the main source of human dignity in East Germany, special education is clearly directed toward preparation for work. This means the development of motivation and skill to undertake work that corresponds to the limitation or disability that such a person might bear.

In West Germany, on the other hand, treatment of the disabled has been moving in the direction of more complex diagnoses for the disability (physical, social, psychological, etc.). The society itself is seen as one of the origins of disabilities. In addition, greater efforts are being made to integrate disabled children into normal environments, despite some resistance in the schools.[46]

Academic selectivity, where it exists in the GDR, appears almost to embarrass officialdom. Under the Education Act of 1965, the *Erweiterte Oberschule* (Academic Senior High School) is barely mentioned and described as one of the "educational institutions which prepare for university admission [Hochschulreife]."[47] Nevertheless this two-year school is the principal educational route (two-thirds) to the university and academic professions. Yet, as admission to the Academic Senior High School does not take place until students have completed the full ten years of the Polytechnic School, it bears little resemblance to the West German *Gymnasium*. Furthermore, as the number of students who are admitted to the EOS and prepared for admission to universities must be adjusted "according to societal needs," the size of this future academic elite was reduced from 11.4 percent of all 18-year-olds in 1964 to 8.4 percent in 1977.[48] By contrast, in the less planned West German system, the number taking the *Abitur* increased rapidly during this same period, even when it became apparent that the economy could not absorb all those with academic training in professional positions.

In the 1980s, about 10 percent of the graduates from the Polytechnic School were permitted to enter the EOS (Academic Senior High School). Criteria for admission include a second foreign language and "solidarity with our state, which shall be proved by social attitude and activities."[49] The admissions commissions, which must include representatives of the Party Youth Organization (FDJ), are instructed "to ensure in their decisions that children of parents who perform particularly notable service in the building [*Aufbau*] of Socialism shall be privileged in admission to the EOS."[50] Furthermore, a quota system must be used to ensure that workers will be adequately represented among those selected for this school. Thus, the government has established criteria that not only ensure the intellectual qualifications of its future academic elite, but the social and political dependability of this group as well. This is quite consistent with the principle of "partisanship" (*Parteilichkeit*), which governs many aspects of decision-making in the GDR, even in the courts.

Yet, the whole concept of an academic elite is regarded with great suspicion in the GDR, as it is in most socialist/communist states, It is strongly reminiscent of a bourgeois society and seems to diminish the importance of productive labor. Vocational training, therefore, continues to occupy a salient position in educational thinking. Even the ideal "intellectual" is the "worker-philosopher" (*Arbeiterphilosoph*) who was described by the great Soviet pedagogue, P. P. Blonskij (1884–1941). The "worker-researcher" (*Arbeiterforscher*) was proclaimed as the goal of GDR education in 1960.[51]

A conflict exists, however, between the manpower needs of a modern industrial society and this ideal of an intellectual elite drawn from the ranks of vocationally trained workers. The need for highly skilled technicians mitigates against spending many years in learning and practicing a more traditional agricultural or industrial skill. Yet, one-third of all of those who take the *Abitur* for university admission in the GDR come from vocational training backgrounds. Even these, however, have usually spent three years in special *Abitur* classes, which are offered in vocational schools.[52]

For the vast majority of youngsters in the GDR, however, vocational training follows their completion of the Polytechnic School rather than preparation for an academic career. This is not only regarded as a constitutional right, but is also seen as one of the most important elements in socialist personality development: "By providing and strengthening general and vocational knowledge to abilities and skills as well as developing socialist attitudes and behaviors, vocational education and training (*Berufsbildung*) makes an important contribution to the formation of fully developed personalities."[53] Describing "future skilled workers," the government and the FDJ declared in 1976, "Their Marxist-Leninist view of life and their striving for high communist ideals permeate their personal convictions and behaviors. They feel, think and act as patriots of their socialist motherland. . . ."[54]

Not surprisingly, therefore, given its perceived importance, vocational education and training is under the centralized control of a State Secretary for Vocational Education (since 1970). The traditional dichotomy, which still persists in West Germany, between private and public vocational training, has been abolished and a highly organized and rationalized government system has been created in its stead. A network of 720 "Factory Vocational Schools" has been established in conjunction with "socialist units of production." The Vocational Schools are thus linked directly to the factory or "production unit" itself. In small industries, crafts, and farming, some traditional apprenticeships continue, but these have been decreasing. By 1983, 80 percent of all apprentices were being trained in large, "people-owned" productive units, and more than one-fourth of these apprentices were living in 1,360 dormitories, where both technical training and ideological instruction could be more effectively conducted.

While in West Germany vocational training continues to be carried on in rather haphazard fashion with private industrial organization (for example, craft guilds, manufacturers associations, etc.) exercising greater influence than either the government or the universities, in the East central planning is the rule. Vocational training and education are seen as the key to planned scientific and technical progress. Vocational guidance and career planning are therefore geared to long-term state needs. Vocational information is provided through the youth organization, FDJ, as well as County Vocational Guidance Services. Training is offered in 318 skilled occupations with about 600 identified specializations (1983); apprenticeships in "basic occupations" (*Grundberufe*) normally require about 18 months, with specialization taking six more. Thus, an apprentice might spend 18 months learning the skills of a construction worker (*Baufacharbeiter*), then six more months learning to become a bricklayer or a plasterer.[55]

To the U.S. observer whose occupation is a matter of free choice, even whim, and where "vocational planning" is at best a result of the pressures of the marketplace, vocational guidance, and slightly controlled chaos, East German planning appears terribly restrictive. It should be remembered that East Germany is a relatively small country firmly committed to an ideology that entails careful planning. Both German states are heir to a tradition that has not always regarded one's profession or occupation (*Beruf*) as a matter of free choice. East German educators and planners point with pride to a system that harmonizes vocational aspirations and public need. The result, they claim, is full employment and a sense of dignity that only socially useful labor can give. Nothing could be more humane, GDR educators argue, and they proudly proclaim: "Our educational system is ahead of that of the BRD by one entire historical epoch."[56] To their Western cousins, however, freedom and human dignity cannot be achieved through rigorous planning and guidance of the state.

NOTES

The first epigraph to Chapter 7 is from Rainer Winkel, "Alternative Schulen — Ausweg aus der Schulmisere?" in *Alternative fuer die Schule,* edited by Georg Auernheimer and Karl Heinz Heinemann (Koeln, 1980), p. 29.

The second epigraph is from Thomas Mann, *Buddenbrooks,* translated by H. T. Lowe-Porter (New York, 1952), p. 580.

1. Johann Wolfgang von Goethe, *Goethes Werke in sechs Baenden* I (Leipzig, 1940), p. 234. Translation by Stephen Spender in *The Permanent Goethe* (New York, 1948), p. 655.
2. Statistics in this chapter are quoted from Bundesminister fuer Bildung und Wissenschaft, ed., *Grund- und Strukturdaten 1982/83* (Bonn); see also Hans Hermann Groothoff and Martin Stallmann, *Paedagogisches Lexikon* (Stuttgart, 1961).
3. Charlotte Werhahn in *Zeitmagazin,* no. 26 (June 21, 1985): 20.
4. Paul Ziertmann, *Das amerikanische College und die deutsche Oberstufe* (Wiesbaden, 1950).
5. Hansgert Peisert, *Soziale Lage und Bildungschancen in. Deutschland* (Muenchen, 1967).
6. Wolfgang Klafki et al., *Funkkolleg Erziehungswissenschaft I* (Frankfurt, 1970), p. 169.
7. "Stamoschul" (June 26, 1985), p. 25.
8. Ralf Dahrendorf, *Bildung ist Buergerrecht* (Hamburg, 1965); see also Dahrendorf, *Society and Democracy in Germany* (Garden City, NY, 1967).
9. Heinrich Weinstock, *Realer Humanismus* (Heidelberg, 1955).
10. Saul B. Robinsohn, *Bildungsreform als Revision des Curriculum* (Neuwied, 1967).
11. Raimond Poignant, *Das Bildungswesen in den Laendern der EWG* (Frankfurt, 1966). German edition of "L'enseignement dans les pays du Marché Commun" (Paris 1965).
12. Georg Picht, *Die deutsche Bildungskatastrophe* (Muenchen, 1965).
13. Willy Starck, *Die Sitzenbleiber-Katastrophe* (Stuttgart, 1974).
14. Cf. Robert Pedley, *Die englische Gesamtschule* (Bad Heilbrunn, 1966). Translation of Pedley's *The Comprehensive School* (Hammondsworth, n.d.); also see Diether Hopf, *Uebergangsauslese und Leistungsdifferenzierung* (Frankfurt, 1970); Karl Heinz Ingenkamp, ed., *Die Fragwuerdigkeit der Zensurengebung* (Weinheim, 1972).
15. Cf. Deutscher Bildungsrat, *Reform der Sekundarstufe II* (Braunschweig, 1971).
16. Deutscher Bildungsrat, *Zur Neuordnung der Sekundarstufe II. Konzept fuer eine Verbindung von allgemeinem und beruflichem Lernen* (Stuttgart, 1974).
17. It is almost axiomatic in the history of education that national crises (for example, World War II, Sputnik, etc.) precipitate educational soul-searching and reform (for example, the Butler Act of 1944 in England, etc.).
18. See Diether Hopf, Lothar Krappmann, and H. Scheerer, "Aktuelle Probleme der Grundschule," in *Bildung in der Bundesrepublik Deutschland,* vol. 2, edited by

Max-Planck-Institut fuer Bildungsforschung (Reinbek, 1980), pp. 1113–76.

19. Bund-Laender-Kommission fuer Bildungsplanung, *Bildungsgesamtplan*, vol. 1 (Stuttgart, 1973), p. 25.

20. See Walter Twellmann, ed., *Handbuch Schule und Unterricht*, vol. 5, 1 (Duesseldorf, 1981), p. 232.

21. Adalbert Rang and Wolfgang Schulz, eds., *Gesamtschule. Bilanz ihrer Praxis*, 2nd ed. (Hamburg, 1976).

22. *Grund- und Strukturdaten*, pp. 22, 37.

23. W. Keim, "Die Gesamtschule und ihre Didaktik," in Twellmann, *Handbuch Schule und Unterricht*, p. 193.

24. Helmut Fend et al., *Leistungsvergleich zwischen Gesamtschulen und Schulen des traditionellen Schulsystems* (Hildesheim, 1981); Wottawa, *Gesamtschule: Was sie uns wirklich bringt* (Duesseldorf, 1982).

25. Albert Reble, *Zur Geschichte der Hoeheren Schule*, vol. 2 (Bad Heilbrunn, 1975), p. 233.

26. Starck, *Sitzenbleiber-Katastrophe*, p. 20; *Grund-und Strukturdaten*, p. 26.

27. In one representative survey from about 11 percent of the class to about 8 percent. See Hannelore Gerstein, *Erfolg und Versagen im Gymnasium* (Weinheim, 1972), p. 80.

28. Erich Geyer, ed., *Differenzierung der Realschuloberstufe in Nordrhein-Westfalen* (Hannover, 1976), p. 13.

29. Ibid., p. 27f.

30. March 2, 1984.

31. Deutscher Ausschuss fuer das Erziehungs- und Bildungswesen, *Rahmenplan zur Umgestaltung und Vereinheitlichung des allgemeinbildenden oeffentlichen Schulwesens* (Stuttgart, 1959), p. 26.

32. Cf. Deutscher Bildungsrat, *Zur Neuordnung der Sekundarstufe II* (Stuttgart, 1974).

33. For instance in the *Kollegschule*. See Kultusminister NW, ed.,Schulversuch Kollegschule NW (Koeln, 1976).

34. Akademie der Paedagogischen Wissenschaften der DDR, ed., *Das Bildungswesen der Deutschen Demokratischen Republik*, 2d ed. (Berlin, 1983), p. 26f.

35. Ibid., p. 34.

36. Ibid., p. 36ff.

37. Karl-Heinz Guenther et al., *Geschichte der Erziehung*, 11th ed. (Berlin, 1973), p. 626ff.

38. Ibid., p. 693.

39. Helmut Klein, *Bildung in der DDR* (Reinbek, 1974), p. 116.

40. Guenther et al., *Geschichte der Erziehung*, p. 630ff.

41. Klaus Dieter Mende, "Schulreform und Gesellschaft in der DDR, 1945–1965," in Saul B. Robinsohn et al., *Schulreform als gesellschaftlicher Prozess*, vol. 1 (Stuttgart, 1972), p. 57ff.

42. Ministerium fuer Volksbildung, ed., *Sozialistisches Bildungsrecht: Rechtsvorschriften und Dokumente* (Berlin, 1973), p. 33.

43. March 19, 1985.

44. Mende, "Schulreform und Gesellschaft," p. 59.

45.   *Bildungswesen der DDR,* p. 74ff. See also L. Hammer, "Early Identification of Handicaps and Early Special Education in the German Democratic Republic," *Prospects,* 11, no. 4 (1981): 460–68.

46.   Hans Dennerlein and Karlheinz Schramm, eds., *Handbuch der Behindertenpaedagogik,* 2 vols. (Muenchen, 1979).

47.   In Paragraph 21.

48.   *DDR Handbuch* (1979), p. 315.

49.   Government Instruction of June 10, 1966. See also Mende, "Schulreform und Gesellschaft," p. 61; *Bildungswesen der DDR,* p. 80ff.

50.   Ibid.

51.   Guenther et al., *Geschichte der Erziehung,* p. 651.

52.   See Gerlind Schmidt, *Sekundarabschlusse mit Hochschulreife im Bildungswesen der DDR* (Weinheim/Basel, 1976).

53.   *Bildungswesen der DDR,* p. 91.

54.   Ibid., p. 92. See also GDR Youth Law of January 28, 1974; Staatssekretariat fuer Berufsbildung, ed., *Sozialistisches Bildungsrecht — Berufsbildung* (Berlin, 1979), p. 44ff.

55.   *Sozialistisches Bildungsrecht — Berufbildung,* p. 80f.

56.   Guenter et al., *Geschichte der Erziehung,* p. 664.

8

THE CURRICULUM: FREE CHOICE AND DIVERSITY VERSUS NO CHOICE AND REQUIREMENTS

> I have been poring over Marx and Lenin all day long and it has now become 11 o'clock. At last I have thrown it all into the corner. In contrast to you I don't like it at all. To spend my time doing something like that! When there is such a miserable obligation hanging over your head, you really can't even get excited about getting started. . . . We always say in a joking way that, after graduation, you could design your own padded cell.
>
> Letter of a nineteen-year-old East German student to a friend in West Germany

> It wouldn't be so bad if they put some Kafka into the curriculum.
>
> From a story by an East German student, Thorsten Schulz

THE PROBLEM OF THE CURRICULUM IN OUR TIME

One of the axioms most often repeated in the nineteenth century was: "The Battle of Waterloo was won on the playing fields of Eton." Never mind that Eton had not yet adopted team sports (and playing fields) into its curriculum prior to Wellington's defeat of Napoleon in 1815, the maxim expresses one of the great truths of modern times, that the great successes or failures of modern states, whether on the battlefield, in the laboratory, or in the marketplace, are to a great extent a result of what is taught in its schools. When Prussian armies defeated the French in 1871, the vanquished French dispatched a commission to Prussia as soon as feasible to study Prussian schools, and when the Soviets launched their Sputnik into space in 1957, it precipitated a crisis among U.S. educators and curriculum planners, to say nothing of the public and the politicians. And certainly the success of Japanese industrial products in world markets has caused other industrial states to re-examine what is taught in their schools. A plethora of studies and proposals has been the result of this "crisis" in the United States.

Most recent curriculum debates, therefore, have been precipitated by a sense of national anxiety. In the United States, this has usually provided support for those who favor a "back to basics" approach, those who believe there is a common core of subject matter that every student should master. This was true in the late 1950s, when Sputnik evoked renewed stress on math, science, and languages, and has also been the case in the 1980s, when a lagging economy coincided with lower scores on standard achievement tests to produce such widely discussed documents as Mortimer Adler's *Paideia Proposal* and the Carnegie Foundation's *Nation at Risk*.

The debate, however, is not a new one. What to teach and whether to permit the pupil any choice among subjects has, perhaps, been placed in a new context, although it certainly dates from the time of Plato and Aristotle. Nor did the medieval notion of basic knowledge as enshrined in the *Septem Artes Liberales* ever settle the issue. Even in an age when the sum of human knowledge was relatively small and the learned world was remarkably homogeneous, scholars and schoolmasters repeatedly challenged the basics; indeed, Renaissance learning was largely the result of such a challenge.

In more recent times, the incredible proliferation of knowledge as well as the advent of popular education has shifted the focus. If there are *basic subjects* that *everyone* should know, how much and how well should they be learned? How much math is enough, how much history, or literature, or foreign languages? At different times and in different places these questions have been addressed and answered in different ways. The U.S. tradition has been, for example, to teach the three R's in elementary school, to offer an increasing number and variety of electives in high school, and to mix requirements of a general nature with electives in colleges and universities. The German tradition, on the other hand, was to provide a basic general education in primary school, offer virtually no electives in the different types of secondary schools, and then grant university students unlimited freedom of choice (*Studienfreiheit*).

The curriculum choices that a society makes reveal a good deal about that society. Not only does the curriculum say something about what knowledge is most prized, it also discloses other values of a society as well. The German twins are no exception. The students in these two states are confronted with highly dissimilar subjects and differing amounts of choice in selecting subjects. It is, therefore, to the curricula of these estranged twins that we must now turn.

TWO DIFFERENT WEEKLY SCHEDULES

What then are the weekly schedules of the school systems in East and West Germany and what do they tell us? Of course, the schedule simply gives us the titles of courses and how many hours are devoted each week to them. It does not disclose what is actually taught. Thus, a course such as history or any other social science will undoubtedly differ dramatically in content in the Federal Republic and the GDR; nevertheless, the weekly schedules in themselves provide a useful base for comparison. We start with the curriculum plan for the East German Polytechnic School (Table 1).

What will immediately strike most readers about Table 1 is how little choice is afforded students of the Polytechnic School in East Germany. The ideal citizen of this socialist state is the product of a highly standardized curriculum. With the exception of a single course in needlework in grades four and five and the option of a second foreign language in grades seven to ten, no electives are offered in the entire ten years of matriculation.

The subjects that all students must take, however, fall into three major groups. The first contains those that are designed to impart a socialist view of history and contemporary society as well as provide a sense of solidarity with the Soviet Union. It includes, in addition to German, Russian for everyone, history, civics, and geography. The second group could be called the math-science group, and indicates the high priority that educational planners give to these subjects. Not only does this reveal the emphasis placed on technological and industrial development, it also derives from the ideology of Marxism-Leninism, which stresses both the scientific nature of socialism and its dialectical relationship to changes in means of production. Social and ideological progress are directly dependent on industrial progress.

And last are those subjects that are the pride of socialist/communist curriculum planners, the polytechnic subjects. The first of these is already required in grade one, *Werkunterricht* (practical instruction), which

TABLE 1
Weekly Schedule of the 10-Grade General Polytechnic High School (GDR)

Subject					Grade					
	1	2	3	4	5	6	7	8	9	10
German	10	12	14	14	7	6	5	5	3	4
Russian	—	—	—	—	6	5	3	3	3	3
History	—	—	—	—	1	2	2	2	2	2
Civics	—	—	—	—	—	—	1	1	1	2
Geography	—	—	—	—	2	2	2	2	1	2
Mathematics	5	6	6	6	6	6	6	4	5	4
Physics	—	—	—	—	—	3	2	2	3	3
Astronomy	—	—	—	—	—	—	—	—	—	1
Chemistry	—	—	—	—	—	—	2	4	2	2
Biology	—	—	—	—	2	2	1	2	2	2
"Werkunterricht" (wood work, metal work, etc.)	1	1	1	2	2	2	—	—	—	—
School garden instruction	1	1	1	1	—	—	—	—	—	—
Polytechnic instruction	—	—	—	—	—	—	4	4	5	5
Introduction into socialist production	—	—	—	—	—	—	1	1	2	2
Technical drawing	—	—	—	—	—	—	1	1	—	—
Productive work	—	—	—	—	—	—	2	2	3	3
Art/drawing	1	1	1	2	1	1	1	1	1	—
Music	1	1	2	1	1	1	1	1	1	1
Physical education	2	2	2	3	3	3	2	2	2	2

Optional									
Needlework	—	—	—	1	1	—	—	—	—	—
2nd foreign language	—	—	—	—	—	—	3	3	3	2
Lessons per week (including options)	21	24	27	30	32	33	35	36	34	35
Plus: Obligatory premilitary service in grades 9 and 10										

Source: Adapted from Akademie der Paedagogischen Wissenschaften der DDR, ed., *Das Bildungswesen der Deutschen Demokratischen Republik*, 2d ed. (Berlin, 1983), p. 62.

includes learning to work with materials such as wood and metal, and school garden instruction. By grades seven to ten, students take courses in "Socialist Production" and "Productive Labor," which bring them directly into factories and agricultural production units. The significance of these polytechnic courses is indicated by the fact that the schools derive their name from this portion of the curriculum. As we have described in Chapters 4 and 5, polytechnic education is deeply rooted in the Marxist ideological commitment to productive labor and its efficacy in providing human dignity and shaping the "socialist personality."

Beyond these three main groups of subjects there is little else. Art, music, and physical education occupy a very limited role in the curriculum. Schools are not expected, however, to provide for all the social and emotional needs of East German children, and occupy only the morning part of the "full day educational process." Afternoons and evenings are supposed to be spent doing homework, but also engaging in political and youth group activities, whose importance is deemed very great.

Many if not most of the trends of the Polytechnic School can be traced further in the Academic Senior High School (EOS) which, it should be recalled, provides two additional years of schooling for those destined for academic professions.

Table 2 confirms the emphasis placed on the math/science and historical/ideological groups of subjects. By comparison to this level in most Western states, including West Germany, elective courses are still very restricted. Students may select one lesson in art or music per week, a second foreign language, and have a rather vague possibility of taking three hours per week of study groups sometimes offered in conjunction with required courses. When compared to a typical menu of courses offered to juniors and seniors in U.S. high schools, this fare seems bland and monotonous.

Polytechnic education does not cease in the Academic Senior High School, either. It takes the form of the "scientific-practical work," which is included in the curriculum of both years of this school. Students are channeled into a variety of programs such as electrotechnics, data processing, chemotechnics, and agrotechnics. These courses serve a significant vocational function and help to guide students into those (often) regional fields, which state planners have designated as most important for state economic development.

In the GDR, this was the state of required and elective courses in the curriculum in the mid-1980s.

TABLE 2
Weekly Schedule of the EOS (Upper Secondary School — Academic)

	Grade			
	11		*12*	
Subject	*1st half*	*2nd half*	*1st half*	*2nd half*
German	3		4	
Russian	5	3	3	5
2nd foreign language	3	2	3	4
History	3		—	
Civics	1		2	
Geography	2		—	
Mathematics	5		5	
Physics	3		3	
Chemistry	2		3	
Biology	2		3	
"Scientific-practical work"	—	4	4	—
Art or Music (optional)	1		1	
Physical education	2		2	
Optional courses	up to 3		up to 3	

Source: Adapted from Akademie der Paedagogischen Wissenschaften der DDR, ed., *Das Bildungswesen der Deutschen Demokratischen Republik,* 2nd ed. (Berlin, 1983), p. 82.

In West Germany no pair of tables, such as Tables 1 and 2, could begin to encompass the variety of courses, elective as well as required, that are offered in the schools. In the first place, each of the eleven *Laender* provides its own curricula. Then we have seen that, beyond primary school, students attend a wide variety of schools, each with its own distinctive curriculum. Thus in 1980, 25.2 percent of all fifteen-year-old students were attending the *Hauptschule,* 24 percent the *Realschule,* 22.7 percent the *Gymnasium,* and 3.3 percent the Comprehensive School. An additional 18.5 percent were attending Vocational Schools, and about 6 percent were in a variety of private schools with "alternative" curricula. Some of these private schools are committed to very specific curriculum concepts; the well-known

Waldorfschule, for example, derives many of its courses from the ideas of Rudolf Steiner and his followers (see Chapter 10).

For purposes of comparison, however, we shall use the weekly class schedules of the most populous West German *Land,* North Rhine-Westphalia. In most respects these schedules are typical of what would be found in other *Laender*. Table 3 provides the weekly schedule for the North Rhine-Westphalian Primary Schools (grades one to four).

In comparing this weekly schedule with that of the same school years in the GDR, the following points of comparison and difference emerge:

1. As in the GDR, the education ministers of West German *Laender* provide a single weekly schedule for all schools. This undoubtedly derives from the common heritage of the two German states (quite different, for example, from the decentralized regulations of the English Primary Schools). The notion of a sound, common, basic education for all children prevails.

2. In the absence of a single *Weltanschauung,* as exists in the GDR, West German primary schools provide more courses geared to personal development in "specific environments" of children. This takes the form of religious instruction by denominational religious teachers as well as

TABLE 3
Weekly Schedule of the Primary School (Grades 1–4) in North Rhine-Westphalia

Subject	Grade			
	1	*2*	*3*	*4*
Language (German)	4	4	4	4
"Sachunterricht"	2	3	4	5
Mathematics	4	4	4	4
Physical education	3	3	3	3
Music	1	1	1	2
Art/"textile work"	1	2	3	3
Religious instruction	2	2	3	3
Supportive lessons (*Förderunterricht*)	3	3	3	3
Hours per week	21	22	25	27

Source: Kultusministerium of North Rhine-Westphalia.

Sachunterricht, which stresses regional and hometown themes. In addition, West German children spend a good deal more time in art, music, and physical education than their GDR cousins; conversely, East German children spend more hours learning math and other subjects that will prepare them for polytechnic education.

3. *Foerderunterricht* or "supportive instruction" is offered in the primary schools of North Rhine-Westphalia so that teachers can undertake remedial work with small groups of children. The purpose of these classes is to overcome individual differences caused by handicaps and social deprivation and to help all children reach similar general goals of achievement. Certainly, the East Germans would regard these classes as unnecessary in their state, where "equality of condition" already exists and where cooperation to achieve collective goals is part of Marxist-Leninist basic pedagogy in all schools.

Following grade four, the children of North Rhine-Westphalia enter the traditional tripartite school system, like most West German children, some going to each of the three schools, *Hauptschule, Realschule,* and *Gymnasium.* This is not only a matter of school organization, but also has important curricular implications as well. Certainly the heavy emphasis on Latin and academic achievement in the *Gymnasium,* for example, has made it difficult in the past for students to transfer to this school. It has especially made moving from the *Hauptschule* to the *Gymnasium* virtually impossible. As we have seen in Chapter 7, efforts at curricular reform in order to improve this situation have only been partially successful.

The general curricular rule that prevails at the secondary level is: the higher the academic standards of the school type, the more differentiated the curriculum and the greater number of choices that are available to the students. An examination of the courses and programs offered in grades nine and ten of the *Realschulen* of North Rhine-Westphalia illustrates this point (Table 4).

What this table does not reveal, however, is that many of the courses given in grades five to eight were taught as a preparation for the informed choices students could then make in grades nine and ten. Also it is clear that elective courses are offered in the context of a particular branch of study, such as "language branch" or "math/science branch." Students are not free merely to choose elective subjects at random. In addition, a common "core" of subjects is retained, which all students must take. The two weekly hours reserved for *Arbeitsgemeinschaften* (group work)

TABLE 4
Weekly Schedule of the *Realschule* (Here Only Grades 9 and 10) in North Rhine-Westphalia

Courses	Hours	Supplementary subjects	Hours
Language branch			
English	4	Mathematics	4
French	4	Social and economic science	1
		Physics, chemistry, biology	4
Math/science branch			
Mathematics	5	English	4
Physics, chemistry, biology	7	Social and economic science	1
Social science branch			
Social/economic science		Mathematics	4
or Social pedagogy		English	4
or Social care	5	Physics, chemistry, biology	4
Art/music branch			
Art or Music	4	Mathematics	4
		English	4
		Social/economic science	1
		Physics, chemistry, biology	4
Core			
Religious instruction	2		
German	4		
History/geography	3		
Physical education	2		
Domestic science			
or Technical work	2		
Art or Music	2		

Plus: 2 hours elective course (*Arbeitsgemeinschaften*) from a large variety of additional subjects varying in different schools.

This is the heart of the curricular differentiation in the *Realschule* in North Rhine-Westphalia. It is preceded by what has been termed "predifferentiation" in grades 5 to 8, mainly consisting in the offer of an elective French course, beginning in grade 7.

Source: Kultusministerium of North Rhine-Westphalia.

permit students to select from a wide array of alternatives that meet their personal interests (for example, photography, computer science, Latin, sports, etc.).

If schools in West Germany have moved increasingly in the direction of offering more courses and more choices for students in the 1970s and 1980s, this has paralleled developments in the schools of other Western democracies as well. In France, for example, a similar change has been occurring. In the Federal Republic the *Deutsche Bildungsrat,* the reform committee of the 1970s and 1980s, laid the foundation for these changes by the exhaustive research it published, and its commitment to promoting principles of individualization as a key to democracy and as a prime source of motivation and effective learning. Yet, the principle of retaining "major areas of concentration" has permitted administrators to maintain some control over the curriculum, at least in the *Realschule.*

It is in the hoary halls of the *Gymnasium,* however, that the most dramatic curricular changes have occurred. Under the "Bonn Agreement" (*Bonner Vereinbarungen*) of 1972, the education ministers of the various *Laender* agreed to dispense with the traditional compulsory curriculum in the upper levels of the *Gymnasium.* Early twentieth century reformers had successfully introduced the idea of "major areas of concentration" into these elite schools, but virtually no choice was permitted other than this. Following the Bonn Agreement, students in grades eleven to thirteen were permitted virtually to create their own program of two major (five to six hours weekly) and two minor (three hours weekly) subjects. Although a variety of requirements were retained, a great deal of personal discretion was granted to students where previously none had existed. By introducing this change, a weekly class schedule was virtually abolished in the upper secondary level of the *Gymnasium.* A typical mixture of majors and minors might resemble the following:

	Majors (each 5–6 hours p.w.)	*Minors* (each 2–3 hours p.w.)
Student A	Mathematics, Physics	Geography, English
Student B	Biology, Chemistry	Latin, History
Student C	German, English	History, Biology
Student D	French, History	Mathematics, Art
Student E	History, Geography	English, Biology

(one hour equals 45 minutes)

As might be imagined, controversy over the *Gymnasium* curriculum has not disappeared, but its locus has now shifted to the 20 basic half-year courses (three hours weekly) which are still required of *Gymnasium* students. "Progressives" have argued that students should be allowed greater discretion in selecting alternatives in this area, while "conservatives" have maintained that students be required to continue taking courses in German, Math, History, and so on. In the 1980s the conservative position has been predominant.

Nevertheless, the overall trend in West German schools since the early 1970s has been in the direction of increasing personal choice and responsibility in matters of curriculum. The freedom to choose has increased as students progress through the school system to the upper secondary level. This clearly reflects a pluralistic creed where no single view of personality or knowledge prevails; it mirrors both a tolerance of many views as well as an ambiguousness about values. The school curricula of the GDR reflect no such ambiguousness or tolerance. In West Germany students are prepared to meet an unknown future where flexibility has a significant value of its own; in East Germany, the future is foretold and students only need to learn what is needed to arrive and to survive there.

Of course, it would be nice to conclude this section with a paean for freedom and free choice in the schools. The educators who introduced the elective system in West Germany saw themselves as advancing the cause of democracy and freedom; they even involved students in drawing up the plans for reform in the upper secondary level.[1] Yet, freedom, however precious and desirable, lends itself to abuse; freedom of the press, for example, seems to lead to pornographic excesses as well as more desirable goals. Many critics of the broader use of electives have noted that students often make their choices on the basis of what they believe is easiest rather than what is best. Many doubts have been raised in the Federal Republic about entrusting students with so much free choice, and there are those who would like to return to a much more standardized and compulsory curriculum. It seems hardly believable, however, that in the Western twin, a rigid standardized curriculum for all will ever be forced on students again.

WHAT TEACHERS TEACH IN THE FEDERAL REPUBLIC

Weekly lesson plans tell us little about what is actually taught in the classrooms of the German twins. The content of classes is derived from textbooks and the knowledge the teachers possess; the former is, of course, more readily available and easier to analyze than the latter. Yet in

West Germany, where pluralism reigns, the gathering of texts and classroom materials is, in itself, a limitless task. The reasons for this variety of materials are the following: (1) the federal structure of government; (2) the openness of ministerial regulations about selection of teaching materials, which corresponds with; (3) the freedom of teachers to select materials and; (4) the right of students and parents to influence the choice of materials and finally; (5) the free market in the publication of textbooks and teaching materials. A closer examination of these factors is in order.

1. West German pluralism derives in large measure from the federative nature of the polity. As in the United States, where a great deal of power resides in the states, especially pertaining to educational policy, the same is true in the Federal Republic, where the power is in the hands of the *Laender.* One great difference is that in West Germany there are 11 *Laender* rather than 50 states as in the United States. In each of these *Laender* a minister of education retains a good deal of policymaking power, especially where value decisions must be made. Civics, for example, goes by a different name in each of the 11 *Laender.* Terms such as "community studies" (*Gemeinschaftskunde*), "political instruction" (*Politikunterricht*), "social studies" (*Sozialkunde*), and "global studies" (*Weltkunde*) are in use in various *Laender.* Nor are these only differences in title; differences in values are frequently reflected in different nomenclatures. Thus traditionally conservative Rhineland-Palatinate emphasizes an understanding of the existing political order and its preservation in its civics instruction, while social-democratic Hesse stresses an appreciation of conflict and change in society. Hamburg, on the other hand, accentuates politics as a process of finding consensus and cooperating in self-determination.[2] Such fields as math (new math or old math), geography (physical geography or economic geography), history, and literature are not exempt from broad differences between *Laender.*

2. Yet even such large differences between *Laender* do not matter much in a country where ministers of education provide only broad principles of interpretation. In addition, ministerial directives do not carry the weight they once had. Traditional Germany prided itself on the power of authority and the need to obey official orders. Such fearsome authority has gradually diminished in the Federal Republic. Thus, when the minister of education of North Rhine-Westphalia propounds directives about the goals and content of courses in the upper secondary level (*Oberstufe*) of the *Gymnasium,* these serve notice on teachers, parents,

and textbook editors as to what the orientation of courses should be and what minimal requirements will be expected for examinations, but the actual content of the course is left to those who are engaged in the teaching of it in schools. Parents, students, and interested members of the public may also be included in this process. The minister of education in this state even defined a part of his function as being fulfilled when he "provides curricular free space (*Freiraeume*) for independent decisions and activities."[3] This is a far cry from both Old Germany and the New Germany of the East.

Of course, there are teachers who wish to be guided by administrative regulations and be supplied with prescribed educational texts and materials for their classes. For such teachers an abundance of suggested lesson plans and readings come from the ministry of education. But these are all in the form of suggestions and proposed titles that seem to suit the majority of teachers and students quite well. In the general introduction to the "Instruction Guide for History in the Upper Secondary Level of the Gymnasium," (1982) the minister of education in North Rhine-Westphalia explained why this open system was so desirable: "Historical-political education must aim at an open . . . self-determined discourse, and it should promote the recognition that a variety of viewpoints are desirable in order to further the rational solution of conflicts."[4]

This multifaceted approach to history is, of course, characteristic of a pluralist society. As no single view of the past is officially sanctioned, a variety of interpretations must be taught. According to the minister of education, this creates the proper conditions for the student "to understand various values and value systems and to make personal judgments and decisions." In addition, it helps the student gain the "ability to understand critically the reality of present existence . . . in the face of a background of alternative . . . historical possibilities." It assists the student in finding his/her own personal identity while granting full respect and tolerance to the identities of others. Given the horrors of recent German history, virtually all West German authors, pedagogues, and politicians endorse, in principle, these goals of openness and tolerance toward other cultures.

If democracy is indeed enhanced by such an undogmatic approach to questions of school curriculum, then skeptics have little to fear for the survival of democracy in West Germany. The education ministries of the various *Laender* suggest subject themes to teachers, provide examples of outlines for dealing with these themes, suggest possible texts and instructional procedures, but then leave the rest to teachers, students, and parents. Of course, curricular freedom also depends on the character of subjects. It is greater, for example, in German than in math. In general, however, diversity is the order of the day.

3. and 4. The power of teachers to make curricular decisions actually predates the founding of the Federal Republic. Even in the nineteenth century, when "authority" and "obedience" were bywords of the Prussian state, teachers had gained the right to oppose arbitrary government regulations regarding the curriculum. In the Federal Republic these rights have been elaborated and ensured in a number of ways. Most significant in this respect was an imbroglio stemming from Hesse that eventually involved many leading West German figures.

In 1973 the Social Democratic minister of education in Hesse issued a set of "Curriculum Guidelines for the Teaching of Civics" (*Rahmenrichtlinien fuer Gesellschaftslehre*) at the lower secondary level. The courses involved were history, geography, and politics. Ostensibly, according to the guidelines, the purpose of teaching civics was to assist students in learning to make choices, both by themselves and in concert with others. In fact, according to many who read these guidelines, their purpose was to propagate a particular neo-Marxian point of view. World history, for example, was supposed to be taught as a series of social class conflicts. Students were to be instructed in how to unmask the existing social structure and see how the ruling class used authority to maintain itself. Essentially, the ideas of the well-known Frankfurt school of sociology were incorporated into the civics curriculum of the Hessian school system.

A vehement and sometimes volatile discussion followed, a discussion that soon involved leading West German educators, philosophers, academics, and representatives of trade unions, business groups, and churches. According to Bernhard Vogel, who was minister of education in the neighboring *Land* of Rhineland-Palatinate, the results of this heated debate were the following:

> Official curricular guidelines may not be allowed to put the teacher in a position of being merely a "fulfillment agent" [*Erfuellungsgehilfe*] or make a student merely an object of a predetermined instructional concept. . . .

> Education must have as its goal . . . the autonomy of the young adult, autonomy with respect to knowledge, judgment, and action. . . .

> Curricular guidelines and school regulations are merely components whose purpose is to guarantee the free educational scope [*Freiraum*] which is required

in a school, an atmosphere in whch not everything can be regulated nor everything in the curriculum be operationalized if the real educational goal of the school is to be reached.[5]

Thus, the Hessian civics controversy concluded by confirming the independence of teachers in matters of curriculum and ensuring the right of students to be confronted with a plurality of methodologies and approaches to knowledge.

This particular controversy did not, however, resolve all the curriculum questions facing the educators of the Federal Republic. How much, for example, should curriculum planning be the work of students, parents, and the public, as well as scholars, teachers, and administrators? Clearly some subjects, such as math and science, were less controversial with respect to curriculum than the liberal arts and social studies. The theoretical works of both Erich Weniger and Saul B. Robinsohn played a significant role in the framing and discussion of these questions. Weniger examined the democratic interaction of various "educational powers" in curriculum formation, and Robinsohn introduced U.S. ideas of curriculum reform to Germany (especially the earlier curricular work of Ralph W. Tyler).[6]

All in all, the 1970s were filled with lively debates over curriculum questions. Proponents of the idea that learning objectives and curricular elements should be derived from real-life situations challenged the traditional notion of subjects taught in schools being merely appendages to university disciplines. In addition, curriculum planners began to use teachers as members of curriculum commissions as well as asking teachers to develop and test new ideas concerning subject matter and instructional methods.[7] Both West German and U.S. curriculum experts came to share the view "that in the last analysis there is no substitute for the intelligent participation of the teacher in curriculum improvement." "The most striking aspect of the teacher's curriculum development role is its inevitability."[8]

West Germany, once a relatively listless zone with respect to curricular theory, became one of the most active centers for curriculum debate and research.

5. Freedom of the press does not, in itself, guarantee pluralism in the publishing of textbooks. Other factors may inhibit a multiplicity of texts or the expression of multiple points of view in the textbook publishing industry. As has frequently been the case in the United States, one publisher or one text may come to dominate a particular field, or,

more frequently, the text adoption practices of one populous state (for example, Texas) may influence the manner in which all texts are written, thus virtually precipitating voluntary censorship. Publishers in a capitalist society are, after all, trying to maximize their sales and profits.

Yet, when compared to the carefully scrutinized, ideologically pure textbooks of the Soviet Union or the GDR, the free market texts of the United States and the Federal Republic provide teachers with a multiplicity of works and viewpoints from which to choose. This does not guarantee that teachers will make wise choices or that students will always receive the most up-to-date information available. In the hands of those who are conscientious and responsible, free choice is exhilarating and exhausting and builds democracy; in the hands of those who are lazy, it is merely a sham.

WHAT TEACHERS TEACH IN THE GDR

East Germany is a paradise for the curriculum planner who believes in the possibility of the "scientific" construction of curricula and their controlled and consistent application in every classroom of the country; conditions are ideal for such a person. The leaders of this state adhere to a "scientifically proven" set of principles, which are to be inculcated into every citizen as part of forming "the all-around educated socialist personality" and building the socialist/communist society. The classic works of Marx, Engels, and Lenin provide a theoretical basis for these views, and the state and Party provide the means for their propagation and actualization. The school system is uniform, the teachers are supposed to follow directives "creatively," and students, if they wish to succeed, must accept the content and goals of the standard curriculum.

And who produces this curriculum and from where does it emanate? The curriculum planners of the GDR are all trusted and reliable Marxists, all working to shape a new generation of socialist personalities. They are, for example, members of the *Akademie der Paedagogischen Wissenschaften,* whose main building is located near the old Brandenburg Gate in East Berlin. In 1973 the head of the *Akademie,* Gerhart Neuner, described the theoretical basis of curriculum planning in the GDR in his *Lehrplanwerk:*[9]

1. There is a "unity" that exists between "science and socialist ideology." "Marx, Engels and Lenin have founded the ideology of the

working class as a science. . . . It is a scientific ideology, a strict science which is built on the objective laws of reality." The acceptance of Marxism-Leninism is, therefore, "the unalterable precondition for the finding of scientific truth." It is this dogma that gives the quality of unquestionable truth to all decisions pertaining to educational goals, subjects of instruction, and contents of learning. It is this quality of being "true" that differentiates the curriculum of GDR schools from those of West Germany.

2. Consequently, the curriculum planners of the GDR, when they determine curriculum content and goals, are not only dealing with matters of instruction; they are directly involved in planning and shaping the personalities of a future generation. The state has, therefore, appropriated a much more important role for itself and its curriculum planners than the Federal Republic would claim.

3. East German planners assume the existence of a "regular connection between goal, content, and method of instruction" in matters of curriculum. They see an especially close relationship between goal and content, which "form a unity," but do not regard educational methods as "isolated means" either. This dogma of unity derives as a logical consequence of the Marxian assumption of a natural law of history that determines every aspect of the material world. "Didactic and methodological questions," writes Neuner, "must be judged from the point of view of substance and ideology with regard to the goal and content of socialist general education."[10] West German theorists would regard this kind of statement as bureaucratic and ideological jargon and argue that a precise deduction of curriculum elements from broad educational goals is impossible: Contents can serve different purposes.[11]

4. The "socialist personality" is not to be created with an ideal of "scientific objectivity" in the Western sense of such a phrase. The socialist ideal of knowledge and personality grows out of a belief in the unity of socialist knowledge with socialist conviction and socialist thinking, which produces socialist partisanship (*Parteilichkeit*) as the outstanding trait of the socialist personality. The following statement from the official curriculum for the teaching of chemistry in grades nine and ten exemplifies this unity between knowledge and ideology or conviction:

Students must learn to realize the different uses of chemical products under capitalistic and socialistic conditions. Under historic considerations, for example, it must be emphasized that under monopoly capitalism ammonia and its derivatives were manufactured by I. G. Farben to prepare for wars and genocide. By contrast, it must be made clear that in socialist states the products of the chemical industry serve peace and a better life for the working people.[12]

Some Western observers have expressed doubts about whether these principles of curriculum development and implementation can be applied as strictly and fully as claimed. Do teachers, for example, teach their subjects in the prescribed ideological fashion? Are such means successful in producing the proper socialist attitudes and actions in students — the "socialist personality"? In the final analysis there are no satisfactory answers to these questions. Most Western pluralists would like to accept Friedrich Schiller's view of human nature as "free even if born in chains." East German monists prefer to cast their lot with Marx and Lenin, whose science of society must be taught and accepted.

With their fixed goal in mind, curriculum plans in the GDR are numerous and voluminous. A number of West German specialists have expressed admiration at the care with which they are done and have marveled at their thoroughness.[13] Between 1966 and 1972 GDR authorities published 125 grade- and subject-oriented curricula, the majority of which adhered to the following structure:

1. General instructions, with a description of educational goals for teaching the particular subject in a particular grade; also general directions for the teacher.

2. Instructions on how the subject should be organized and taught, including the instructional materials to be used.

3. A synopsis of themes and content, with the amount of time allotted per lesson and the number of lessons allotted for particular topics.

4. A more detailed description of "content of instruction," accompanied by additional remarks on the purpose of teaching the particular unit, some teaching hints, and detailed descriptions of learning materials.

Once completed, the main emphasis with respect to these curricular plans has been their implementation; only minor changes and additions were made in the 1970s. In fact, curriculum specialists have now provided similar thorough and detailed plans for preschools and 315 occupations as well as curricular plans for the further education of teachers.

Undoubtedly, some subjects lend themselves better than others to forming the attitudes and convictions of the socialist personality. History, for example, would appear better suited to this purpose than math; yet this is not entirely so. A comparative description of the curricular plans for these two subjects gives some idea of both the thoroughness of such plans and how ideology suffuses every aspect of education.

For the most part, mathematics is not usually regarded as a subject area that is very amenable to ideology. Yet we know that in subtle ways it has been taught with a particular ideological emphasis. Basic math in Catholic schools may have, in the past, involved adding and subtracting votive candles. Erika Mann has shown in her book, *School for Barbarians,* that Nazi primers taught young Germans how to multiply by calculating how many bombs a fleet of German bombers could drop on enemy cities if each bomber carried a given weight of bombs. [14] Indeed, socialist/communist educators have no difficulty in finding examples of how capitalist states teach math as a means of buttressing the capitalist system.

Basically, however, the purpose of mathematics instruction is to teach the young all the subject matter that is normally associated with this field. In this respect, East Germany is no exception. Curriculum guidelines for the teaching of math make it quite clear that young students in the Polytechnic Schools are expected to learn at least as much math in their ten required years of instruction as children anywhere in the world. Yet these same obligatory guidelines also make it clear that math instruction is a means of ideological education. The "unity of knowledge and communist ideology" is fully accepted, and "the potential of mathematics for the development of socialist convictions and behavior" is explicitly stated in the curriculum guidelines in the following ways:

• Mathematics is highly important in all aspects of societal life. "A high level of mathematical knowledge and abilities" is especially necessary in the natural sciences and in the development of technology and the economy.

• According to Marx's philosophy of materialism, the level of development of such indicators as math, science, and technology are measures of the historical progress of a society.

• For the individual, the attainment of a high level of mathematical skill enhances his/her value for society which is one of the foremost educational goals of communism. The individual has more to contribute to solving problems and changing the world.

• Mathematics provides not only direct educational benefits, but indirect ones as well, such as teaching diligence and self-control, and a respect for accuracy, orderliness, and careful work.

In summary, then, mathematics is clearly regarded in the GDR as a means of "developing those personality traits that a citizen of our socialist state must possess." Math also provides "a precondition for the student's later active participation in the construction of socialism in the realm of production and other areas of our societal life."[15]

Yet, however forcefully the case is made for the ideological importance of mathematics, it appears at times somewhat oblique and far-fetched. That teachers are so frequently admonished not to neglect the ideological potential of mathematics probably signifies how easily they could forget to do so. Such is not the case, however, with a subject such as history, where a particular interpretation is absolutely central to Marxism.

Every event in the past has its particular place and meaning in the Marxist interpretation of history. This inexorable process of historical development is, of course, fully accepted and taught in the schools of the GDR. Each student is expected to learn and understand not only the laws of historical development, but the special significance, for "the struggle of the working class," of such events as medieval feudalism, the Peasants' Wars, capitalism and colonialism, the French Revolution, the origins of the socialist movement, the development of international workers' movements, the Great October Revolution, and the defeat of Nazi Germany. Of course, special emphasis must be placed on the "historical mission" of the Soviet Union and the founding of the first "German Workers' and Peasants' State." Students are to be instructed about the continuing struggle of capitalism and socialism, and to be deeply convinced of the "ultimate victory of socialism." The continuing external as well as internal threats to the GDR must be stressed.

Perhaps one additional example should be provided to illustrate how curriculum planners in East Germany are able to infuse even a minor subject of instruction with ideological significance. Even a subject such as art must have its place in the forming of a "socialist personality."

In grade eight, for example, one hour each week is devoted to art. During the course of this instruction, the following themes must be covered:

- The making of pictures using such events for subject matter as holidays, the local landscape, and the revolutionary struggle of the working class (12 hours).
- Art appreciation: Soviet artists as models in the presentation of revolutionary subjects (3 hours).
- Forming the environment: shaping rooms for life and work in the socialist society (4 hours).
- Art appreciation: proletarian-revolutionary artists in their struggle against exploitation and oppression, fascism, and war (5 hours).
- Visual agitation: posters (*Schautafel*) or wall newspapers as a means of political propaganda (4 hours).
- Art appreciation: landscape painting both as cultural heritage and in the production of contemporary socialist art (2 hours).[16]

Undoubtedly, West German art teachers would regard such a thorough and fully developed curriculum guideline as a straitjacket. Where, they would ask, is there any room for the teacher to take any initiative or demonstrate his/her creative talents as a teacher? GDR definitions of initiative and creativity are to be exercised within the confines of predefined and predetermined socialist/communist activities. The official guidelines that accompany the art curriculum emphasize repeatedly the ideological goals that must be pursued: "The development of the ability to appreciate and evaluate an aesthetic experience is considered as an art-specific contribution to the forming of the socialist personality. . . ." Art must be considered a "weapon" in the worldwide class struggle.[17]

Thus, with respect to such traditional school subjects as mathematics, history, and art, curriculum planning is centralized, obligatory, detailed, and ideological in the GDR. The same is true in all subjects, even physical education. Yet there is one group of subjects that cannot be found in West German schools, but which are absolutely central to the East German curriculum. These are the subjects that constitute the polytechnic curriculum and which GDR students must take for the full ten years of their compulsory schooling.

The principles of *Polytechnic Education* can be traced to the writings of Marx and Engels which, therefore, endow it immediately with the highest priority in the GDR. Indeed, in no other European communist state has polytechnic education assumed such importance as in East Germany; not even in the Soviet Union. According to Marx and Engels, polytechnic education would heal those injuries that capitalism had caused (for example, the alienation of the worker from the productive process, etc.) and thereby develop a new type of worker personality. The new communist worker is, in Marx's own words, to be endowed with "absolute *Disponibilitaet*" (that is, is "the master of the productive process"). At the same time, the "productive force" of such personalities will prove the superiority of communism over capitalism.[18]

With this in mind, GDR curriculum planners have introduced polytechnic education in grade one in the form of practical instruction (*Werkunterricht*) and school garden instruction (*Schulgartenunterricht*). In grade seven this becomes polytechnic instruction proper, and includes such subjects as Introduction to Socialist Production, Technical Drawing, and Productive Work. In addition, polytechnic education continues for those going into the Academic Senior High School (EOS). It is also prescribed as a guiding principle for *all* instruction and should have an influence in the teaching of the sciences, civics, and so on. Clearly its importance to GDR education is paramount.[19]

A closer examination of the curriculum of these polytechnic courses provides a somewhat predictable picture of what GDR ideological planners want their citizens to be. Practical instruction, for example, which pupils are required to take in grades one to six, goes beyond traditional classes in woodwork or metalwork and instructs students in the use of winches, engines, circular saws, transistors, and so on. Similarly, "Introduction to Socialist Production," which all ninth-graders must take, provides a general introduction to the *Betrieb* or small industrial organization. The semester is then broken down into 30 hours divided as follows:

4 hours — The Production Task of the *Betrieb*
4 hours — Economy of Materials and Energy
6 hours — Principal Stages of Production
10 hours — Rationalizing Production
6 hours — Workers' Tasks in the *Betrieb*

Polytechnic education is designed to include a good deal of practical experience as well as theoretical training. Each student is introduced directly into the various areas of productive work. As Friedrich Engels wrote in his *Fundamentals of Communism (Grundsaetze des Kommunismus)*: "Young People should be trained in the whole system of production. . . . This will then remove the one-sided character that the present division of labor now stamps on each individual."[20]

Clearly, practical work cannot be planned and prescribed as rigorously as school-based instruction; nevertheless, polytechnic education follows the same pattern as all other subjects. Curriculum guides provide standardized and compulsory units of instruction, which are then subdivided into even smaller units with detailed instructions as to how each element is meant to contribute to the overall goal of forming the "socialist personality."

Polytechnic education holds a unique place in the GDR educational curriculum. Not only does it provide technical knowledge and start students on the path to socially useful work, it inculcates "socialist attitudes and disciplines" as well. It convinces students of the superiority of a socialized economy and socialized means of production, and creates an appreciation for the role of the working class in society and for the Party that represents it.

Such a uniform, tightly structured, rigidly administered curriculum as that of the GDR certainly raises questions about the goal of such a system. Is it the aim of East German education to form the true "masters of the means of production" as socialist leaders claim, or is it the goal to produce highly competent, but obedient and docile factory and farm workers, as West German critics allege?[21]

NOTES

The first epigraph to Chapter 8 is from Norbert Haase, Lothar Reese, and Peter Wensierski, eds., *VEB Nachwuchs: Jugend in der DDR* (Reinbek, 1983), p. 40.

The second epigraph to Chapter 8 is ibid., p. 67.

1. Deutscher Bildungsrat, ed., *Reform der Sekundarstufe II. Teil A* (Braunschweig, 1971); see also Wolfram Floessner et al., *Theorie: Oberstufe* (Braunschweig, 1977); J. Gzresik, *Perspektiven fuer die weitere Entwicklung der gymnasialen Oberstufe* (Bad Heilbrunn, 1984).
2. H. H. Knuetter, "Historisch-politische Bildung in der Schule — Die Richtlinien in den Laendern der Bundesrepublik Deutschland . . ." *Engagement* (1983): 146–57.
3. Kultusminister NW, *Richtlinien fuer die gymnasiale Oberstufe — Geschichte* (Koeln, 1982), p. 11.
4. Ibid., p. 28.
5. Bernhard Vogel, *Schule am Scheideweg* (Muenchen, 1974), p. 16f.
6. Erich Weniger, *Theorie der Bildungsinhalte und des Lehrplans*, 6th ed. (Weinheim, 1965); Saul B. Robinsohn, *Bildungsreform als Revision des Curriculum* (Neuwied/Berlin, 1967).

7. Peter A. Clark, *Action Research and Organizational Change* (London/New York, 1972); S. Gerbaulet et al., *Schulnahe Curriculumentwicklung* (Stuttgart, 1972); Wolfgang Klafki, "Handlungsforschung im Schulfeld," *Zeitschrift fuer Paedagogik* 19, no. 4 (1973): 487–516.

8. Daniel Tanner and Laurel N. Tanner, *Curriculum Development* (New York/London), p. 623.

9. Gerhart Neuner et al., *Allgemeinbildung — Lehrplanwerk — Unterricht* (Berlin, 1972), p. 39f.

10. Ibid., p. 57.

11. H. Meyer, *Einfuehrung in die Curriculummethologie* (Muenchen, 1972); Herwig Blankertz, *Theorien und Modelle der Didaktik* (Muenchen, 1972).

12. Neuner et al., *Allgemeinbildung*, p. 66.

13. Hartmut Vogt, *Theorie und Praxis der Lehrplanrevision in der DDR* (Muenchen, 1972).

14. "But we have been warned. At least now the problems in arithmetic cannot surprise us. They all have to do with aeroplanes, bombs, cannons, and guns." *School for Barbarians: Education Under the Nazis* (London, 1939), p. 61.

15. Neuner et al., *Allgemeinbildung*, p. 171.

16. Ibid., p. 366.

17. Ibid., p. 361ff.

18. See especially Marx, *Das Kapital*, vol. 1; see also our Chapter 3.

19. Dirk Bode, *Polytechnischer Unterricht in der DDR* (Frankfurt/New York, 1978); Heinz Frankiewicz, *Technik und Bildung in der Schule der DDR* (Berlin, 1968); Helmut Klein, *Polytechnische Bildung und Erziehung in der DDR* (Reinbek, 1962); Willi Voelmy, *Polytechnischer Unterricht in der Zehnklassigen allgemeinbildenden polytechnischen Oberschule der DDR seit 1964* (Frankfurt, 1969).

20. Friedrich Engels, *Grundsaetze des Kommunismus*.

21. See Bode, *Polytechnischer Unterricht*, p. 176ff.

9

TEACHING AND LEARNING IN THE SCHOOLS OF EAST AND WEST

It is not only important *what* pupils learn, but also *how* they learn.

An often stated pedagogical dictum

Get up everybody! — Sit down! — Sit straight! — Open your reader! — Read! — Shut up! — Turn over! — Go to the blackboard! — Go back to your seat! Go on reading! — Close your books! — More quickly!

Typical examples of directive behavior of teachers, collected by Reinhard and Anne-Marie Tausch

THE PROBLEM

Having compared the value systems of the two Germanys, having compared their laws pertaining to education, their official educational goals, school structures, and curricula, what then remains to be described and compared? What remains is the actual life and work of teachers and students in schools: teaching and learning; the ways by which knowledge, values, attitudes and behavior are formed and changed; how students are examined and graded; how they are guided and counseled. What remains is also the general feeling or atmosphere that characterizes school life in the two states before, during, and after classroom sessions.

This, of course, comprises an immense and vitally important dimension of schooling, but one that is exceedingly difficult to research and describe. The complex life and interaction in schools, classrooms, and schoolyards cannot be found in lesson plans and structural patterns of the school system. It represents the *qualitative* aspects of the school day, which may only be experienced and described as a result of direct observation. And both of our estranged twins are reluctant to admit participant observers into their schools; this is especially true in the GDR, where Westerners are not allowed access to classrooms for research purposes. Teachers everywhere are, however, reluctant to have strangers in their midst; the outsiders often disturb the very thing they have come to observe. Indeed, even given the opportunity to visit schools freely, what kind of valid generalizations is it possible to draw; does one come away with anything more than a memory and a notebook filled with anecdotes?

All, however, is not in vain. School ethnography is not hopeless. The interactions between teachers, students, principals, and counselors can be observed and described. So too can the ways that teachers teach and students learn, as well as the way that examinations are given and whether they provoke fear and dread. So too can matters of "style" be described. Despite the impediments to such research, despite the difficulty of describing *das Schulklima,* and drawing generalizations about it, such research is not only possible, it is necessary if one is to compare fully the differences between society and education in the two Germanys.

Given the immensity of this final topic of concern, however, we must limit ourselves to comparing East and West in a few important areas.

THE "PROJECT METHOD" VERSUS THE "SYSTEMATIC TRANSMISSION OF KNOWLEDGE"

> I wouldn't believe it. That dumb, lazy, noisy, recalcitrant and annoying bunch of behaviorally disturbed kids that I had to teach in my class. . . . all of a sudden, they were decent, diligent, motivated and intelligent. It was a miracle.

What had caused this incredible change in the classroom of a West German teacher? Her seventh-grade class in the *Hauptschule* of a small town was notoriously difficult; 26 boys and girls between twelve and fourteen, one-third "repeaters," one-third from foreign families — Turks, Greeks, and Portuguese. Nothing seemed to matter. Whether she became stricter or more lenient, punished or praised, nothing seemed to change the negative nature of this class. They were an agony for teachers and parents.

The teacher went to a counseling session, where it was suggested that she might try the project approach. Although she knew little about this method — her university courses and intern training had barely touched on it — she began to gather and study materials pertaining to it. She was surprised to discover how much was available, even in the curriculum guides of the ministries of education of the various *Laender*. Following the reform movements of the late 1960s, teachers were not only permitted, but even encouraged to organize a good deal of their class work in each school year in projects.[1]

Her students were surprised when she suggested the change; suddenly they found themselves choosing subjects and goals as well as modes of studying, learning, examining, even grading. Some students made ridiculous proposals, in part because they did not seriously believe that they were being given so much responsibility in their classroom. Gradually, however, they accepted their charge and decided to find something interesting and agreeable on which to work. They combined their hours in German, history, and geography and came up with "The History of Our Families — Five Generations, If Possible." It also became immediately apparent that this was not just a choice of subject matter, but involved methodology and other educational issues as well.

What followed was the most exciting teaching experience of this teacher's career — she had been teaching in *Hauptschule* for 15 years. In fact, it seemed more like mutual learning than teaching, she reported. The students discussed their goals, organized groups, divided their tasks, and prepared and delivered reports. They used the teacher as their "resource person" and their audience. They talked with parents, wrote letters, collected materials like family photos, maps, and articles, used reference books, and, in some instances, turned to their textbooks as well.

They put together lively descriptions of the geography and culture of the Portuguese Atlantic coast, of the villages and towns of Anatolia, the mountains of Macedonia, and the forests and lakes of East Prussia. They created illustrated reports describing the lives of fishermen, factory workers, and shopkeepers in four countries for the last hundred years. One group even collected the songs that people sang in their homes, which the class eventually used for an evening program for parents, friends, and teachers. In order to understand the various factors that affected the lives of their families, the students gathered information about rulers, wars, and other political and economic events. They dealt with religion and native languages as well. The project turned out to be not only a very valuable educational experience, it also provided the first model of intercultural understanding for the people involved.

Of course, the project method is not new, nor is it German in its origin. It dates from the turn of the century, when William Heard Kilpatrick and others sought to develop a method of teaching that would be appropriate for a democratic society. It was also seen, by innovators such as Charles R. Richards of Teachers College, Columbia University, as a means of breaking the dull routine of learning in most classrooms. Richards proposed in 1900 that students be involved in work that was truly meaningful to them and that they take responsibility for planning and producing "projects." The thrust of this method of teaching and learning as it was developed by educators (for example, J. A. Stevenson, David Snedden, M. J. Stromzand, and N. L. Bossing) was to counteract the traditional school style of the Herbartians, which stressed abstract learning. Instead, they advocated that students commit themselves to meaningful tasks, involve themselves in planning and executing their project, and achieve tangible results.

It was, however, John Dewey and Kilpatrick who especially provided the philosophical support for this new method, Dewey in his work, *How We Think* (1910), and Kilpatrick in his effort to define a methodology appropriate for a technological and democratic society. Kilpatrick observed that the rapidity of change in the industrial world of the twentieth century obviated traditional bodies of codified knowledge. How could teachers prepare students for an unknown future by teaching the curriculum of the past? Kilpatrick noted that this changing society had caused the breakdown of autocratic structures. Young people were going to be less likely to accept fixed principles or modes of acting without questioning them. Indeed, Kilpatrick felt that students in a democracy should be urged to think for themselves, to raise questions and search for answers that would help them to deal with their world, the world of the future. In a celebrated article, which Kilpatrick published in *Teachers College Record* in 1918, "The Project Method,"[2] he set forth his theories regarding learning, habit formation by doing, and motivation achieved through "wholehearted purposeful activity."

Fifty years later, in the 1960s, student unrest and critical attacks by professionals on West German schools focused the attention of educators on the hypocrisy and inconsistencies of the old system. The question repeatedly asked was whether a state-mandated curriculum and teacher-planned classes were consonant with a society that proclaimed the principles of individual freedom, self-reliance, and personal responsibility for one's career and life goals. On the one side were the old dogmatic views of knowledge and teaching, on the other were new definitions of the role of youth and citizenship in society. Could the aim of schooling be docility, passivity, and obedience when the aim of society was active participation? No one who has read the school novels of the German past could truly believe that one could build a healthy and vibrant democracy with the repressed matriculants of the old schools (even if their repression was somewhat exaggerated for literary effect).[3]

In searching for a new pedagogy appropriate to their industrial democracy, West German educators sifted many "democratic" and "emancipatory" teaching methodologies. Such plans as "Theme-Centered Interaction," "Self-Initiated Learning," "Open Instruction," "Adaptive Instruction," and "Student-Centered Group Work" gained advocates and were debated and tried. Many theorists were attracted by the project method. It seems to combine so many of the qualities that other plans possess separately.

But it is not on the theoretical level that changes in the schools take place. In teacher training programs, teachers of teachers must give credence to new ideas and, in schools, teachers themselves must seek to apply them. It was not enough that professional journals began to publish theoretical discussions of the project method or that school authorities sanctioned its use; it took the willingness of classroom teachers to adopt it in the end, such as the *Hauptschule* teacher whose experiences we have described. The successes this teacher reported were echoed in many parts of the Federal Republic and influenced others to experiment on their own. "It is only when we do projects that they really study hard and there are no behavioral problems," the *Hauptschule* teacher reported.[4]

What then, are the principal characteristics of the project method, and how have these characteristics gained a place in the school regulations of the various *Laender* and in a growing number of classrooms?

1. *Student initiative and responsibility.* This dimension of the project method is reflected in the school regulations of many *Laender*.[5] In Hamburg, for example, teachers are urged to provide "free space for initiative," and in North Rhine-Westphalia "to respond to the individual interests of students" and "show that school life contains free space." Educational theorists are especially enthusiastic about this aspect of project theory:

> Project-oriented instruction [is] ... not a method that can be used arbitrarily like other methods, but rather is a completely different kind of instruction. ... [Its] central feature [is] the self-organization of learning groups ... which allows students co- and self-determination in choice of content and learning, in the definition of instructional goals, in the decision about methods of realization, solution of the problem, and evaluation of the results.[6]

2. *Differentiation of learning groups according to interest and abilities.* The fundamental principle here is that learning groups should not be formed on the basis of test results, sex, or age. Instead, the project itself is supposed to stimulate students to form their own groups and to distribute tasks among themselves in much the same way as young people form a team to play soccer or baseball. Individuals are given various assignments according to their abilities, personal interests, and goals.

3. *Social learning.* The project method enhances virtually every aspect of social learning. As Karl Frey has noted: "curricular legitimation of project instruction largely depends on ... communication and meta-interaction," in which "individual and group motives of action" lead to a differentiated, broadly accepted agreement about a sensible way of handling the project. Indeed, at the very outset, students learn to negotiate with each other about what constitutes a worthwhile project, how to structure and manage it, to "put plans into reality," how to "develop patterns of future actions," how to "exchange information about interim results," "plan new steps," and "bring the project to completion."[7] Throughout the process the emphasis is on free, spontaneous, self-determined and self-responsible social interaction in the interest of achieving a mutually accepted goal.

4. *Learning by participating in real-life activities.* Project work is supposed to grow from real and "meaningful" life situations, as opposed to traditional scholastic learning, which is based on mastering established disciplines in a prescribed fashion. The importance of this aspect of the project method not only derives from motivation, which is increased as a result, but from an enhanced sense of dignity as well; young people discover that their own problems, plans, and desires are taken seriously.

Some administrators in the Federal Republic still seem to fear this aspect of the project method as inducing students to be hypercritical and too anti-authoritarian. Even a democratic society requires individuals to accept a certain level of authority in their lives. Thus curricular plans and school regulations of the various *Laender* frequently prefer to stress the "interdisciplinary character" of projects, or the opportunity they provide to develop "holistic perspectives" (*ganzheitliche Sichtweisen*). The Hamburg regulations, for example, note that project learning gives young people the opportunity to "put acquired knowledge and abilities in meaningful coherence."[8]

5. *Learning by doing and judging.* This is perhaps the most widely shared and highly valued aspect of the project method. Not only does this kind of learning occupy a significant place in the work of Dewey and Kilpatrick, it has German roots as well. At the turn of the century, Munich school reformer and educational philosopher Georg Kerschensteiner (1854–1932) made this idea central to his *Arbeitschule* (activity school). The terminology of Kerschensteiner and his associates has found its way into the school regulations of virtually every West German *Land*. In Schleswig-Holstein, for example, such phrases as "learning by doing," "extending the experience of students," "cooperative planning," and "achieving results in a concrete product," are applied to project instruction and bear testimony to the importance of Dewey, Kerschensteiner et al.

As so much of the value of this method is thus derived from participation of "doing" and honest "judgment" (that is, evaluation of efforts, methods, and results), the project method may succeed even when the activity fails to achieve its goal. Indeed, failure also compels students to confront a life situation that may enhance learning. Allowing students to be involved in such real-life problems, permitting them to act in meaningful ways, is regarded as a matter of human dignity, which must be accorded to young people in a democracy.

In summary, it should be noted that the project method is only one concept of instruction among many that are gaining considerable popularity in West Germany. It is, however, characteristic of a general tendency or direction in West German educational theory and practice. The direction of pedagogy has been toward concepts such as open instruction, self-initiated learning, and problem-centered instruction. These trends have been characteristic, not only of West German education, but of other Western democracies as well. The highly specialized, self-selected studies of the British sixth form and the complicated elective system of the U.S. high school are examples of the same tenor of change. Certainly the concept of nondirective, client-centered counseling that has not only swept through Western societies, but penetrated the schools as well, is an indicator of the same spirit.

This does not mean, however, that West Germany is a paradise of democratic education, and that self-initiated, self-determined, self-planned, self-executed, and self-assessed learning has won the day and transformed every school in the Federal Republic into a hothouse of democratic learning. Far from it. In fact, numerous West German critics complain that the democratization of school life in the Federal Republic has barely begun, and that an authoritarian climate still prevails, as in some other Western democracies. One purpose of this work, however, is to show the directions in which the two Germanys are moving. Certainly project instruction, with its emphasis on nondirective learning, has gained a wide and apparently growing following in West Germany among teachers, educational theorists, and curriculum planners in the various ministries of education.

This trend has, however, gained no adherents in the GDR or in any of the nations of the Eastern bloc. In fact, one must observe the dramatically different reception given to the project method by the pedagogues of the East to understand not only theoretical differences, but differences in the classroom as well.

The first official reaction to the increasing popularity of this educational theory in the West issued from the prestigious Academy of Pedagogical Sciences of the USSR in 1967. At that time, two members of the Academy edited "the first official description of pedagogical theory from the perspective of Marxist-Leninist science."[9] The tone was highly critical:

> In the pedagogical system of Pragmatism, the important principle of student activity was actualized in the form of the Project Method. . . . This kind of instruction led to chaotic conditions and, in the final analysis, to superficial knowledge. . . . In this way, students can be kept occupied with merely utilitarian tasks, while a large part of the children, particularly those of the common people, can be denied a sound education because imparting true knowledge to the children of the working class would give them a strong weapon in the struggle against capitalism.[10]

Why, one might ask, should Marxist theorists be so critical of a method whose goal is to motivate students and to stimulate their sense of initiative and responsibility as well as to bridge the gap between school and life, of a philosophy of instruction that seeks to enhance social learning?

Perhaps the answer can be found in the way the project method confronts systematic knowledge. The project method grants only relative value to traditional subject areas; these do not receive special methodological attention. Indeed, the most difficult task for the teacher employing a project mode of instruction is to integrate systematic knowledge into the project. While the stress in the project method is on learning to live in a changing world, the direction of that change is not dogmatically presented. The future is not yet known. If anything, students learn to challenge their elders, rather than to accept a view of history that is wholeheartedly committed to "the objective truth" found in the writings of Marx and Lenin. It appears that the project method undermines dogma.

In the GDR, and elsewhere in the socialist/communist countries, methods of instruction are closely linked to the goals and content of instruction. As the head of the Pedagogical Academy of the GDR, Gerhart Neuner, noted: "In the organization of instruction, teachers must proceed consistently from the goals and content defined in the curriculum."[11]

When the goal is the systematic inculcation of a world view, methodology becomes an instrument of that goal. The choice of an instructional method is determined by the "objective" historical progress of the world's development toward communism. This is what communist educators call the "law of the unity of goal, content and method."[12] The project method may be appropriate for a decadent bourgeois society; it is not appropriate for a socialist/communist one.

According to contemporary Marxist educational theory, students are both receivers and active learners of "scientifically proven" knowledge (that is, Marxist-Leninist theories). Interestingly, this was not the case in the early 1920s immediately following the Bolshevik Revolution. In those heady days, Soviet educators experimented with a variety of child-centered theories of learning and were enamored of Western reform movements that blossomed everywhere following the Great War. It was Anton S. Makarenko, a Russian-born educator who had never been an emigré or traveled in the West, who ultimately laid the foundation for a return to an authority-centered system. Makarenko ridiculed those Western "pedological" concepts and experimented himself with a disciplined form of collective education. Rather than focusing his pedagogy on personal growth and the development of the individual personality, Makarenko made the needs of society paramount and maintained that the individual actualized himself/herself within that framework. The collective is more important than individuals can ever be. The function of the teacher is to assist the Party and the state in the development of communism. Methods of teaching and learning, according to Makarenko, must be directed toward that goal rather than being determined by the personal needs or goals of students or teachers.

The spirit and tone of Makarenko and his followers pervade the pedagogy of the GDR. In the official newspaper, *Neues Deutschland,* for example, frequent descriptions of schooling appear, especially in the weekend edition, to underscore the efficacy of authorized educational practices. More direct accounts by teachers and principals appear in the *DLZ (Teachers' Weekly Newspaper)*; testimonials to the efficacy of the official methodology appear frequently:

> In our school we have a political climate which permits the creation of clear political horizons. It not only allows ideological knowledge and insights to be conveyed, above all it makes our scientific ideology the compass for the actions and behavior of every single teacher and every single student.[13]

But East German pedagogy does not derive entirely from Soviet sources; it has its own German past as well. The systematic transmission of moral and political truths was the hallmark of the Herbartians (the rather dogmatic followers of Johann Friedrich Herbart, 1776–1841) and the Prussian system of the nineteenth century. While certainly not directly acknowledged by GDR educators, this tradition has been a powerful one in East Germany.

According to the Academy of Pedagogical Sciences of the GDR, the following instructional pattern should be followed in all schools, with the "all-round development of socialist personalities" constantly kept foremost in mind as the ultimate goal of GDR education:[14]

1. *Setting goals for students.* Not only are the defined goals in the curriculum "obligatory," they must be described to students to keep them on the straight road toward the "socialist personality." Teachers "are obliged to put this plan into effect in order to achieve the desired goal of personality development." Systematic repetition of acquired knowledge is also deemed necessary.

2. *Presentation of new material.* This should be lively, stimulating, concise, and concentrated. "Omit everything that is unessential; permit no digressions." According to this point of view, any detour is unacceptable as nothing is gained by chance. The forming of the "socialist personality" is clear and deliberate.

3. *Consolidating, exercising, applying, and systematizing.* All of the traditional steps in acquisition of knowledge are followed here: accuracy

of memorization, repetition, "anchoring" knowledge in the consciousness of students, training the memory, forming habits, and so on. The inculcation of ideology is seen as part of this process: "The task of systematization . . . also leads to a qualitative enrichment of ideological convictions." Application is part of the process of systematization — application in similar situations and in daily student life circumstances. Results must always be controlled.

4. *Assessment and examination.* In this final step teachers must "examine how well students have achieved the goal and how energetically they will continue to strive to achieve it." "The examination documents the success of the teacher's planning and guidance and permits him/her to direct further progress systematically."

In order to appreciate fully the manner in which teaching and learning are supposed to occur in the GDR, an example from an East German text will illustrate the point. The particular class is devoted to differences between socialist and capitalist production. The goal is to reinforce communist convictions:

> The teacher directed the discussion in such a way that the students themselves, i.e., especially the "active core," . . . had an opportunity to practice partisan communist evaluation of modern capitalism and to maintain their point of view in discussion. The "active core" of students . . . had to gain the experience of defending the stronger position — which would increase their self-confidence and authority in the group. On the other hand students with questionable or clearly negative points of view had to suffer "defeat," which, as a form of disapproval, would exercise an influence on their inner conflict. In this way, the entire process of appropriation [*Aneigung*] and the acquisition of knowledge during lessons became a factor in the social process of the class as a collective — the development and consolidation of collective relationships.[15]

Interestingly, the successful lesson depends on the "core" espousing the proper point of view in a discussion and being triumphant. Not only must those with the wrong point of view fail, they must internalize the defeat as well and feel what it means to be ambiguous or to champion a false position. The system is quite similar to what is prescribed for Jesuit teachers in the *Ratio Studiorum* of 1599. Discussion is encouraged and seen as desirable, but the correct point of view must prevail in the end. This method of teaching and learning is clearly consistent with a system where the "truth" is known, either through science or faith.

And yet certain aspects of educational theory and reality of teaching are common to both East and West Germany. Even some of those elements that are part of the project method are accepted and encouraged in GDR schools. It would be wrong to assume that East German theoreticians only want to create a passive citizenry, an army of fellow-travelers (*Mitlaeufer*) who merely legitimate the social and political system by their passivity. Nothing could be further from the truth. Passivity itself is seen as an impediment to the ultimate realization of a communist society. Moreover, passivity may easily become passive resistance.

The aims of East German education, therefore, are commitment, involvement, and enthusiasm. The use of educational rhetoric in attaining these goals is not dissimilar from that employed in the Federal Republic. As the reader peruses East German educational journals such as *Paedagogik*,[16] he/she encounters many words and phrases that can be found just as frequently in West German journals: "Motivating and stimulating students for extracurricular tasks," "self-directed problem-solving," "school books as a means of active learning," "increasing the self-responsibility of students," "conscious creative activity for students in the development of their dialectical-materialistic thinking," and so on. In fact, terms like "motivation," "creativity," "active learning," and "responsibility" are almost as much a part of the discourse of East German polytechnic education as they are of the West German project method.

This does not mean, however, that East German educators subscribe in any way to such tenets of project instruction as individual interests, personal responsibility, self-directed learning, finding creative solutions to unknown problems, or development of personally meaningful values and attitudes. An example from *Paedagogik* best describes the "project instruction" that the East Germans hope to foster through polytechnic education.

The goal of this "project" was established by a factory for a group of "young technical designers": to construct a model of a "Meliomat," which is a machine used for laying irrigation and drainage pipes. Initially, student enthusiasm was "not really great." They "would have much preferred to build a machine according to their own fantasy or desires." For this reason the teacher showed them the actual machine and demonstrated how it worked. Then the students were permitted to operate the machine, "which brought their youthful enthusiasm to a peak." Then workers told them how badly a model constructed to scale was needed in order to provide workers in a partner factory in the Soviet Union with a complete model, thus permitting them to introduce new technology. The students, now motivated, began to measure the machine and examine the material from which it was built. "This was the proper beginning," writes the author of the article, "in their search for a technical solution. . . ."[17]

Clearly this idea of a "project" is quite different from what is meant by the term in the educational lexicon of the Federal Republic. So too are the other related terms like "creative," "motivated," and "responsible." In the GDR, the goals are given, and motivation and meaning are provided by demonstrating how socially useful the task at hand is (such as constructing a model pipe-laying machine). "Creativity" and "initiative" are terms used to describe how one learns to contribute to achieving the goal given by the communist state and the Party of the workers.

Another article in *Paedagogik* in which the author, W. Szalai, used this terminology, illustrates the dissimilarity of meaning even more dramatically. "Creative activities" are necessary, writes Szalai, in order to overcome the many situations in a classroom that might hinder or obstruct the effective use of official textbooks and learning materials and the realization of the stated goals of instruction. Szalai finds that instruction is most effective, "the more thoroughly the official materials (curriculum, textbooks, and instructional materials) are used."[18] Clearly, "creativity" as employed here has the same meaning as in the fine arts, when artists are directed to employ their imagination for the propagation of Marxism-Leninism, that is, "socialist realism."

ASSESSMENT, SELECTION, AND GUIDANCE COUNSELING IN THE TWO GERMANYS

How far, then, can this comparison of the methods of instruction applied in the Two Germanys be extended — and does the comparison remain consistent? Is the general trend in West Germany (toward open and less directed forms of learning, with an emphasis on development of the individual's personality) also characteristic of such processes as assessment, selection, and guidance counseling? And in East Germany, on the other hand, does the tendency toward centralized planning and control and cultivation of ideological and societal concerns permeate every aspect of educational activity?

It is, of course, quite logical in a state committed to a planned economy and development, that the schools be systematically used to fulfill these plans, and that the tools of assessment, selection, and guidance be employed directly for this purpose. The Academy of Pedagogical Sciences of the GDR frankly admits this: "An assessment is pedagogically correct if it promotes the further development of students and student collectives toward the goals that are set by the socialist society."19

Yet, it is precisely in these areas of assessment, selection, and guidance that we can observe how complicated the comparison of society and education is between the estranged twins. Whereas West Germany would appear to place greater emphasis on individual personality development in its schools than the GDR, it takes less account of personality differences in making assessments of student achievement and in selection procedures. Schools in the Federal Republic rely much more heavily on "objective standards" (usually exam scores and grades) than does East Germany, for example, in determining who will receive a higher education. The reasons for this are themselves the result of an open society where parents may resort to the courts to challenge any subjective standards used by teachers and administrators; this leaves the schools no recourse but to employ demonstrably equitable standards of assessment and selection.

The GDR, on the other hand, does employ criteria that are partisan in every respect. The assessment and selection of students for various careers is no exception, and there is no recourse to the courts for equity. Thus, there exists a wide gap between such procedures in East and West, with "personality" assessment more likely to be used in the GDR than in West Germany.

Traditionally, in Old Germany, the evaluation of moral behavior and maturity of personality occupied an important role in the assessment of students. Categories such as *Fuehrung* (conduct), *Betragen* (bearing), and *Aufmerksamkeit* (attentiveness) stood at the top of student report cards. Indeed, one of the traditional terms for the *Abitur* (leaving exam) was *Reife-Zeugnis,* which emphasized the maturity of the student rather than his/her intellectual achievement. In some exceptional instances, the *Abitur* was granted or withheld on the basis of personality assessment. As late as the 1960s, in fact, some students, who received the grade of *mangelhaft* (deficient) in a major subject on their *Abitur* examination, might be granted this coveted certificate because their personal maturity warranted it.

For a number of reasons, however, teachers have gradually been divested of this aspect of assessment in the Federal Republic. The element of "arbitrariness" was always present in such assessments. Under earlier German authoritarian regimes, "arbitrariness" could hardly be contested; it was not even a suitable subject for discussion. In West

Germany, where all such matters have become a part of public discourse, parents have used the courts to protect their children from the use of such indefensible criteria in deciding their futures. The courts, in turn, have consistently ruled that personal traits, social behavior, and political opinions, for example, may not be used by educators in making their assessments of students. As a result, the old *Kopfnoten* (personality grades) have been dropped from report cards, and the computer rather than the teacher has become the preferred mode of selection for universities and careers.

It should be noted that this development has not received universal acclaim in West Germany. Critics have challenged the brutality of such a narrowly based evaluation system for young people. It has been left to private schools, however, such as the *Waldorfschule,* and to primary schools to develop instruments for describing student personality traits on their reports. The problem of evaluating students in other than purely measurable ways, while still equitable, troubles many educators in West Germany and elsewhere.

In East Germany educators justify and use a much broader base than grades in their student assessments. Teachers are expected to write exhaustive reports on all their students, evaluating their moral, social, and political behavior. According to the guidelines provided by the Academy in East Berlin: "The goal and content of the curriculum demand that teachers take the whole personality of the student into account." In particular this means:

- achievement and behavior in productive labor, attitude toward work and working people,
- order and discipline,
- evidence of social activity through participation in the pioneer organization and FDJ,
- level of political and ideological convictions as well as moral traits,
- attitude toward the collective, position held in the collective, and influence on the development of the collective.[20]

If, in the Federal Republic, the danger exists of reducing student evaluations to the most narrowly defined achievement results, in the GDR the threat exists that annual reports on student attitudes and activities will make every student "transparent." Every moral lapse or political reticence will find its way into the files of state administrators and/or Party functionaries. Furthermore, such reports will reflect not only teacher evaluations, but as one teacher described: "I place great importance on consultation with FDJ leaders. In general they evaluate their fellow students quite critically and correctly [*treffend*]."[21]

Not only are the means by which students are evaluated in the two Germanys vastly different, and the reports and files which are amassed thereby, but the use that is made of this material as well. In the Federal Republic strict laws protect the privacy of persons and the use of personal data. The Federal Surpeme Court has, for example, even ruled against one form of computer-readable passports for this reason. In the GDR the interest and well-being of the collective far outweigh the personal privacy of individuals. A student's attitude toward collectives or level of activity in FDJ are regarded as important information in making any decision about his/her qualifications for higher education or a career. This is, of course, quite logical in a country where commitment to the workers and their Party and state is regarded as the *sine qua non* for advancement, and where economic and social planning restrict the number of those who may be advanced. Thus the selection of students for the Academic Senior High School (EOS) in East Germany depends on a much broader inventory of personal information than selection of higher secondary level students in the Federal Republic.

The overall impact of these contrasting procedures of assessment and selection in the two Germanys directly affects such matters as equal opportunity and social justice in education. Clearly, the narrow emphasis on grades in the Federal Republic and severe restrictions imposed on the use of social and cultural data, as well as personality factors, make plans for social reform difficult, if not impossible, to implement. As one might expect, the result is that the higher the level of education, the fewer are the children from the working-class and foreign families.

The GDR, on the other hand, guarantees balanced representation of various social groups in the Academic Senior High School (EOS) and universities, "according to the social structure of the population." In order to achieve this goal, harsh measures and a strict quota system are frequently used to assure working-class representation. (Party functionaries are incidentally classified as "working class.") However bright a student, if his/her father happens to be a clergyman or if he/she is not deeply involved in the FDJ, little opportunity exists for academic advancement and a high-status career.

Therefore, in the West, efforts to overcome social deprivation are painfully slow, while in the East a different form of political discrimination has become the order of the day. Such is the continuing dilemma of social justice in Germany and, indeed, in the two halves of the northern hemisphere of this planet.

One additional and interesting area of comparison is guidance counseling. Here, too, we find dramatic differences between East and West, which underscore the growing gulf that exists in virtually every area of social and educational policy and school life.

Counseling in schools by specially trained personnel was a U.S. invention. It is rooted in a pluralistic world view, which emphasizes personal development and individual choice.[22] There is no single pattern of problem-solving underlying the development of guidance counseling; rather, there are many different and frequently competing approaches that have been used.[23] Virtually all of them, however, regard the individual, with all of his/her capacities and abilities, as central to the process, and the future is seen as open. Each stresses the right of the individual to lead his/her life and to use the school as a means to self-fulfillment. Handicaps, social conflicts, and problems of choice frequently provide the frustrations that guidance counselors help students to confront and, if possible, surmount. This is a helping service which, according to its proponents, is necessary for schools to provide. Guidance counseling does not provide solutions to problems for students, but helps them to develop self-knowledge and grow and thereby solve problems themselves.

This system, which stresses the individual as the bearer of human dignity, has found a growing body of supporters among Western educators in recent decades. Even in European states, such as West Germany, where schooling has not traditionally emphasized such quasi-academic services, guidance counseling has made a good deal of headway. Insofar as it addresses the difficulties of individual freedom and growth in a pluralistic society, guidance counseling, like the project method, is frequently regarded as an additional effort in the democratization of education and society.

Thus, guidance counseling had achieved a significant and growing role in West German schools by the mid-1980s. Not only have some 750 counseling services been established to help students to confront emotional and social difficulties as well as learning problems, some 10,000 teacher-counselors, who do counseling on a part-time basis as part of their teaching commitment, have been trained as well.[24]

Yet the history of guidance counseling in the Federal Republic reveals not only how democratic innovations have been introduced into the school, but how slowly matters change as well. German schools and teachers were traditionally authoritarian; their function was the transmission of a traditional culture to a younger generation. Counseling, like the project method, involves a redefinition of the role of the teacher vis-à-vis students and parents. In addition, counseling costs money, in training, retraining, and so on. As a result of both the need to redefine the function of schools and teachers as well as the costs involved, the progress of guidance counseling, however desirable, has been uneven if not slow in West Germany. Other West European countries also move slowly ahead in this area.

Among the various modes of counseling that have blossomed in North America, the one that has found that greatest resonance in the Federal Republic is that associated with Carl Rogers and his followers. Methodologically, the Rogerian approach emphasizes a nondirective style, with the counselor establishing a relationship of trust, warmth, respect, and empathy in order to heighten the student's self-respect and self-esteem. This Rogerian form of counseling seeks to improve the students' own problem-solving capacities rather than directing young people toward goals and behaviors prescribed by society.[25]

Nothing could be more alien to East German social and educational philosophy than West German guidance counseling, to say nothing of the Rogerian approach. Guidance procedures in the GDR do not support the Western notion that society as a whole will profit if the capacities and aspirations of individuals are served and satisfied. In East Germany, human dignity is attained through the collective and by joining the individual to the "objective historical process." Indeed, the prevailing belief regards the personal needs of the individual as an obstacle to societal development, or as Anton S. Makarenko wrote: "We are not concerned with the individual."[26]

For this reason, such matters as learning difficulties, poor social relationships, and the like are not regarded as problems to be handled in confidential sessions with trained professionals, but are matters to be confronted with the help of the collective (for example, the school class or the youth group, etc.). Frequently, this involves helping students to overcome their selfish individualism and to coordinate their behavior as well as their values to the group.

With repect to vocational guidance, the same differences in approach prevail. In West Germany vocational guidance is provided by guidance counselors whose primary concerns are supposed to be the desires and capabilities of the individual student. Good guidance counseling also takes account of market factors as well, but is not part of a larger planning apparatus.

In the GDR, the "objective needs of society" take precedence over personal ambitions — at least they are supposed to do so. The "Decree [*Verordnung*] on Vocational Guidance" of April 15, 1970, makes schools, particularly school principals, responsible for the orientation and guidance of students, but the term "orientation" in East German lexicons means "to steer or direct someone toward a given goal."[27] This goal is provided by regional vocational training officers, universities, productive units, and the army. A "careers teacher" in the school is responsible for overseeing "the school's planned contribution to the fulfillment of recruiting plans for skilled workers, higher occupations and academic professions."[28] Assistance in fulfilling this function is provided by homeroom teachers, the FDJ, parents' committees, and local productive units (*Betriebe*).

This does not mean, however, that state authorities are bluntly forcing students into vocations that are not consonant with their own interests and plans. The goal is to make young people want what the government and the people's industries and people's army need, or as an East German educator described it, "to enable students to have a choice of occupations which corresponds to their personal interests and societal necessities."[29]

In case of a conflict between these two, the "socialist personality" obeys the demands of society.

The entire educational system of the GDR prepares the student to act in this way. Vocational preparation in the polytechnic school is presumably geared to state planning and needs, as are actual training and work in factories and on farms. Vocational orientation also takes place in classrooms, FDJ meetings, and with workers.

One can hardly imagine a greater gulf than what exists between the two Germanys with respect to vocational counseling and guidance. It, as much as anything, illustrates the different directions in which these two societies are moving. In East Germany, "orientation" and "guidance" are geared toward the needs of the workers' state. In the West, "counseling" is for personal growth and self-development, although not without considerations of social responsibility.

This, too, is one of many indicators of the historic process of the estrangement of the German twins. The notion of this estrangement is not very popular with many Germans who hope that their divided country will be reunited some day. However, East German rulers use their educational system quite effectively to strengthen their own separate communist state. And, of course, a firm democratization of West German education must widen the gap, too. More than by educational laws, ideologies, and organizations, the actual process of estrangement appears to be advanced by the everyday life and activities in schools.

NOTES

For the first epigraph to Chapter 9, see, for example, E. Weber, *Erziehungsstile*, 3rd ed. (Donauwoerth, 1972), p. 267.

The second epigraph to Chapter 9 is from Reinhard Tausch and Anne-Marie Tausch, *Erziehungspsychologie*, 7th ed. (Goettingen, 1973), p. 204.

1. See *Bildung und Erziehung* 37 (1984): 1.
2. Pp. 319–35. A German translation was published in John Dewey and William Heard Kilpatrick, *Der Projekt-Plan-Grundlegung und Praxis* (Weimar, 1939); see, for example, Karl Frey, *Die Projektmethode* (Weinheim/Basel, 1982); Annemarie Kaiser and Franz Josef Kaiser, eds., *Projektstudium und Projektarbeit in der Schule* (Bad Heilbrunn, 1977); Bernhard Suin de Boutemard, *Schule, Projektunterricht und soziale Handlungsperformanz* (Muenchen, 1975).
3. For an excellent discussion of these works and a bibliography, see W. R. Hicks, *The School in English and German Fiction* (London, n.d.).
4. Cf. also Manfred Bayer, "endlich ist der Tag gekommen, an dem die Schueler der Hauptschule einmal gerne in die Schulen gehen," in *Westermanns Paedagogische Beitraege* 34 (1982): 62–65. (At last the day has come when pupils of the Hauptschule like to go to school.)
5. Kurt Riquarts, "Hinweise auf 'Projektunterricht' in Lehrplaenen und Richtlinien der Laender der Bundesrepublik Deutschland und Berlin (West)," *Bildung und Erziehung* 37, no. 1 (1984): 37–46.
6. Peter Bonn, "Projekt-Projektorientierter Unterricht-Projektstudium," in *Woerterbuch der Erziehung*, edited by O. Wulf (Muenchen, 1974), p. 472.
7. Karl Frey, "Die Projektmethode im historischen und konzeptionellen Zusammenhang," *Bildung und Erziehung* 37, no. 1 (1984): 3 ff.
8. Riquarts, "Hinweise," p. 29ff.
9. Quotation from the cover of the West German edition of Fedor Filippovich Koroljow and Vladimir Efimovich Gmurman, *Allgemeine Grundlagen der marxistischen Paedagogik* (Pullach, 1973).
10. Ibid., p. 322.
11. Neuner et al., *Allgemeinbildung* (Berlin, 1972), p. 492.
12. Ibid., p. 56f.
13. I. Friedrich in *DLZ* 31 (November 2, 1984): 1.
14. Neuner et al., *Allgemeinbildung*, p. 459ff.
15. Ibid., p. 54.
16. See Volume for 1982.

17. R. Kludas, "Erziehung zum kulturvollen Verhalten in der Freizeit," *Paedagogik* (1982): 34ff.

18. *Paedagogik* (1982): 1007.

19. Neuner et al., *Allgemeinbildung,* p. 483.

20. Ibid., p. 491.

21. Neuner reports this as the "opinion of many teachers in our schools." Ibid., p. 491.

22. See, for example, Edwin L. Herr, *Guidance and Counseling in the Schools* (Falls Church, VA, 1979); Leona Elizabeth Tyler, *The Work of the Counselor* (New York, 1969).

23. See Herbert M. Burks and Buford Stefflre, *Theories of Counseling* (New York, 1979).

24. For details see Lothar R. Martin and J. De Volder, "Guidance and Counseling Services in the Federal Republic of Germany," *The Personnel and Guidance Journal* 61, no. 8 (1983): 482–87.

25. For several decades Reinhard and Anne-Marie Tausch have been strong and successful advocates of this approach to counseling and education. See their *Erziehungspsychologie,* 8th ed. (Goettingen, 1977).

26. For a systematic comparison of guidance counseling in the United States, the Soviet Union, and the Federal Republic of Germany, see Lothar R. Martin, *Schulberatung: Anlaesse, Aufgaben, Methodenkonzeption* (Stuttgart, 1981), pp. 68–110.

27. See Hartmut Vogt, "Berufsbildungsberatung in der DDR," in *Handbuch der Bildungsberatung I,* edited by Kurt Heller (Stuttgart, 1975), p. 75ff.

28. Ibid., p. 82.

29. A. Siebel, "Berufs — und Studienberatung," *Paedagogik* (1983): 226ff.

10

CONCLUSION: ALTERNATIVE SCHOOLS — HOSPITALS OR LABORATORIES

Then the boy said: "But you don't learn anything?"

And I replied: "No, we don't have arithmetic and stuff like that — that's true. Except when we like, and that's rare."

Then he asked me: "Don't you do anything at school?"

And I told him: "Of course we do. The other day we built a *Lichtorgel* (an electric organ with colored flashing lightbulbs) or wove cloth on orange crates, or made apple juice (that was stupid), and we took a bike trip along the River Main and we slept in our school overnight, and tomorrow we are going to take a TV set apart."

Then he was quiet.

A ten-year-old girl from the
Frankfurt Free School

AN UNCOMMON COMPARISON

In writing the preceding work we have taken a certain risk. The works that attempt a comprehensive comparison of two systems of education are few; in itself this attests to the difficulty of the problem. Systems of education are incredibly complex. They are, at best, difficult to describe and, in their totality, virtually impossible to measure and compare. They are books, buildings, and budgets, and they are innumerable sets of human interactions, between parents, teachers, government officials, and pupils. How then can one begin to draw a comparison between two such systems? Is it possible?

Comparative educators have usually focused their research on one or a few aspects of educational systems and compared such matters as teacher education, university admissions, achievement testing, and so on, in two or a number of countries. Other comparativists have researched and written about the educational system of a distant country, its structure, history, and ideological underpinnings. Frequently, they have tried to devise new methodological techniques in doing so.

Perhaps one of the principal reasons comparative educators have seldom undertaken a comparison such as ours is the difficult and sometimes controversial question of what methodology to employ. Should one use a historical-hermeneutical approach or an empirical-statistical analysis? Or both? Our contention is that, given the nature of what is being compared, such controversies may be futile. Certainly, the material bases of an education system (buildings, books, salaries, etc.) may readily be measured and compared. But education is also a group process that might best be examined through behavioral observation and structural analysis of organizations. Indeed, a broad range of social and psychological tools must be used in order to understand, and then compare, "learning" in two or more different systems. We contend, however, that any such study will fail if it does not take into acocunt the human and humane dimension of rearing and teaching — educating. Education, as we have described it, does take place in a "system," but it does, in the final analysis, deal with people.

In general, we have adhered to a systems approach for our comparison.[1] Given the innumerable elements that we might have compared and the complexity of interactions within these two educational systems, we have attempted to identify a number of elements that we judged as particularly vital to the life and meaning of these systems. We feel confident that this approach not only permits a better understanding of things as they are, but may even allow us to venture some opinions about what *may* happen in the future. As our chapter titles indicate, we have been interested in the "whole" system rather than in an abundance of details. The following graph (Figure 7) illustrates how we see the various elements of the educational systems we have discussed. It also expresses our conviction that, despite their complexities, educational systems can be meaningfully compared.

Thus, our task, given all of these factors, is complex and endless. The risks are great; critics will probably be able to feast on their particular bones of contention. Yet, we believe that our goal of describing and comparing the educational systems of these estranged twins is worth the risk. Living as we do in two competing and frequently hostile worlds, we need a constant flow of information, a constant effort at understanding.

FIGURE 7
**Interrelation of Main Subsystems of Educational Systems
(main paths of influence; in reality each subsystem
influences all the others.)**

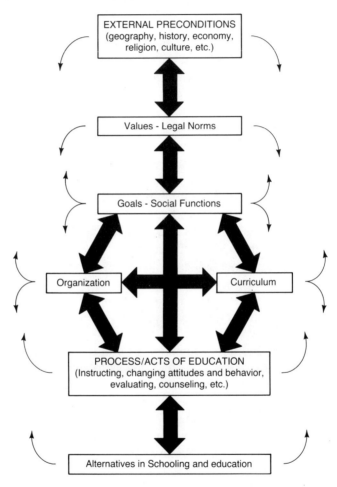

Yet, we still have one important part in this picture to complete, one element that we believe is vital to an understanding and comparison of education and society in the two Germanys. That element is alternative schools and alternative educational practices. It is with this theme and its significance that we will complete this work.

ALTERNATIVE SCHOOLS IN THE FEDERAL REPUBLIC

There is hardly a better way to examine the long history of educational thought than through the prism of alternative schools and the alternative educational theorists who founded them. Where else do we find the educational problems and shortcomings of an age better represented? Where can we find more cogent criticism of the existing state of things, of the contemporary and conventional wisdom concerning education? Among the alternative educators of the past stand such legendary figures as Socrates, Comenius, Rousseau, Pestalozzi, Dewey, and Makarenko. In addition, schools such as Yverdun, Summerhill, and the Gorki Colony, as well as many lesser-known ones, are vivid reminders of educational needs that were not being met by the traditional schools of the time.

Of course, alternative schools not only reveal the educational shortcomings of their age; they also serve as experimental stations or laboratories by providing a society with an opportunity to test and observe avant-garde notions about education. Whether alternative schools serve as "hospitals" for the casualties of traditional schools or as "laboratories" for future innovations, they are valuable sources of information for researchers.

In the West German twin, alternative schools hold a prominent place in the educational spectrum. In guaranteeing the existence of private schools, the *Grundgesetz* has certainly opened the way for alternative schools as well. In addition, various court decisions have held that the *Laender* governments must assist private schools with subsidies from their education budgets. Of course, not all private schools are alternative schools. The largest majority of private institutions are denominational, 1,070 Catholic and 171 Protestant schools, while the so-called "Deutsche Privatschulen" constitute an additional 253; most of these latter schools, while privately controlled, offer a curriculum similar to that of most public schools.[2] Alternative schools in the narrower sense are much fewer in number. Indeed, some writers would only apply this term to a small number of "free," "liberated," "experimental schools" like the School Hannover Glocksee or the Bielefeld Laborschule.[3]

For our purposes, we shall use the *Waldorf-Schulen* (Waldorf Schools) as our looking-glass. These schools represent one of the most common and popular types of alternative school in West Germany; by 1983, 80 were operating, with more being planned. Waldorf Schools have also gained prominence in the United States and other Western countries. These schools trace their origin to the pedagogical ideas of Rudolf Steiner (1861–1925) and his philosophy of *Anthroposophie,*[4] which holds that education should be determined by "true knowledge of the human being." What does this mean in practice, and how have the Waldorf people used this precept as a means of finding fault with the public schools of the Federal Republic? These are the criticisms that the Waldorf proponents make of the state schools.[5]

1. State schools submit students to a biased, narrow, and purely cognitive concept of education. This, of course, is a universal reproach of reformers, but it is particularly apt in Germany. One reason for this is the half-day character of the typical West German school, the school day occupying only the morning hours. This means that the curriculum must be compressed into thirty 45-minute lessons, and leaves little time for "unimportant" subjects. Traditional subjects such as math, science, and languages dominate the curriculum and make the school a place for "serious" learning. Little time remains for social life and fun. Moreover, the teacher must become a task master who not only fills the childrens' morning hours with instruction and examinations, but ruins the afternoons and evenings of his charges as well with heavy doses of homework. To be sure, some time is allotted for art and athletics, but only the "hard-core" cognitive subjects really count when it comes to advancement. Pestalozzi's dictum that education should be for the "*Kopf, Herz, und Hand*" (head, heart, and hand) is virtually ignored.

2. State schools are also generally achievement oriented, which is not only "unnatural," but which intensifies the tendency toward a narrow, cognitive approach. What counts is achievement as measured by tests in cognitive core subjects. Failure means not only *sitzenbleiben* (staying behind to repeat a school year), it may mean exclusion from the *Realschule* and *Gymnasium,* as well as higher education, which in turn limits one's job opportunities. Schools thus become pressure cookers that create anxieties in children and conflicts in families and even teach children to cheat in order to succeed. What this prevents is the

identification of personally chosen, meaningful goals that would provide a sense of genuine and humane achievement.

3. As a result of the above, state schools ignore the physical and emotional needs of children as well as their creative capacities. Their desire to do, to create, to produce, to act, and to enjoy is frustrated by the public schools. Wholeness in thinking, feeling, believing, and willing is sacrificed in order to produce "data collectors and data processors." Thus, this system, which prizes cognitive learning so highly, misses the mark in this realm by not appreciating how much cognitive achievement springs from the full involvement of the human personality with all of its dimensions.

4. State schools ignore individuality. Despite such trends as individualization of instruction and the introduction of electives, state schools still tend to treat children as an anonymous mass who are classified and organized according to rules of bureaucratic and budgetary efficiency and whose performance is assessed according to its deviation from average norms. The uniqueness of a child is ignored, as are its special needs, whether these be physical, emotional, social, or spiritual. Thus the real task of education is missed, which is supporting the development of active, growing personalities who will be able to achieve their goals and gain happiness in a changing world.

5. State schools ignore the process of child and adolescent development. For example, many of the major steps in school matriculation occur in ways and at times that are harmful to the developing child (for example, school entrance at age six or seven and transition to various secondary schools at age ten). Furthermore, teaching methods and the curriculum as well as school organization hinder the natural growth of "personalities." Where is there a place for fantasy and imagination, for feeling and creating? The "rhythm" of growing and learning is disregarded. According to Rudolf Steiner and his followers, human development can be actualized by a certain rhythm of changing activities, alternating each day between the cognitive-rational, the imitative-practical, and the creative-artistic. The school year, indeed the entire school life of the child, should be in harmony with the phases of child and adolescent development. This has all been carefully studied and sensitively described by Rudolf Steiner.

6. State schools tend to ignore the social dimension of a child's life and thereby also limit the important contribution that parents and others can make to a child's education. By using such criteria as intelligence, achievement, and social class as means of grouping students, teachers

and administrators deprecate human relationships in favor of bureaucratic criteria. Despite recent efforts to promote the participation of parents in state schools, their contribution is relatively small and often not highly valued.

Indeed, in all of these areas of concern, the Waldorf Schools do offer alternatives. Their curriculum goes far beyond cognitive learning and is richly endowed with creative arts and crafts.[6] "Eurythmie," a subject that is unique to these schools, promotes the physical development of the body, muscles and limbs, while also stimulating expression by means of rhythmic movements, gestures, and mimicry. All of the capacities of a human being are supposed to be developed to be in harmony with the "soul" of the person. Traditional subjects are taught as well, but not in the traditional manner. For example, the child begins foreign language study early, but not by means of grammatical training or translation; instead the emphasis is placed on self-expression and communication, and later on language as a means to develop moral attitudes. Language study thus leads not to a "cold" but to a "warm" intelligence.[7]

Thus, in the Waldorf Schools, "achievement" is not seen as the result of imposed tasks, but as an expression of personal ideas, will, and self-actualization. Students are never held back; there are no grades. Instead of grade cards or transcripts with academic results, comprehensive characterizations of a student's personality development during the school year are recorded. The Waldorf Schools aim to provide an atmosphere where students "learn without fear and act with self-reliance."[8]

Proponents of the Waldorf Schools also claim that their teachers are particularly well prepared to promote the individuality of students and to elicit their humane qualities. The entire timetable of the schools — day, year, and overall program — is formed in such a way as to be in harmony with the psychological laws of human development. In addition, the curriculum rests on a strong psychological and artistic base. The schools also promote a healthy social climate. Students become deeply involved in governing their school (there is no traditional principal) and tend to identify deeply with the philosophy and methods of the Waldorf Schools. Constancy is also encouraged by having the same teacher (*Klassenlehrer*) for the first eight school years.

Thus the Waldorf Schools in West Germany seek to solve many of the problems confronting state schools in industrial societies. They offer alternatives for some students whose needs are not well met in the state schools. In addition, the Waldorf Schools have stimulated new modes of educational thinking. This does not mean that these schools are without problems. For example, some students who are successful and well adjusted in the Waldorf Schools find it quite difficult to adjust to a society where routine work and externally imposed tasks are common, and where seemingly senseless achievements are valued and rewarded.

One additional problem for the Waldorf Schools stems from the clientele they have attracted. When Steiner founded the first of these schools in the Waldorf-Astoria cigarette factory near Stuttgart in 1919, most of the students came from working-class backgrounds. Success has, however, brought with it children who are largely from prosperous middle-class homes. Not only does it require money for tuition at the Waldorf Schools, but the pedagogy of Steiner and his followers has largely appealed to educated people, especially those whose children are having difficulties in state schools. In addition, the Waldorf Schools now have a "snob" appeal for some parents and their children. Needless to say, Steiner would not have approved of this motive for sending students to his schools.

Not only the Waldorf Schools, but many other alternative schools that began as pedagogical experiments and barely survived, have found that success has brought them acclaim as well as an elite clientele. The German country boarding schools (*Landerziehungsheime*) are another case in point.[9] This has elicited a great deal of criticism from Marxist and other radical social reformers, both West and East, who regard this as additional evidence of the dominance of the bourgeoisie. For them, true "alternative schools" are only those that aim to change the class structure of society. In West Germany in the 1980s only a few schools of this type exist — another sign of the fairly stable and conservative structure of schools and school life in the Federal Republic.

In the East German twin, alternatives such as the Waldorf Schools do not exist; nor, in fact, does one find any "free schools," "anti-authoritarian schools," or any kind of church or private school. Of course, this does not mean that there are no problems in GDR education and that the needs of all children are adequately served. Rather, it means that schooling is a state monopoly and that competition from whatever source is not permitted. Any changes or improvements that will occur in the organization, curriculum, or methods of the state schools must originate, therefore, with the government or the Party. According to the GDR Constitution (Article 21, Paragraph 2), citizens have the "right of participation and cooperation in the shaping of institutions" and may address "state authorities and institutions with their concerns and proposals." Citizens are not, however, given the right to found and maintain schools.

We have seen in previous chapters (for example, Chapter 8) that young East Germans complain about dull, rote learning in their schools and even long for "some Kafka in their curriculum," and that some of these students refuse to study or cooperate in "building their padded cells."[10] There are, in fact, many indications that the problems that alternative schools in West Germany seek to remedy find their counterpart in the East: the hierarchical organization of schools, lack of communication, overvaluing of cognitive achievements, neglect of individuality and creativity, and stifling of humane social relations. If anything, some of these grievances are even more acute in the GDR, where an enormous, highly centralized state mechanism conveys only officially approved knowledge, ideology, attitudes, and behaviors.

Yet, none of these grievances may be expressed by the founding of alternative schools. Citizens who criticize the system too freely or who refuse to cooperate are labeled as bourgeois, individualistic, or anti-progressive (reactionary). Their fate is silence, isolation, and "nonexistence." We do not make this harsh judgment in order to heap praise on West German educators. Frequently, they have not been open and receptive to new ideas and programs. Yet, the GDR school system can hardly be surpassed in its monitoring and stifling of "alternative ideas." The concept of *Einheit* is everywhere dominant.

Yet, a very careful scrutiny does reveal some flexibility in the GDR monolith. Although the official ideology does call for *Einheitsschulen* that are comprehensive and fully integrated in every way (for example, socially as well as intellectually), this does not appear to satisfy fully the needs of society or individuals in the GDR. For example, how can academically gifted students be properly prepared for the Academic Senior High School (EOS) or how can special talents in music, sports, sciences, or languages be properly trained and utilized by the state under such a system? Thus, in spite of the proclaimed nature of the *Einheitsschule,* the GDR has for several decades permitted a considerable number of students in grades eight and nine to attend so-called preparatory classes in which they prepare for the EOS by studying a second foreign language and by engaging in a more intensive study of subjects in the general curriculum. Despite rhetoric to the contrary, they are "segregated." Yet, in order to qualify for these special classes, students must not only have demonstrated high academic performance, they must have also displayed the right "political-social attitudes." And children from working-class backgrounds or whose parents rank high in the socialist/communist hierarchy are given preference.[11] It should be noted, however, that in the mid-1980s these preparatory classes are being eliminated. This may indicate either that the number of students entering the EOS is being reduced or that a sufficient number of politically reliable and academically proficient students are available for the EOS without resort to special classes.

Another group of students who qualify for special schools in the GDR are those with special gifts in mathematics, science, technology, Russian language, sports, and fine arts. Clearly, these areas are considered significant enough to warrant special training for those who manifest special talents in them. The GDR Education Law of 1965 provides for "Special Schools ... to serve the particular needs for the development of junior staff for the economy, the sciences, sports and culture." "High achievement and special giftedness" are required for "admission to these schools."[12] The inclusion of the Russian language as one of the special areas that qualify for a special school attests, of course, to the close relationship of East Germany to the Soviet Union, a relationship that is defined in the Constitution (Article 6, Paragraph 2) as "forever and irrevocable."

One of these special schools, the School of German-Soviet Friendship (*Schule der deutsch-sowjetischen Freundschaft*) has been described in *Paedagogik,* a leading educational journal of the GDR.[13] Interestingly, this school occupies the site of one of Germany's most famous pre-Nazi alternative schools, the Free School Community (Freie Schulgemeinde) of Wickersdorf. Wickersdorf had been founded as a boarding school in 1906 by Gustav Wyneken (1875–1964), a controversial school reformer, who deplored the rote learning and stifling authoritarian atmosphere of Wilhelminian schools. East German educators criticize Wyneken's ideas as bourgeois and "reformist," yet praise the humanistic elements in his theories as forerunners of socialism/communism.

As with all private schools in the GDR, Wickersdorf was integrated into the state school system and eventually became a special school for Russian studies with an emphasis on Russian language. The author of the *Paedagogik* article describes how future teachers of Russian develop a love of the Soviet Union and how in the future they will be able "to deepen friendship and fraternal cooperation with the principal force in the socialist community of states, i.e., the Soviet Union." Students will be expected to provide good examples of the "new kind of human being" currently being created in the GDR. Insofar as the school pioneers in new educational modes, it is involved in the study of "famous champions of German-Soviet friendships" (for example, Clara Zetkin and Nadesha Krupskaja). Students will also read the works of Wasili Suchomlinski and Anton S. Makarenko.

Special schools, such as the German-Soviet Friendship School, thus serve a number of the functions in the GDR that alternative schools satisfy in West Germany and other pluralistic states. Not only do these schools take care of the needs of a special group of students, they also undertake some innovations with respect to curriculum and teaching methods. Clearly, the differences between these schools and alternative schools in Western societies are obvious. Unlike the alternative schools, which tend to develop a broad range of options to the state system in West Germany, the special schools in the GDR are planned alternatives to the *Einheitsschule* with careful state and Party supervision. The talented students who attend these institutions are destined for outstanding careers. Having been carefully selected, they are virtually consecrated to their new schools in a solemn ceremony of the Party Youth Organization. They will be expected to make "high achievements in the service of the socialist society and the Party."[14]

Thus, the "alternative schools" of the German twins provide an additional lens by which to observe these two societies. In the West they are part of that delicate mechanism by which freedom and human dignity are promoted through pluralism. In the East they are part of the dedicated process of forming the "new human being" through centralized planning and control. Both states proclaim their fealty to humanity, however much they differ in the roads they have chosen to follow. We can only hope that the purposes of humanity will be served and will succeed.

NOTES

The epigraph to Chapter 10 is from L. van Dick, *Alternativschulen* (Reinbek, 1979), p. 187.

1. See Ludwig von Bertalanffy, *General Systems Theory: Foundations, Development, Applications* (London, 1971); also George G. Klir, *Trends in General Systems Theory* (New York, 1972), and Niklas Luhmann, *Soziologische Aufklaerung* (Opladen, 1972).

2.   R. Winkel, "Alternative Schulen — Ausweg aus der Schulmisere?" in *Alternativen fuer die Schule,* edited by Georg Auernheimer and K. H. Heinemann (Koeln, 1980), pp. 29–44.

3.   Ibid.

4.   See especially A. C. Harwood, *The Recovery of Man in Childhood. A Study of the Educational Work of Rudolf Steiner* (London, 1958). Of Steiner's many works, see especially *The Roots of Education* (London, 1968) and *The Modern Art of Education* (London, 1972).

5.   For example, see Stefan Leber, ed., *Die Paedagogik der Waldorfschule und ihre Grundlagen* (Darmstadt, 1983); Christoph Lindenberg, *Waldorfschulen: Angstfrei lernen, selbstbewusst handeln* (Reinbek, 1975), and George Rist and Peter Schneider, *Die Hiberniaschule* (Reinbek, 1977).

6.   Some Waldorf Schools offer a full general education plus training for an occupation.

7.   B. Morgenstern, "Fremdsprachenunterricht," in Leber, *Die Paedagogik der Waldorfschule,* p. 223ff.

8.   Lindenberg, *Waldorfschulen.*

9.   See Sterling Fishman, "Hermann Lietz and the Founding of the German Country Boarding School Movement," *Paedagogica Historica* 8, no. 2 (1968): 351–71.

10.   Norbert Haase, Lothar Reese, and Peter Wensierski, eds., *VEB Nachwuchs— Jugend in der DDR* (Reinbek, 1983), pp. 40, 65f, 83, 115, 190.

11.   Gerlind Schmidt, *Sekundarabschluesse mit Hochschulreife im Bildungswesen der DDR* (Weinheim Basel, 1976), p. 16.

12.   Ministerium fuer Volksbildung, ed., *Sozialistisches Bildungsrecht-Volksbildung. Rechtsvorschriften und Dokumente* (Berlin, 1973), p. 33.

13.   *Paedagogik* 36 (1981): 14–26.

14.   See Ministerium fuer Volksbildung, ed., *Sozialistisches Bildungsrecht-Volksbildung: Oberschulen* (Berlin, 1982), p. 190ff (regulation of the cooperation of music schools and Polytechnic Schools, 1962).

BIBLIOGRAPHY

Abusch, A. *Der Irrweg einer Nation,* 8th ed. (Berlin, 1960).

Achinger, G. *Die Schulreform in der UdSSR* (Muenchen, 1973).

Ahrbeck, R. *Die allseitig entwickelte Persoenlichkeit* (Berlin, 1979).

Akademie der Paedagogischen Wissenschaften der DDR, ed. *Erziehung sozialistischer Persoenlichkeiten* (Berlin, 1976).

_____. *Das Bildungswesen der Deutschen Demokratischen Republik,* 2nd ed. (Berlin, 1983).

Anweiler, O. et al. *Bildungssysteme in Europa,* 3rd ed. (Weinheim, 1980).

Arnove, R. F. "Comparative Education and World Systems Analysis." *Comparative Education Review* 1980: 48–63.

Auernheimer, G. and K. H. Heinemann, eds. *Alternativen fuer die Schule* (Koeln, 1980).

Autorenkollektiv: B. Bittighoefer et al. *Moral und Gesellschaft* (Berlin, 1968).

Backer, J. H. *The Decision to Divide Germany* (Durham, N.C., 1978).

Baker, K. L. *Germany Transformed: Political Culture and the New Politics* (Cambridge, MA, 1981).

Baylis, T. A. *The Technical Intelligentsia and the East German Elite: Legitimacy and Social Change in Mature Communism* (Berkeley, CA, 1974).

Beaumont, M. *The Origins of the Second World War* (New Haven, 1978).

Benner, D. *Entgegnungen zum Bonner Forum "Mut zur Erziehung"* (Muenchen, 1978).

Berger, M., ed. *Kulturpolitisches Woerterbuch,* 2nd ed. (Berlin, 1978).

Bertalanffy, L. v. *General Systems Theory: Foundations, Developments, Applications* (London, 1971).

Bidwell, P. W. "Emphasis on Culture in the French Zone." *Foreign Affairs* 27 (1948): 78–85.

Blankertz, H. *Theorien und Modelle der Didaktik,* 11th ed. (Muenchen, 1980).

Blonskij, P. P. *Trudovaja skola* (Moskva, 1919).

_____. *Die Arbeitsschule* (Paderborn, 1973).

Bode, D. *Polytechnischer Unterricht in der DDR* (Frankfurt/New York, 1978).

Bodenman, P. S. "Education in the Soviet Zone of Germany." *School Life* 41 (December 1958): 14–17.

Boehme, W. et al., eds. *Kleines politisches Woerterbuch,* 2nd ed. (Berlin, 1973).

Bollnow, O. F. *Existenzphilosophie und Paedagogik* (Stuttgart, 1959).

Bundesminister fuer Bildung und Wissenschaft, ed. *Grund-und Strukturdaten* (Bonn, 1982/83; 1985/86).

Bundesminister fuer innerdeutsche Beziehungen, ed. *DDR-Handbuch,* 2nd ed. (Koeln, 1979).

Bundesverfassungsgericht, ed. *Entscheidungen des Bundesverfassungsgerichts (BVerfGE)* (Tuebingen). Published annually.

Bund-Laender-Kommission fuer Bildungsplanung. *Bildungsgesamtplan,* 2 vols. (Stuttgart, 1973).

Burks, H. M. and B. Stefflre. *Theories of Counseling* (New York, 1979).

Caldon, M. "Strangely Conservative." *Times Educational Supplement,* December 30, 1977, pp. 8–9.

Childs, D. *East Germany* (London, 1969).

_____. *The GDR: Moscow's German Ally* (London, 1983).

Childs, D. and J. Johnson. *West Germany: Politics and Society* (London, 1981).

Christofferson, A. C. "Educational Reconstruction in Land Hesse, Germany." *Educational Forum* 13 (March 1949): 313–19.

Clark, P. A. *Action Research and Organizational Change* (London/New York, 1972).

Cohn, E. *The Economics of Education* (Cambridge, MA, 1979).

Croan, M. *East Germany: The Soviet Connection* (Beverly Hills, CA, 1976).

Dahrendorf, R. *Bildung ist Buergerrecht* (Hamburg, 1965).

_____. *Society and Democracy in Germany* (Garden City, N.Y., 1967).

Dennerlein, H. and K. Schramm, eds. *Handbuch der Behindertenpaedagogik*, 2 vols. (Muenchen, 1979).

Deutscher Ausschuss fuer das Erziehungs-und Bildungswesen. *Rahmenplan zur Umgestaltung des allgemeinbildenden oeffentlichen Schulwesens* (Stuttgart, 1959).

Deutscher Bildungsrat, ed. *Lernziele der Gesamtschule* (Stuttgart, 1969).

_____. *Strukturplan fuer das Bildungswesen* (Stuttgart, 1970).

_____. *Reform des Sekundarstufe II* (Braunschweig, 1971).

_____. *Zur Neuordnung der Sekundarstufe II. Konzept fuer eine Verbindung von allgemeinem und beruflichem Lernen* (Stuttgart, 1974).

Development of Education in the German Democratic Republic (Berlin, 1981).

Dewey, J. *Democracy and Education* (New York, 1916).

Dewey, J. and W. H. Kilpatrick. *Der Projektplan — Grundlegung und Praxis* (Weimar, 1939).

Dornberg, J. *The New Germans: Thirty Years After* (New York, 1976).

_____. *The Other Germany* (New York, 1968).

_____. *Schizophrenic Germany* (New York, 1961).

"East-West Education Contrasted." *Virginia Journal of Education* (May 1965): 24.

Education for Today and Tomorrow (Dresden, 1973).

The Educational System in the German Democratic Republic (Berlin, 1979).

Engels, F. *The Peasant War in Germany* (New York, 1966).

Falk, M. R. *History of Germany* (New York, 1957).

Fend, H. et al. *Leistungsvergleich zwischen Gesamtschulen und Schulen des traditionellen Schulsystems* (Hildesheim, 1981).

Fishman, S. "The Berlin Wall in the History of Education." *History of Education Quarterly* 22, no. 3 (Fall 1982): 363–70.

____. "Hermann Lietz and the Founding of the German Country Boarding School Movement." *Paedagogica Historica* 8, no. 2 (1968): 351–71.

Flitner, W. *Die gymnasiale Oberstufe* (Heidelberg, 1961).

Frankiewicz, H. *Technik und Bildung in der Schule der DDR* (Berlin, 1968).

Frey, K. *Die Projektmethode* (Weinheim/Basel, 1982).

____. "Die Projektmethode im historischen und konzeptionellen Zusammenhang." *Bildung und Erziehung* 37 (1984): 3ff.

Fuehr, C. and W. D. Halls, eds. *Educational Reform in the Federal Republic of Germany* (Hamburg, 1970).

Galton, F. *Inquiries into Human Faculty and its Development* (London, 1883).

Gerbaulet, S. et al. *Schulnahe Curriculumentwicklung* (Stuttgart, 1972).

Gerstein, H. *Erfolg und Versagen im Gymnasium* (Weinheim, 1972).

Geyer, E., ed. *Differenzierung in der Realschuloberstufe in Nordrhein-Westfalen* (Hannover, 1976).

Gimbel, J. *A German Community Under American Occupation: Marburg 1945–52* (Stanford, 1961).

Glowka, D. and D. Waterkamp. "Das Schulwesen der DDR aus westdeutscher Sicht." In *Handbuch Schule und Unterricht,* vol. 3, edited by W. Twellmann (Duesseldorf, 1981).

Grace, A. G. *Basic Principles of Educational Reconstruction in Germany* (Frankfurt, 1948).

Grandke, A. et al. "Zur Wirksamkeit des Erziehungsrechts des FGB." *Neue Justiz* 8 (1979): 345–49.

Grant, N. *Society, Schools, and Progress in Eastern Europe* (Oxford, 1969).

____. *Soviet Education* (Baltimore, 1964).

Groothoff, H. and M. Stallman. *Paedagogisches Lexikon* (Stuttgart, 1961).

Guenther, H., C. Willeke, and R. Willeke. *Grundlegung einer bejahenden Erziehung* (Muenchen, 1977).

Guenther, K. H. et al. *Geschichte der Erziehung,* 11th ed. (Berlin, 1973).

Grzesik, J. *Perspektiven fuer die weitere Entwicklung der gymnasialen Oberstufe* (Bad Heilbrunn, 1984).

Haase, N., L. Reese, and P. Wensierski, eds. *VEB Nachwuchs: Jugend in der DDR* (Reinbek, 1983).

Haeberle, L. *Erziehungsziele und Orientierungswerte im Verfassungsstaat* (Frieburg/Muenchen, 1981).

Hammer, L. "Early Identification of Handicaps and Early Special Education in the German Democratic Republic." *Prospects* 11 (1981): 460–68.

Hanhardt, A. M. *The German Democratic Republic* (Baltimore, 1968).

Harwood, A. C. *The Discovery of Man in Childhood. A Study of the Educational Work of Rudolf Steiner* (London, 1958).

Hearnden, A. *The British in Germany: Educational Reconstruction after 1945* (London, 1978).

____. *Education in the Two Germanies* (Oxford, 1974).

____. *Education, Culture and Politics in West Germany* (Oxford, 1976).

____. "Individual Freedom and State Intervention in East and West German Education." *Comparative Education* 10, no. 2 (1974): 131–35.

Hegel, G. W. F. *Philosophy of Right* (Oxford, 1942).

____. *Philosophy of History* (New York, 1956).

Herr, E. L. *Guidance and Counseling in Schools* (Falls Church, VA, 1979).

Herspring, D. R. *East German Civil-Military Relations: The Impact of Technology, 1949–1972* (New York, 1973).

Hettwer, H. *Das Bildungswesen in der DDR — strukturelle und inhaltliche Entwicklung seit 1945* (Koeln, 1976).

Hicks, W. R. *The School in English and German Fiction* (London, n.d.).

Hocking, W. E. *Experiment in Education* (Chicago, 1954).

Hollander, P. *Soviet and American Society* (New York, 1973).

Holm, H. A. *The Other Germans: Report from an East German Town* (New York, 1970).

Holmes, B. *Problems in Education: A Comparative Approach* (London, 1965).

Hopf, D. *Uebergangsauslese und Leistungsdifferenzierung* (Frankfurt, 1970).

Huebener, T. *The Schools of West Germany: A Study of German Elementary and Secondary Schools* (New York, 1962).

Hylla, E. J. and F. Kegel. *Education in Germany: An Introduction for Foreigners* (Frankfurt, 1954).

Ingenkamp, K. *Die Fragwuerdigkeit der Zensurengebung* (Weinheim, 1973).

Jaeggi, U. *Kapital und Arbeit in der Bundesrepublik Deutschland* (Frankfurt, 1973).

Jensen, A. R. "Social Class, Race, Genetics." *American Educational Research Journal* 9 (1968): 1–42.

Johnson, P. G. "Secondary Education in the Schools of Germany." *School Life* 30 (October 1947): 12–14.

Kaiser, A. and F. K. Kaiser, eds. *Projektstudium und Projektarbeit in der Schule* (Bad Heilbrunn, 1977).

Kazamias, A. M. and K. Schwartz. "Intellectual and Ideological Perspectives in Comparative Education: An Interpretation." *Comparative Education Review* 21 (1977): 153–76.

Kienitz, W. and W. Mehnert. "Ueber Gegenstand und Aufgaben der marxistischen Vergleichenden Paedagogik." *Vergleichende Paedagogik* 2 (1966): 225–46.

King, E. J. *Communist Education* (Indianapolis, 1963).

____. *Comparative Studies and Educational Decision* (London, 1968).

Kitzinger, U. *German Electoral Politics: A Study of the 1957 Campaign* (Oxford, 1960).

Klafki, W. et al. *Funkkolleg Erziehungswissenschaft,* 3 vols. (Frankfurt, 1970).

____. "Handlungsforschung im Schulfeld." *Zeitschrift fuer Paedagogik* 19 (1973): 487–516.

Klein, H. *Bildung in der DDR* (Reinbek, 1974).

____. *First-Hand Information: Education in a Socialist Country,* 2nd rev. ed. (Dresden, 1976).

____. *Polytechnische Bildung und Erziehung in der DDR* (Reinbek, 1962).

Klir, G. G. *Trends in General Systems Theory* (New York, 1972).

Kludas, R. "Erziehung zu kulturvollem Verhalten in der Freizeit." *Paedagogik* (1982): 34ff.

Knoll, J. H. *The German Educational System* (Bad Godesberg, 1967).

Knuetter, H. H. "Historisch-politische Bildung in der Schule — Die Richtlinien in den Laendern der Bundesrepublik Deutschland." *Engagement* 1983: 146–57.

Koroljow, F. F. and V. E. Gmurman. *Allgemeine Grundlagen der marxistischen Paedagogik* (Pullach bei Muenchen, 1973).

Krieger, L. *The German Idea of Freedom* (Chicago, 1972).

Krisch, H. *The German Democratic Republic* (Boulder, 1985).

____. *German Politics Under Soviet Occupation* (New York, 1974).

Kultusminister des Landes Nordrhein-Westfalen, ed. *Schulversuch Kollegschule NW* (Koeln, 1976).

____. *Richtlinien fuer die gymnasiale Oberstufe — Geschichte* (Koeln, 1982).

Lawson, R. F. "English Approach to Educational Reorientation in Postwar Germany." *Comparative Education Review* (June 1974): 58–64.

____. *The Reform of the West German School System* (Ann Arbor, 1965).

Leber, S., ed. *Die Paedagogik der Waldorfschule und ihre Grundlagen* (Darmstadt, 1983).

Lennert, R., ed. *Das Problem der gymnasialen Oberstufe* (Bad Heilbrunn, 1971).

Leonhard, W. *Child of the Revolution* (Chicago, 1958).

Lilge, F. "German Educational Reforms in the Soviet Zone of Occupation." *Harvard Educational Review* 18 (January 1948): 35–46.

Lindenberg, C. *Waldorfschulen: Angstfrei lernen, selbstbewusst handeln* (Reinbek, 1975).

Lindgren, A. M. *Germany Revisited: Education in the Federal Republic* (Washington, D.C., 1957).

Lingens, H. G. and B. Lingens. *Education in West Germany: A Quest for Excellence* (Bloomington, IN, 1980).

Littman, U. *An Introduction to the Confusion of German Education* (Bonn, 1974).

Ludz, P. C. *The Changing Party Elite in East Germany* (Cambridge, MA, 1972).

_____. *The German Democratic Republic from the Sixties to the Seventies: A Socio-Political Analysis* (Cambridge, MA, 1970).

_____. "Discovery and 'Recognition' of East Germany." *Comparative Politics* 2 (July 1970): 681–92.

Luhmann, N. *Soziologische Aufklaerung* (Opladen, 1972).

Makarenko, A. S. *Werke V* (Berlin, 1964).

Mallinson, V. *An Introduction to the Study of Comparative Education* (Melbourne, 1957).

Mann, E. *Schools for Barbarians: Education under the Nazis.* (London, 1939).

Mann, G. *The History of Germany Since 1789* (New York, 1968).

Martin, L. R. *Schulberatung: Anlaesse, Aufgaben, Methodenkonzeption* (Stuttgart, 1981).

_____. "Sekundarstufe II im internationalen Vergleich." *Handbuch Schule und Unterricht,* edited by Walter Twellman. 5, no. 1 (Duesseldorf, 1981):168–79.

_____. "Benachteiligtenprojekt N. — ein modernes Stans?" *Westermanns paedagogische Beitraege* (in print).

Martin, L. R. and B. Wehrly. "Counseling, School and Society: Interdependent Systems — The Example of the Federal Republic of Germany." *Counseling and Human Development* 12, no. 2 (1979): 1–12.

Martin, L. R. and J. DeVolder. "Guidance and Counseling Services in the Federal Republic of Germany." *Personnel and Guidance Journal* 61, no. 8 (1983): 482–87.

Marx, K. *Das Kapital* (Hamburg, 1874–1894).

Marx, K. and F. Engels. *Basic Writings on Politics and Philosophy*, edited by L. S. Feuer (Garden City, N.Y., 1959).

____. *Werke 23* (Berlin, 1972).

Max Planck Institut fuer Bildungsforschung, ed. *Bildung in der Bundesrepublik Deutschland*, 2 vols. (Reinbek, 1980).

____. *Between Elite and Mass Education: Education in the Federal Republic of Germany* (Albany, 1983).

McCauley, M. *East Germany: The Dilemmas of Division* (London, 1980).

____. *Power and Authority in East Germany: The Socialist Unity Party* (London, 1981).

____. *The German Democratic Republic Since 1945* (New York, 1983).

Mende, K. D. "Schulreform und Gesellschaft in der DDR, 1945—1965." In *Schulreform als gesellschaftlicher Prozess*, vol. 1, edited by S. B. Robinsohn (Stuttgart, 1972).

Merelman, R. M. and C. R. Foster. "Political Culture and Education in Advanced Industrial Societies: West Germany and the United States." *International Review of Education* 24 (1978): 443–65.

Ministerium fuer Volksbildung, ed. *Sozialistisches Bildungsrecht: Rechtsvorschriften und Dokumente* (Berlin, 1973).

____. *Sozialistisches Bildungsrecht, Volksbildung: Allgemeinbildende polytechnische Oberschule* (Berlin, 1973).

Ministerrat der Deutschen Demokratischen Republik (Minsterium fuer Volksbildung), ed., *Lehrplaene* and *Praezisierte Lehrplaene* (Berlin, 1970–1981).

Mitter, W. "Education in the Federal Republic of Germany: The Next Decade." *Comparative Education* 16 (1980): 257–65.

Mittler, P. *The Study of Twins* (Middlesex, England, 1971).

Moore-Rinvolucri, M. J. *Education in East Germany* (Hamden, CT, 1973).

Nettl, J. P. *The Eastern Zone and Soviet Policy in Germany, 1945–1950* (London, 1951).

Niermann, J. *Lehrer in der DDR* (Heidelberg, 1973).

_____. *Woerterbuch der DDR-Paedagogik* (Heidelberg, 1974).

Neuner, G. *Zur Theorie der sozialistischen Allgemeinbildung* (Berlin, 1973).

_____. *Sozialistische Persoenlichkeit — ihr Werden, ihre Erziehung* (Berlin, 1975).

Neuner, G. et al. *Allgemeinbildung-Lehrplanwerk-Unterricht* (Berlin, 1972).

Noah, H. J. and M. A. Eckstein. *Toward a Science of Comparative Education* (New York, 1969).

OECD. *Planning Education for Economic and Social Development* (Paris, 1963).

Ollmann, B. *Alienation* (Cambridge, MA, 1971).

Paedagogik, Zeitschrift fuer Theorie und Praxis der sozialistischen Erziehung. Edited by Deutsches Paedagogisches Zentralinstitut, Berlin.

Peisert, H. *Soziale Lage und Bildungschancen in Deutschland* (Muenchen, 1967).

Picht, G. *Die deutsche Bildungskatastrophe* (Muenchen, 1965).

Poignant, R. *L'enseignement dans les pays du Marché Commun* (Paris, 1965).

Polzin, J. "Ueber Ziel, Inhalt und Methoden der sozialistischen Allgemeinbildung." *Paedagogik* 22 (1967): 31–42.

Rang, A. and W. Schultz, eds. *Gesamtschule, Bilanz ihrer Praxis,* 2nd ed. (Hamburg, 1976).

Reble, A., ed. *Zur Geschichte der Hoeheren Schule,* 2 vols. (Bad Heilbrunn, 1975).

Recum, H. v. *Bildungsoekonomie im Wandel* (Braunschweig, 1978).

_____. "Education in the Affluent Society: Problems and Conflicts." *International Review of Education* 27 (1981): 3–14.

Riquarts, K. "Hinweise auf Projektunterricht in Lehrplaenen und Richtlinien der Laender der Bundesrepublik Deutschland und Berlin (West)" *Bildung und Erziehung* 37 (1984): 37–46.

Rist, G. and P. Schneider. *Die Hibernia-Schule* (Reinbek, 1977).

Robertson, E. M., ed. *The Origins of the Second World War* (London, 1971).

Robinsohn, S. B. *Bildungsreform als Revision des Curriculum* (Neuwied, 1967).

Roth, H. "Educational Organization in Germany." *Journal of Teacher Education* (December 1950): 274–78.

Rust, V. D. *Education in East and West Germany: A Bibliography* (New York, 1984).

Samuel, R. H. and R. H. Thomas. *Education and Society in Modern Germany* (London, 1949).

Schacht, R. *Alienation* (Garden City, N.Y., 1970).

Schleiermacher, F. *Paedagogische Schriften*, edited by E. Weniger and T. Schulze (Duesseldorf/Muenchen, 1966).

Schmidt-Bleibtreu, B. and F. Klein. *Kommentar zum Grundgesetz fuer die Bundesrepublik Deutschland*, 3rd ed. (Neuwied, 1973).

Schmidt, G. *Sekundarabschluesse mit Hochschulreife in der DDR* (Weinheim/Basel, 1976).

Schmitt, K. "Education and Politics in the German Democratic Republic." *Comparative Education Review* (1975): 31–50.

Schneeweiss, M. L. "German Schools and Democracy." *Modern Language Journal* 34 (February 1950): 111–25.

Schueler, H. "Education in West Germany." *Education* 76 (February 1956): 384–89.

Schwaenke, U. *Die Interdependenz von Bildungswesen und Gesellschaft* (Weinheim/Basel, 1980).

Schwarze, W. *The GDR Today: Life in the "Other" Germany* (London, 1973).

Senf, H. "Cooperation Between School and Family in the German Democratic Republic." *Prospects* 10, no. 3 (1981): 340–45.

Shafer, S. M. *Postwar American Influence on the West German Volksschule.* (Ann Arbor, MI, 1964).

____. "The Socialization of Girls in the Secondary Schools of England and the Two Germanies." *Int. Rev. of Education* 22 (1976): 5–23.

Shirer, W. L. *The Rise and Fall of the Third Reich* (New York, 1960).

Siebel, A. "Berufs-und Studienberatung." *Paedagogik* (1983): 226ff.

Smith, J. E. *Germany Beyond the Wall: People, Politics, . . . and Prosperity* (Boston, 1967).

Sommerville, J. *The Philosphy of Marxism* (New York, 1967).

Staatssekretariat fuer Berufsbildung, ed. *Sozialistisches Bildungsrecht-Berufsbildung* (Berlin, 1979).

Starck, W. *Die Sitzenbleiber-Katastrophe* (Stuttgart, 1974).

Steiner, R. *The Roots of Education* (London, 1968).

————. *The Modern Art of Education* (London, 1972).

Suin de Boutemard, B. *Schule, Projektunterricht und soziale Handlungsperformanz* (Muenchen, 1975).

Tanner, D. and L. U. Tanner. *Curriculum Development* (New York/London, 1980).

Tausch, R. and A. M. Tausch. *Erziehungspsychologie*, 7th ed. (Goettingen, 1973).

Tent, J. F. *Mission on the Rhine: Reeducation and Denazification in American-Occupied Germany* (Chicago and London, 1982).

Twellman, W., ed. *Handbuch Schule und Unterricht*, vols. 1–5 (Duesseldorf, 1980–1981).

Tyler, L. E. *The Work of the Counselor* (New York, 1969).

U.S. State Department of Public Affairs, ed. *Germany, 1947–1949* (Washington, D.C., 1950).

Van Dick, L. *Alternativschulen* (Reinbek, 1979).

Vergleichende Erziehungswissenschaft, edited by A. Busch et al. (Pullach bei Muenchen, 1974).

Voelmy, W. *Polytechnischer Unterrricht in der DDR seit 1964* (Frankfurt, 1969).

Vogel, B., ed. *Schule am Scheideweg* (Muenchen, 1974).

Vogt, H. *Theorie und Praxis der Lehrplanrevision in der DDR* (Muenchen, 1972).

____. "Berufsbildungsberatung in der DDR." In *Handbuch der Bildungsberatung I*, edited by K. Heller (Stuttgart, 1975), 75ff.

Warren, R. L. *Education in Rebhausen, A German Village* (New York, 1967).

Waterkamp, D. *Lehrplanreform in der DDR* (Hannover, 1975).

Weber, E. *Erziehungsstile*, 3rd ed. (Donauwoerth, 1972).

Weniger, E. *Didaktik als Bildungslehre*, 2 vols. (Weinheim, 1952).

Weinstock, H. *Realer Humanismus* (Heidelberg, 1955).

Willis, F. R. *The French in Germany, 1945–1949* (Stanford, 1962).

Wottawa, H. *Gesamtschule: Was sie uns wirklich bringt* (Duesseldorf, 1982).

Ziertmann, P. *Das amerikanische College und die deutsche Oberstufe* (Wiesbaden, 1950).

Zink, H. *American Military Government in Germany* (New York, 1947).

____. *The United States in Germany, 1944–1955* (Princeton, N.J., 1957).

INDEX

ABOUT THE AUTHORS

Sterling Fishman is a Professor of History and Educational Policy Studies at the University of Wisconsin in Madison. Professor Fishman received his BA from Washington University (St. Louis) and his graduate degrees from the University of Wisconsin. Earlier in his career he taught at SUNY-Binghamton and Douglass College of Rutgers University. Professor Fishman has spent a considerable amount of time in Germany and in 1979 was appointed as Fulbright Professor at the University of Bonn. His major research interests have been in the history of European education and the history of childhood and adolescence. In addition to numerous articles, he has published a book on German adolescence, *The Struggle for German Youth, 1890–1914* (New York, 1976) and co-edited *Teacher, Student and Society* (Boston, 1974).

Lothar Martin is Studien Professor at the Institut fuer Erziehungswissenschaft, University of Bonn, Federal Republic of Germany. He is a Doctor of Philosophy of the University of Marburg, Germany. As an undergraduate exchange student he studied at Hobart College, Geneva, New York. Professor Martin has visited the United States numerous times and lectured at various universities. During the spring term 1983 he taught Comparative Education at the University of Wisconsin-Madison, as a Visiting Professor.

Professor Martin's main fields of research and teaching are Comparative Education and Guidance and Counseling, particularly Comparative Schooling and Counseling. He has published a number of books, articles, and book reviews in these fields. He is also editor of the *International Journal for the Advancement of Counseling*.

As a member of various international associations, he has tried to promote school education, helping services, and international understanding.

REVOLUTION THROUGH REFORM: A Comparison of
Sarvodaya and Conscientization
Mathew Zachariah

NONFORMAL EDUCATION IN LATIN AMERICA
AND THE CARIBBEAN: Stability, Reform, or Revolution
Thomas J. La Belle

EDUCATIONAL POLICIES IN CRISIS: Japanese and American
Perspectives
William K. Cummings, Edward R. Beauchamp, Shogo Ichikawa,
Victor N. Kobayashi, Morikazu Ushiogi

EDUCATION AND REVOLUTION IN NICARAGUA
Robert F. Arnove